"A work of searing eloquence and moral fire, informed by a scholarship that spans forgotten classics and nearly all the best new thinking. All in the service of building a better world. In one word: splendid."

James K. Galbraith, author of *Welcome to the Poisoned Chalice: The Destruction of Greece and the Future of Europe*

"What a passion for the abolition of enslavement by the ruling totalitarian class! What a courage to denounce the role of orthodox economists as the 'intellectual aristocracy' of predators! A true and deep culture is enshrined in this brilliant study, which is Professor Bougrine's modern version of *Das Kapital*. This is the best answer to neoliberals and should be read by everyone."

Alain Parguez, Emeritus Professor, Université Franche-Comté, Besançon, France

"A brilliant exposition of the colonial roots of the Great Divergence. An excellent analysis of the current neoliberal model. Bougrine convincingly argues for a radical reform in the spirits of Keynes, Marx and Karl Polanyi."

Kari Polanyi Levitt, Emerita Professor of Economics, McGill University, Canada. Author of *From the Great Transformation to the Great Financialization*

"An excellent critical review of mainstream academic thoughts on poverty in the contemporary global system; a convincing illustration of the shortcomings of these thoughts on the case of Canada."

Samir Amin, President of the Third World Forum

"Bougrine quotes Nelson Mandela: 'Like slavery and apartheid, poverty is not natural. It is man-made and it can be overcome and eradicated by the actions of human beings.' But what actions? Many have written passionately about these and related topics. What Hassan Bougrine brings to the table is that he is also an expert monetary theorist, and is therefore well able to suggest plausible 'means and ways'."

John Smithin, York University, Toronto

T0358898

The Creation of Wealth and Poverty

There is a failure of governments to provide the citizens of developing countries with the necessary ingredients for growth and development. This can only be explained by their inability to secure the sources of financing which ultimately allow them to "command" these ingredients.

The Creation of Wealth and Poverty is a study of the means and ways by which wealth and poverty are created in both developed and developing countries. It puts a particular emphasis on the role played by economic policy in shaping the stratification of modern societies through specific programmes dealing with issues of job creation, poverty and environmental degradation. This book is concerned with the social effects of the ongoing crisis in finance, development and the environment. By focusing on the political, legal and financial institutions that govern society and the economy, the book provides an analysis of wealth and poverty from a historical perspective. It shows how economic and social policies of the neoliberal model have led to a rise in unemployment, poverty and inequality and, therefore, made societies more polarized.

This volume will be of great interest to policymakers, academics and students who study political economy, development economics and macroeconomics.

Hassan Bougrine holds a PhD from the University of Ottawa and has been teaching at Laurentian University for nearly 30 years where he is currently the Chair of the Economics Department. He has been a Visiting Professor and scholar at many institutions in Latin America, Europe and Africa.

Routledge Frontiers of Political Economy

The Creation of Wealth and Poverty

Means and Ways

Hassan Bougrine

LONDON AND NEW YORK

First published 2017
by Routledge

2 Park Square, Milton Park, Abingdon, Oxfordshire OX14 4RN
52 Vanderbilt Avenue, New York, NY 10017

Routledge is an imprint of the Taylor & Francis Group, an informa business

First issued in paperback 2020

British Library Cataloguing in Publication Data
A catalogue record for this book is available from the British Library

Library of Congress Cataloging in Publication Data
Names: Bougrine, Hassan, author.
Title: The creation of wealth and poverty : means and ways / Hassan
    Bougrine.
Description: 1 Edition. | New York : Routledge, 2017. | Includes index
Identifiers: LCCN 2016030487| ISBN 9781138816756 (hardback) |
    ISBN 9781315745954 (ebook)
Subjects: LCSH: Economic policy. | Economic development—
    Environmental aspects. | Social stratification. | Wealth. | Poverty
Classification: LCC HD87 .B68 2017 | DDC 339.4—dc23
LC record available at https://lccn.loc.gov/2016030487

ISBN: 978-1-138-81675-6 (hbk)
ISBN: 978-0-367-59567-8 (pbk)

Typeset in Times New Roman
by Swales & Willis, Exeter, Devon, UK

To my children Salma Bougrine and Karim Bougrine, with love forever, as you say.

Contents

Illustrations

Figures

Tables

Acknowledgements

I am particularly grateful to my colleague Brian K. MacLean who patiently read the entire manuscript and made thoughtful suggestions. I would also like to thank the following friends and colleagues who read various chapters of the book and provided me with valuable and helpful comments: Fletcher Baragar, Roy Culpeper, Radhika Desai, Adrien Faudot, Marc Lavoie, John Loxley, Thomas Michl, Anthony E. Myatt, Alain Parguez, Steven Pressman, Louis-Philippe Rochon, Sergio Rossi, Mario Seccareccia, John Serieux, John Smithin, Brenda Spotton-Visano and Matías Vernengo.

Introduction

The process by which wealth and poverty are created often escapes most people because the manner in which it works is quite subtle. It is not obvious because its mechanics are intricately woven into the institutions that govern our daily lives, bringing us to accept the outcome as our fate, however unfortunate it might be. But when contradictions between wealth and poverty force social classes into confrontation, the process is exposed: it resides in the power to design and implement particular economic and social policies. Our constructed institutions, from the obligation to pay taxes and honour contracts, through the education system and to the requirement of absolute respect for property rights, simply legitimize that outcome and make the obligations not only morally but also legally binding. Each time a society designs a system to ensure some form of order in the production, distribution and consumption of resources, it always relies on the power of these institutions to enforce the day-to-day workings of that process.

This recognition forces us to study closely the sources of power conferred onto those who are in charge of policymaking. Some of the leading scholars in the study of inequality and poverty have come to the conclusion that the entrenched elite that today dictates its austerity policies on the rest of the population benefits from a strong support of an oligarchy that uses its wealth to gain control of the political process and, therefore, of the making of economic policy (e.g. Galbraith, 2012, 2016; Stiglitz, 2013, 2016; Hudson, 2015). Social stratification, i.e. the division of societies into poor and wealthy – though not peculiar to capitalism – has recently become polarized, and the oligarchy has succeeded in turning government into a "predator state" (see Galbraith, 2008) and economic policy into an instrument of "class warfare"; according to the ILO (2014) and the Organization for Economic Cooperation and Development (OECD) (2012, 2015), the implementation of austerity policies since the 1980s has made long-term unemployment and part-time work the new stylized facts, which resulted in a fall of the share of labour in national income in most OECD countries.

One of the most popular explanations for the existence of poverty is the notion of "scarcity" – meaning that there is not enough to go around, whether we are talking about food or money. Scarcity of money, as it turns out, is the overarching argument used to justify all the ills in society. It justifies hunger and malnutrition, homelessness and illiteracy, lack of healthcare and all other manifestations of poverty.

This book takes the view that poverty is not inevitable. It is not the fate and should not be the destiny of the weak and powerless people in a modern society. Poverty is man-made and as such it can also be eliminated by intelligent economic and social policies.[1] As Stiglitz (2015: 6) stated about inequality, it is the result of "a choice we make with the rules we create to structure our economy".

Even though the fight against poverty in the so-called developing countries has been on the agenda of the United Nations at least since the 1970s and the World Bank's motto has been 'a world free of poverty' for just as long, a cursory assessment indicates that their policies have been a total failure. Indeed, the most recent report of the World Bank (2016) itself informs us that poverty in Africa alone has increased by another 100 million people since 1990 – and blamed that on 'population growth'. Many scholars have questioned the seriousness of such aims to fight poverty and point to the hostility in the dominant political and intellectual discourse to an overall strategy that seeks to *eradicate* poverty.

The existence of wealth and poverty, often literally side by side, is perhaps the most fundamental and long-lasting contradiction in human history. Ownership of vital and productive resources is what sets apart the rich from the poor. In ancient societies, when human needs were basic and wealth meant getting the goods from nature to satisfy these "natural" needs, increased wealth simply translated into increased consumption and improved well-being. Wealth then meant all the things that are useful for satisfying needs and ensuring the well-being of their holder. Possession of these "things" became a necessity. In modern societies, the desire to accumulate wealth is no longer necessarily dictated or justified by such needs.

In his classic study of *Ancient Society*, Morgan (1877: 537) informs us that, in the earlier stages of human evolution, with the exception of some personal articles, the passion for possession of things had not entered the human mind: "Lands, as yet hardly a subject of property, were owned by the tribes in common, while tenement houses were owned jointly by their occupants". Anthropological evidence tells us that in these societies subsistence and well-being were in fact a collective task, and so people organized themselves in a way to maximize the welfare of the whole community. Social values encouraged the ability to gather and produce more goods and services for the community. Members took pride in doing this because protecting their community against the calamities of nature meant their own individual protection. Together they were stronger; and they knew it instinctively. This behaviour was guaranteed – and reinforced – through the democratic practice of *reciprocity* and strict *redistribution* (see Polanyi, 1944). Economic scarcity, i.e. poverty, was not an individual problem. Like natural catastrophes, it was faced collectively and solved through sharing and equal redistribution.

Economic scarcity became an individual problem when redistribution ceased to be equal. That tragic turning point in human history occurred when the *function* of distribution was snatched by "powerful families of influential men . . . the ruling aristocracy, [and] . . . the administrative bureaucracy" (Thurnwald, 1932: 106). For it was then that these 'distributors' secured their direct control over the distribution of fertile land, water rights and other goods and services essential for survival, which then gave them the "power to govern by reward and punishment through providing and withholding" the resources under their control and "to dispossess the means of subsistence from those persons who failed to contribute labor demanded of them, who failed to produce sufficient resources, or who secretly accumulated resources" (Haas, 1981: 96–8). Property, ownership of vital resources, became the instrument of social control.

In this context, Morgan (1877: 560–1) noted that "Property and office were the foundations upon which aristocracy planted itself" and started disturbing "the balance of society by introducing unequal privileges, and degrees of respect for individuals among people of the same nationality, and thus became the source of discord and strife". For sure there was opposition to such stratification, but there is overwhelming evidence that the primitive state that emerged henceforth resorted to the use of brutal force to uphold decisions made by these distributors who enjoyed increasing power by *withholding* resources from their fellow citizens – that is, by creating an artificial scarcity to make them hungry, homeless, cold and so on in order to force them into submission and obedience.

Today, the neoliberal state uses austerity policies, which are based on the notion of scarcity, to achieve the same objective of diverting more resources to the dominant class – which is armed and empowered by its ownership of vital resources, the most important of which is financial capital. Unlike primitive societies, however, in which exclusion and privation from access to resources took a direct physical form and in which one may have relied on henchmen to enforce the unequal distribution, in parliamentary democracies we prefer to do it through the market. In market economies, access to goods and services and the acquisition of assets depend on the person's income so that the unemployed and low-income earners are legally subjected to deprivation and exclusion through market forces.

Since then, the desire to own, the passion for possession and the "greed of gain" have grown so much that they have become such commanding forces in defining the social stratification and in shaping the relations among individuals and between classes. In the last quarter of the nineteenth century, Morgan (1877: 561) wrote that, in modern society, the "outgrowth of [private] property has been so immense, its forms so diversified, its uses so expanding and its management so intelligent in the interests of its owners . . . that the human mind stands bewildered in the presence of its own creation". Obviously, Morgan had not known anything about the esoteric financial products of today, but probably he would not have been surprised given that he had noticed the trend towards a "property career" and hoped that it would not become the final destiny of humankind. Alas, our modern capitalist society is built on a system of private ownership that extends beyond tangible resources to include knowledge and ideas as property rights to 'inventions' or 'innovations', which are now protected by universally recognized standard laws on intellectual property in the form of copyrights, trademarks and patents and have become a source of income and wealth for their owners.

The purpose of property law is to ensure exclusion and provide the guarantee that wealth remains 'in the family' by transmitting it to the heirs. That is why many of the rich families today were also rich several centuries ago (see Barone and Mocetti, 2016). Although there are cases of social mobility as some fortunate rich "can emerge from within the crowd", to use Tocqueville's expression, wealth inheritance continues to play a major role and ensures that children born into rich families remain rich and the poor may even experience worse standards of living than their parents. Poverty, although lived and suffered by individuals, is a collective problem; a social problem in that it affects only certain people and never others. As long as there is no active government redistributive policies the status quo is maintained and can go on for generations, even centuries. Wealth and affluence are the foundations of personal power and influence in society. That is why it is important to insist on democracy in government in order to benefit from the power of policymaking, which can be used as a lever to eliminate poverty and achieve democracy in the economic and social spheres.

Poverty is a wicked form of social retribution, for there is no worse punishment than letting a person suffer until they succumb to death for lack of food. The United Nations estimates that about 3 million children under five years of age die every year because of malnutrition. Despite all the brouhaha of non-governmental organizations (NGOs), which make a lot of money from the business of helping the poor (see Rashid, 2006), there is the tacit acceptance of a seemingly vengeful verdict 'let them die' – so as to reduce population, because of some deeply-seated Malthusian fears. During the heyday of structural adjustment programmes in Africa and Asia, the World Bank had in fact devised an even more radical solution to the 'Malthusian problem' by advocating and financially supporting a programme named 'family planning', which essentially consisted of pushing contraceptive pills among the poor, but often the preferred solution was to literally cut off poor women's fallopian tubes – an operation clinically known as sterilization. These clinical operations were performed in public hospitals 'for free' and presented as evidence of complying with the structural adjustment programme to ensure that governments receive financial assistance from the World Bank (see Connelly, 2008).

Population control through forced sterilization of women in poor countries had its theoretical justifications in a book by Ehrlich (1968: 3, 18) in which he warned of mass starvation because there were "too many people" and "too little food". These claims were sold as facts and quickly a chorus of individuals, organizations and institutions adopted the idea of overpopulation as humanity's number one problem: the United Nations with its UNDP, UNICEF, UNESCO, FAO, the WHO, the OECD and many more all argued that population growth was not sustainable and that something had to be done. To solve the problems of poverty, food scarcity, pollution and damage to the environment, population growth had to be reduced and for that procreation must forcibly be brought under control. Mass murder through permanent 'small' wars (see Amin, 2004) and death by starvation tacitly became acceptable solutions, and surprisingly many people were resigned to this fate and became oblivious to the tragedies – impassibly watching them unfold on their television screens as if the actors and the victims were only elves and trolls.

There is a reason for the spectators' apathy. Since colonial times, missionaries, reporters, novelists and scholars from the West have often portrayed old civilizations of the East and the South with 'their teeming millions' as potential threats. Ehrlich (1968: 1–2, 128–9), for instance, started chapter 1 of his book by stating that he came to understand the problem of population explosion 'emotionally' one night when he and his wife and daughter were returning to their hotel in Delhi. The streets of Delhi, he said, "seemed alive with people. People eating, people washing, people sleeping. People visiting, arguing, and screaming. People thrusting their hands through the taxi window, begging. People defecating and urinating. People clinging to buses. People herding animals. People, people, people, people".

After attributing the problem of abject poverty in India and other countries to "too many people", he then asked "Will they starve gracefully, without rocking the boat? Or will they attempt to overwhelm us in order to get what they consider to be their fair share?" – whence the unspoken words of the sentence 'let them die' or better yet, prevent them from being born. Note, however, that at the same time an extensive public policy of 'baby bonuses' was being generalized in most industrialized countries in order to increase fertility rates, because population there was ageing. Policymakers in these countries have also resorted – and still do – to immigration from Asia, Africa and the rest of the Americas to achieve the desired increase in population because they know that population is good for development, not necessarily an obstacle to it.

In an apparent attempt to diffuse the anger among those who are genuinely concerned with poverty and human development, and perhaps in order to appease the anguish of the poor, some international organizations and their economists have recently turned to the increasing use of the word "happiness" and have developed an "Index of Happiness" to argue that, among others, Africans might be poor but they are happy – and that is what counts (see, for instance, Layard, 2005). As part of its new Sustainable Development Goals,[2] the UN has again given itself another extension and now aims to eliminate extreme poverty by the year 2030. Its 'Sustainable Development Solutions Network' also publishes the *World Happiness Report*, which ironically in 2015 ranked Libya – a destroyed country, torn by war and run by militias – as 63rd, ahead of Greece, which was ranked as 102nd, on the happiness scale (see Helliwell *et al.*, 2015: figure 2.2). But that does not explain why refugees risk drowning in the Mediterranean Sea in the hope of reaching Greece, rather than staying in Libya to enjoy their "happiness".

Using the case of Greece and other peripheral European countries, Galbraith (2016) tells the story of the creation of wealth and poverty with vivid details. He shows how the political elite in Europe, backed by the powerful oligarchs and creditors, succeeds in imposing on Greece policies that determine the course of events – that is, what happens to the livelihoods of the unemployed, the public sector employees, the pensioners and the general mass of the population – mainly because Greece does not have its own money. The main lesson nations should learn is that national sovereignty matters when it comes to the creation of wealth and poverty.

Monetary sovereignty, as long maintained by Post-Keynesians, is indeed crucial for financing domestic development initiatives; and thus for fighting poverty. Along these lines, I argue here that the mechanics of money creation are deliberately shrouded in mystery and that in reality a sovereign (national) government, with its own Central Bank, faces no budget constraints. Using its own currency, the sovereign government can pay for any expenditure – whether it is related to building a new hospital, a school or a highway, or to the hiring of teachers, nurses, engineers or street sweepers – simply by creating new money. Whenever there is a need for improving the public infrastructure or for creating jobs, the government simply orders its Central Bank to debit its account and transfer the funds to the concerned recipients by crediting their accounts at commercial banks with an equal amount. The government becomes indebted to its Central Bank, but the private sector's recipients benefit from an income which they can use to buy goods and services or acquire assets and start building their wealth. Following such an analysis, we discover that the debt owed by the government to its Central Bank is actually a source of private wealth. Understanding money and how public spending is financed are essential because they effectively liberate the government from being subject to an imaginary budget constraint and allow it to actively pursue policies to achieve full employment and eliminate poverty.

It should be noted that the focus of this book is mainly on two interrelated issues: (1) democracy in government, and (2) the power of policymaking, which coincidently also correspond to the two priorities that Rodrik (2011) opts for in his political trilemma – the third being economic globalization. The pursuit of *direct democracy* is crucial because it gives the masses leverage on the political process, allowing them to have a say and participate directly in the design of economic and social policies that affect their lives – or in the rewriting of the rules that govern the economy, as Stiglitz (2015) would say. These are the essential ingredients of national sovereignty. From this perspective, political democracy is necessarily only one component of an *inclusive* democracy that extends to the economic and social spheres – all within the context of respect and care for nature and the environment.

In terms of the political trilemma, however, poor countries cannot afford the luxury of giving up globalization and attempting to grow as closed economies, as this would be venturing down a longer and winding road. They need access to foreign technology for their capital development, but they also need access to financing. These are the two major constraints frustrating developmental projects and they can only be overcome through international cooperation to work out a radical reform of the current international monetary system. Industrialization in developing countries is essential for progress and for the structural transformation of these economies in order to create jobs and fight poverty, but it should not replicate the experience of capitalist industrialization that was based on fossil fuels energy. The book concludes by recommending instead that the democratic state play a crucial role in making it all happen by supporting the green economy through public policy initiatives that are coherently integrated within an overall development strategy.

Notes

1 The late Nelson Mandela also remarked that "Like slavery and apartheid, poverty is not natural. It is man-made and it can be overcome and eradicated by the actions of human beings". In a speech available at the BBC online: http://news.bbc.co.uk/2/hi/uk_news/politics/4232603.stm, accessed 20 March 2016.
2 As officially stated, these goals are: (1) by 2030, eradicate extreme poverty for all people everywhere, currently measured as people living on less than $1.25 a day, and (2) reduce at least by half the proportion of men, women and children of all ages living in poverty in all its dimensions according to national definitions. See https://sustainabledevelopment.un.org/topics, accessed 20 March 2016.

References

Amin, S. (2004) *The Liberal Virus: Permanent War and the Americanization of the World* (New York: Monthly Review Press).

Barone, G. and S. Mocetti (2016) *Intergenerational Mobility in the Very Long Run: Florence 1427–2011*, Banca d'Italia: Working Papers, No. 1060.

Connelly, M. J. (2008) *Fatal Misconception: The Struggle to Control World Population* (Cambridge, MA: Harvard University Press).

Ehrlich, P. R. (1978 [1968]) *The Population Bomb* (New York: Ballantine Books).

Galbraith, J. K. (2008) *The Predator State: How Conservatives Abandoned the Free Market and Why Liberals Should Too* (New York: Free Press).

Galbraith, J. K. (2012) *Inequality and Instability: A Study of the World Economy Just Before the Future of Europe* (New Haven, CT: Yale University Press).

Galbraith, J. K. (2016) *Welcome to the Poisoned Chalice: The Destruction of Greece and the Great Crisis* (Oxford, UK: Oxford University Press).

Haas, J. (1981) "Class Conflict and the State in the New World", in Jones, G. D. and R. R. Kautz (eds), *The Transition to Statehood in the New World* (Cambridge, UK: Cambridge University Press, pp. 80–102).

Helliwell, J. F., Layard, R. and J. D. Sachs (2015) *World Happiness Report*, New York: The Earth Institute, available online: http://worldhappiness.report/, accessed 20 March 2016.

Hudson, M. (2015) *Killing the Host: How Financial Parasites and Debt Bondage Destroy the Global Economy* (Petrolia, CA: Counterpunch Books).

ILO [International Labour Organization] (2014) *Global Wage Report 2014/2015: Wages and Income Inequality* (Geneva: International Labour Office).

Layard, R. (2005) *Happiness: Lessons from a New Science* (New York: Penguin).

Morgan, L. H. (1877) *Ancient Society: Or Researches in the Lines of Human Progress from Savagery through Barbarism to Civilization*, New York: Holt & Co., available online from the *Internet Archive*: https://archive.org/details/ancientsociety00morg, accessed 20 March 2016.

OECD (2012) *OECD Employment Outlook 2012* (Paris: OECD Publishing).

OECD (2015) *OECD Employment Outlook 2015* (Paris: OECD Publishing).

Polanvyi, K. (1944) *The Great Transformation: The Political and Economic Origins of Our Time*, (Boston, MA: Beacon Press).

Rashid, S. (2006) "Watchman, Who Watches Thee? Donors and Corruption in Less-Developed Countries", *Independent Review* Vol. 10, No. 3, pp. 411–18.

Rodrik, D. (2011) *The Globalization Paradox: Democracy and the Future of the World Economy* (New York: W. W. Norton & Co.).

Stiglitz, J. E. (2013) *The Price of Inequality: How Today's Divided Society Endangers Our Future* (New York: W. W. Norton & Co.).

Stiglitz, J. E. (2015) *Rewriting the Rules of the American Economy: An Agenda for Shared Prosperity* (New York: Roosevelt Institute).

Stiglitz, J. E. (2016) *Rewriting the Rules of the American Economy: An Agenda for Growth and Shared Prosperity* (New York: W. W. Norton & Co.).

Thurnwald, R. (1969 [1932]) *Economics in Primitive Communities* (London: Oxford University Press).

World Bank (2016) *Poverty in a Rising Africa: Africa Poverty Report*, authored by Beegle, K., L. Christiaensen, A. Dabalen, and I. Gaddis (Washington, DC: The World Bank).

1 The state, the market and management of class relations

> They demand free enterprise, but are the spokesmen for monopoly and vested interest. Their final objective toward which all their deceit is directed is to capture political power so that, using the power of the state and the power of the market simultaneously, they may keep the common man in eternal subjection.
>
> Henry A. Wallace, Vice-President of the United States, 1944 (9 April)
> *New York Times.* Also quoted in Culver and Hyde (2000)

Introduction

Recent developments in anthropology, ethnography, economic history and various fields of other sciences bear testimony to the complexity and diversity of the ways in which human beings have historically organized their relationships to form communities and build institutions. However, if we focus on certain aspects of the economic life of these communities, it becomes relatively easy to identify at least the essential elements that played an important role in such an evolution. In this chapter, I will concentrate on the study of the emergence and evolution of two major institutions: the state and the market because they represent the centre of power in modern societies. Both the state and the market exert such an enormous influence on the lives of individuals, families and communities by making them healthy or sick, educated or ignorant, rich or poor – not to mention the impact on important character traits such as kindness or antipathy, altruism or selfishness and so on. It is true that *a priori* the state and the market appear as some mystical superstructures that are above everyone and escape the control or manipulation of anyone. But this is not so. As we shall see below, the state and the market are institutions that were *created* by humans and as such they are nothing more than instruments that can be – and routinely are – used by their creators to achieve defined goals and objectives.

In most societies today, the economically dominant class has gained some extraordinary powers and hegemony thereby rendering the state a subservient agent, but still an agent with powers (judicial and military, or the "ministry of police" as Jeremy Bentham (1797) would call it) that are used to assert the ideals of the market and implement the actions and decisions required to achieve those ideals. This scenario is referred to here as the laissez-faire or the neoliberal model of economic and social organization, which in practice translates to a dialectic relationship between power and wealth: concentration of wealth leads to a concentration of power, which in turn reinforces the concentration of wealth – thus supporting the 'rich-get-richer' dynamic. How we can liberate the state from such enslavement by powerful private interests is the main topic of this chapter and the following one. The alternative scenario in which the state emerges as the dominant agent using and directing the market to achieve higher goals of social development and growth for the benefit of all – or at least the grand majority of – the members of the population, will be called the egalitarian model. By studying and comparing the two models, I hope to elucidate the intricacies of the relationship between the state and the market. This is of paramount importance because the main preoccupation today among both intellectuals and grassroots activists is the type of economic model and policies that should prevail in a democratic society.

Even though in the more recent literature the neoliberals talk about small government and invariably attempt to equate the idea of a free, self-regulating market with the absence of the state, in reality they call for a big and omnipresent government with all the powers it needs to ensure that the principles of laissez-faire are adhered to. As Polanvyi (1944: 140, 250) commented, "the road to the free market was opened and kept open by an enormous increase in continuous, centrally organized and controlled interventionism" and that "the market has been the outcome of a conscious and often violent intervention on the part of government which imposed the market organization on society for noneconomic ends". This conscious and tenacious effort to use the state apparatus to promote and impose the market system for more than two centuries now clearly tells us two things: (1) without the state, the market system would not have evolved to be what it is today, and (2) because it is imposed on society by a government that lacks democratic credentials, the ideology of free markets cannot survive if society resorts to universal suffrage as a means of organizing its political system – whence, we are led to the conclusion that the neoliberal model is not compatible with *direct* democracy.

The above observations lead us to examine more closely the emergence of the state and the market as organizing mechanisms of social relations since the early stages of human evolution. Going back to ancient societies is important because it allows us to understand how these two institutions came into existence. The present chapter does not pretend to offer a detailed or comprehensive historical account of the emergence and evolution of the market and the state. I will, however, survey some of the relevant literature to highlight the crucial events and turning points in their long trajectory as they evolved from their archaic primitive form towards their modern manifestations. The purpose is to be informed about the past and use it as a background to compare with the current neoliberal system. In so doing, I will attempt to answer one fundamental question: Why did human beings, even in their primitive communities, ever think about creating a state and a market? In other words, what was their motivation for wanting to create these institutions and for what purpose did they need them?

The primitive state and its economic role

Because they live, and must live, with each other out of necessity, in (small or large) groups, in (close or distant) communities, people necessarily maintain relationships with their fellows at home (to do the household chores), at work (to produce the necessities of life) and at play (to show and display their beliefs, to celebrate life). Anthropological evidence tells us that these relations are not the same everywhere but take various and diverse forms over space and time. People's behaviour towards one another does not remain random and unpredictable. Over time, with custom and perhaps religious belief, it becomes codified, institutionalized in tacit or written agreements, for example, of cooperation and mutual assistance such as by giving help to one another through the supply of free labour or goods. The goods can be exchanged in different ways. For instance, the donor of the goods can bring them to the home of the needy, the receiver or the two can agree to meet in a specified place on a given time, i.e. in a market place.[1] Hence, the market covers only one aspect of the diverse and complex web of human relationships and its emergence cannot be explained by the individual's cold calculations and desire for material gain and profit, as in Adam Smith's (1776: 25) "propensity to barter, truck and exchange one thing for another".

These codes of behaviour are often and even always honoured willingly, but their respect is also ensured by the moral, religious and political authority of the local, regional or national chiefs and leaders who may, of course, impose themselves as despots but are often chosen because of their wisdom, knowledge or courage to look after the good functioning of the system (economic and social relations) and thus protect members of their community from things such as abuse from others or aggression from members of other communities. In addition, the chiefs, i.e. the 'primitive' state, also called for the provision of collective help and relief in the face of threats by natural disasters resulting in a shortage of resources. Economic and social security of the individual members was guaranteed by the whole community. This is what the 'primitive' state has done and this is what the modern state is supposed to do: offer protection, economic and social security to all members of society, including protection against unemployment, exploitation and scarcity. When it fails, or intentionally refuses, to do so, we must understand that social justice and protection no longer constitute a priority on the agenda of our political leaders, the modern chiefs, and that instead they have armed themselves to defend the interests of the powerful economic class. In that case, the choice is clear and the natural human impulse, the urge, for protection calls for the alternative, democratic state.

In addition to its political function, the state has always had an economic role. In fact, as we shall see below, the state came into being primarily for economic reasons. Its much-emphasized role of keeping 'law and order' has always been, and still is, centred on keeping the *economic order*. In his influential book, *The Great Transformation*, Karl Polanyi (1944) noted that no human society can survive for a long time without a system that ensures some form of order in the production, distribution and consumption of resources. Polanyi also noted that an economic order is necessarily determined within its social context, which gives it its particular shape and structure in conformity with the prevailing set of cultural values – hence the diversity of economic and social forms of organization. This is a general observation that applies to modern as well as to primitive societies. To understand the question of how diverse economic and social organizations are formed, how they are reproduced and how they evolve, we must go beyond the arbitrary separation between history and anthropology, sociology and economics. Economic relations are only one aspect of human life and whether they pertain to the production of goods (and services), redistribution and exchange, or consumption of such, they reflect – and necessarily are the product of – the prevailing historical conditions, which include the level of (social, technological) development with its modes of thinking, beliefs, religion and culture (Godelier, 1974).

Anthropologist George Dalton (1961: 21, emphasis added), who studied primitive economies in different parts of the world, concluded that "transactions of material goods in primitive society are expressions of *social obligation* which have neither mechanism nor meaning of their own apart from the social ties and social situations they express". Thurnwald (1932: xiii) put it even more emphatically by stating that "the characteristic feature of primitive economics is the absence of any desire to make profits from production or exchange . . . Generous gifts, however, are unquestionably received with gratitude, although such prodigality has generally to be returned with corresponding lavishness". Thurnwald (1932: 106) added that:

> [t]he idea is that the person receiving his or her share will be ready tomorrow to give the same to the distributor of today. Today's giving will be recompensed by tomorrow's taking. This is the outcome of the principle of reciprocity which pervades every relation of primitive life and is exemplified in many other ways.

Here, the exchange of goods (as well as their production and consumption) is organized along the prevailing customs, habits and the general 'code of behaviour'. The reciprocal gift-giving and the equal distribution of the goods among the members of the community are two important characteristics of the early 'simple', i.e. *not stratified* primitive societies. Following the anthropological works of Thurnwald (1932), Malinowski (1939) and Sahlins (1958, 1972), it is now widely accepted that social organization in primitive societies was based on the principles of *reciprocity* and *redistribution*. Polanyi (1944: 50–53) maintains that in egalitarian and democratic societies, reciprocity and strict redistribution worked as a wonderful system; concluding that "the result is a stupendous organizational achievement in the economic field". Such a system does indeed deserve praise because even though individuals receive no remuneration for their labour and do not get any personal gain or profit from giving away the product of their labour, they still work hard[2] for the common goal of "producing and storing for the satisfaction of the wants of members of the group".

The underlying reasons that ensure the continuous functioning and reproduction of such an organization are nicely summarized by Polanyi (1944: 46, emphasis added) and it is worth quoting him at length:

> The individual's economic interest is rarely paramount, for the community keeps all its members from starving unless it is itself borne down by catastrophe, in which case interests are again threatened collectively, not individually. The maintenance of social ties, on the other hand, is crucial. First, because by disregarding the accepted code of honor, or generosity, the individual cuts himself off from the community and becomes an outcast; second, because, in the long run, all social obligations are reciprocal, and their fulfilment serves also the individual's give-and-take interests best. Such a situation must exert a continuous pressure on the individual to eliminate economic self-interest from his consciousness . . . This attitude is reinforced by the frequency of communal activities such as partaking of food from the common catch or sharing in the results of some far-flung and dangerous tribal expedition. *The premium set on generosity is so great when measured in terms of social prestige as to make any other behavior than that of utter self-forgetfulness simply not pay.*

As for redistribution, it can be said that for as long as it consisted of giving back to the members of the group what *they* have 'produced and stored', it worked very well. Carneiro (1981: 60) wrote that redistribution in the egalitarian communities meant "the complete and equitable reassignment of a village's harvest back to its producers by a chief who is merely a temporary and benign custodian of it". Unfortunately, the dynamics of social relations are such that the outcome of their evolution cannot always be predicted. Redistribution in larger communities would understandably require more than just the diligent work of the benevolent chief. In his study of primitive communities, Thurnwald (1932: 106–8, emphasis added) reported that:

> [a]mong some tribes . . . there is an intermediary in the person of a headman, or other prominent member of the community. He receives and distributes all supplies. The consequences arising from this fact appear to be far-reaching. With these people distribution is still effected on a democratic basis, but in graded and *stratified* societies distribution is the function of powerful families of influential men, of the ruling aristocracy, or of the administrative bureaucracy; and it is often abused. The distributors of any political power *reserve a percentage of the profits for themselves.*

The question, of course, is how big a percentage these distributors keep for themselves.[3] No wonder distribution is arguably *the* most problematic and most debated issue in human societies ever since their primitive stages. Thurnwald also noted that:

[t]he distribution function increases with the growing political power of a few families and the rise of despots. The chief receives the gifts of the peasants, which have now become "taxes", and distributes them among his officials, especially those attached to his court.

He added that "a more extensive area controlled by a despot necessitates an increase in the number of warehouses, granaries, and treasuries, and a corresponding increase in the number of officials required for their management", therefore justifying the calls for more 'gifts' and contributions, i.e. the levy of even higher taxes.

Even though most anthropologists consider 'redistribution' as the basis for the rise of chiefdoms and the state, Carneiro (1981: 58 emphasis added) made the interesting observation that "what a chief gains from redistribution proper is esteem, not power. Power accrues to him only when he *ceases* to redistribute food and goods wholesale and begins to appropriate and concentrate them". In other words, the chief gets power by *withholding* resources from his fellow citizens, i.e. by creating an artificial scarcity to make them hungry, homeless, cold and so on and force them into submission, obedience and allegiance. And when he does give food and other goods through redistribution, he makes them feel not only thankful but mostly indebted to him so that when he comes around next time to collect "the taxes", they all obligingly contribute! In any case, by now taxes are no longer voluntary. Use of force, coercion and violence against the populace to force them to pay taxes to the chief but also to supply labour has been recorded in chiefdoms from various parts around the world. Thus the Pharaohs of Egypt, the Zulu chiefs of South Africa or the Tahitian chiefs of Polynesia had all accumulated "the power to govern by reward and punishment through providing and withholding the economic goods and services they control" (Haas, 1981: 96). Of the Polynesian chief, Sahlins (1958: 19) said that "coercive force was applied by the chief in punishing those who infringed his rights, especially if the transgressors were low in status". Carneiro (1981: 61) noted that:

[b]y the selective distribution of food, goods, booty, women, and the like the chief rewards those who have rendered him service. Thus he builds up a core of officials, warriors, henchmen, retainers, and the like who will be personally loyal to him and through whom he can issue orders and have them obeyed. In short, it is through the shrewd and self-interested disbursement of taxes that the administrative machinery of the chiefdom (and the state) is built up.

Interest in the origin of the state and its nature arose early among philosophers and researchers in various fields of social sciences who have been debating the subject for a long time. A concise historical survey of their views, particularly since the period of Enlightenment, is given by Service (1975) in his book on the *Origins of the State and Civilization*. A more recent review of the vast literature on the subject can be found in Haas (1981) who summarized the debate by categorizing the numerous explanations into two main theories: (1) *conflict* (or coercive, class, radical) theories, and (2) *integration* (or contract, consensus, conservative) theories. Haas (1981: 80) commented that "the basic conflict argument is that the state developed primarily as a coercive mechanism to resolve internal conflict that arises between economically stratified classes within a society", whereas in integration theories the state is seen "as an integrative mechanism to coordinate and regulate the different parts of complex societies. Basically, they see the state as a nonpartisan institution of government that provides organizational benefits to the society as a whole". Haas (1981) put both theories to the test and, citing archaeological evidence from Peru and Mesoamerica, concluded that those who were *governors* and wielded political power were also economically well-endowed, i.e. they were wealthy, had a better diet and lived in lavish houses and palaces whereas the *governed* were poor, with a clear *pattern* of restricted access to basic resources such as food, tools, and protective devices – thus confirming the class explanation to the origin of the state.

Moreover, Haas (1981: 88–95) also gave evidence that the chiefs, governmental rulers, had direct managerial control over the distribution of land, water rights, and other goods and services essential for survival, which gave them the power "to dispossess the means of subsistence from those persons who failed to contribute labor demanded of them, who failed to produce sufficient resources, or who secretly accumulated resources" (Haas, 1981: 98). What is even more important is that the high-status people, the upper class of the wealthy and the governors, had people from the lower status working for them and that there was hostility and antagonism, even rebellion and revolt[4] within society because "persons with restricted access to resources would contest, rather than accept, the unequal distribution of those resources" (Haas, 1981: 90). The antagonism between social classes was the basic premise upon which Karl Marx and Frederick Engels built their theory of the state. Their view is summarized in the following statement by Engels (1884: 160), in his book on *The Origin of the State, the Family and Private Property* where he stated that:

> Because the state arose from the need to hold class antagonisms in check, but because it arose, at the same time, in the midst of the conflict of these classes, it is, as a rule, the state of the most powerful, economically dominant class, which, through the medium of the state, becomes also the politically dominant class, and thus acquires new means of holding down and exploiting the oppressed class.

The main contention of the integration theorists (Service, 1962, 1975) is that the origin of the state is not based on class antagonism, but none of them can deny that once the state had emerged as a political entity with power to control and command the citizens under its jurisdiction, it was then vulnerable to yielding to influence from the economically well-endowed members of the community or to even willingly defend their interests, for these will also coincide with, and help reinforce, the interests and power of the 'politicians'. In any case, the difference in focus among these theories on whether the origin of the state was class-based or not is really not crucial for the purpose of this book, which is concerned with economic policies in today's societies. And today, no one can deny that capitalism is a class-based society and that the capitalist class – represented not only by the industrialists as Godelier (1974: viii) has said but also by the financiers – commands much power over the design and implementation of policies by the present neoliberal state.

The neoliberal state and the policies of pauperization

There is now a large number of books and articles about the meaning, nature and history of neoliberalism. An electronic search for 'neoliberalism' shows several thousands of peer-reviewed scholarly entries. The great majority of these writings examine neoliberalism from a critical point of view – emphasizing various aspects of what neoliberalism does to the workplace, to families, to consumption and culture, to trade and finance and so on. A good account of these ill effects is provided by Smith (2016) in his *Imperialism in the Twenty-First Century*. In spite of the divergent theoretical persuasions of these analyses, they all reach the same conclusion: neoliberalism hurts the poor and the working class, and benefits the rich, the elite and the capitalist class. This conclusion forms the basis for the political opposition to the neoliberal model or agenda, as is often referred to in the leftist political literature. However, a closer examination of this critical literature reveals that there is no agreement about what neoliberalism is. In fact, one often finds vague, ambiguous and even contradictory definitions of neoliberalism – identifying the latter as a higher stage of capitalism, imperialism, globalization, libertarianism, neo-conservatism and conservative right-wing governments (see Kotz, 2015).

The above type of analyses could be sufficient if the aim were only to garner wider support for opposing neoliberalism and decrying what it does. But if the objective is to propose an alternative to it, then we need a more systematic analysis that would lay bare the philosophical foundations of neoliberalism, its principles and ideas and most importantly the manner by which these ideas are turned into concrete economic and social policies, that is, the use of the state apparatus. For this purpose, neoliberalism is defined here as both: (a) a system of thought that exalts individualism and the role of markets, and (b) an ensemble of politically active and committed intellectuals whose aim is to literally *capture* (national and international) institutions and use them to implement their ideas in the form of a policy package (see Ostry *et al.*, 2016).

Does it mean that neoliberalism is a political party? No. A secret society? No. But to be sure, Hayek (1944) and his colleagues did not just put their ideas 'out on the market' and then go to sleep.[5] They sought media coverage to disseminate their ideas and actively courted influential people and corporations to adopt and defend their cause by setting up and financing a dedicated network of right-wing think thanks – thus recruiting an army of intellectuals and politicians, from various parts of the world, who would work on finding ways to transform current social structures into conformity with the neoliberal ideals (see Desai, 1994). In short, they are not only engaged in what Herman and Chomsky (1988) called 'manufacturing consent' but also in policymaking, that is, in using the political power of the state – whether it is a political democracy or a military dictatorship – to implement their ideas and institutionalize their policies. In this respect, it is important to remember that the first experiments with neoliberalism actually took place in Chile under the fascist dictatorship of Augusto Pinochet in the early 1970s (see Monbiot, 2016) and then, from 1979 onwards, were generalized to practically all African countries in the form of 'structural adjustment programmes' sponsored by the World Bank and the IMF – institutions which had already been partly or wholly captured by neoliberal ideologues (see Mirowski, 2013).

In the introduction to the 50th anniversary edition of Hayek's *Road to Serfdom* (Friedman, 1994: xv), Milton Friedman sounded exasperated by what he called "the fact of growing intellectual support of collectivism". After wondering "why is it that intellectual classes everywhere almost automatically range themselves on the side of collectivism – even when chanting individualist slogans – and denigrate and revile capitalism?", he then went on to affirm that the battle must be won and that the socialists must be defeated. This tells us that neoliberalism has a cause. It wants to defeat socialism, collectivism and any form of cooperative social organization.[6] Helping others through the concerted actions of the community such as social programmes must be ruled out because it implies that individuals are forced to pay taxes in order to support such programmes and help others and that is a loss of liberty and freedom (Nozick, 1974). According to Friedman (1962: 190–1), one way to help others:

> [a]nd in many ways the most desirable, is private charity. It is noteworthy that the heyday of laissez-faire, the middle and late nineteenth century in Britain and the United States, saw an extraordinary proliferation of private eleemosynary organizations and institutions. One of the major costs of the extension of governmental welfare activities has been the corresponding decline in private charitable activities.

Moreover, Friedman and Friedman (1980: 5) considered social programmes as part of a paternalistic system in which dominates "the view that government's role is to serve as a parent charged with the duty of coercing some to aid others". This echoes Friedman's (1962: 195) earlier statement on the issue of equality when he wrote:

> He [the egalitarian] will defend taking from some to give to others, not as a more effective means whereby the "some" can achieve an objective they want to achieve, but on grounds of "justice". At this point, equality comes sharply into conflict with freedom; one must choose. One cannot be both an egalitarian, in this sense, and a liberal.

In fact, as argued by Plant (2009: 6–7), neoliberals go further than that. They see the rule of law as "a framework of general rules for the achievement of private ends" and believe that:

> There is no such thing as a substantive common good for the state to pursue and for the law to embody and thus the political pursuit of something like social justice or a greater sense of solidarity and community lies outside the rule of law.

As a system of thought, even though it is not homogenous and is changing as it evolves over time, neoliberalism remains the incarnation of an ideology that openly preaches greed, selfishness and individualism (Hayek, 1944; Friedman, 1962; Nozick, 1974). Neoliberals often, but not always, do it by the book. It is as if their project is not yet finalized, which makes it very flexible, indeed malleable as it is an amalgam of some naïve and some very extreme ideas – hence the seeming discrepancy between theoretical propositions and concrete applications: neoliberalism thrives under benevolent governments with an extensive social welfare system, under military dictatorships with no provisions for workers' and political rights but also under political democracy where the elite still resorts to the use of the state to impose policies such as those based on austerity. Mirowski (2014) is right to call this constantly evolving project a *Neoliberal Thought Collective* of a "political movement that dared not speak its own name". Mirowski's description of neoliberalism echoes Polanyi's (1944) description of classical liberalism. Indeed, the similarity is quite striking since what Mirowski says of the neoliberals' praxis is exactly what Polanyi said about liberals when he argued that they rely heavily on the use of the power of the state to shape the market in order to achieve their desired objectives. Polanyi (1944: 140–1) wrote:

> [t]he introduction of free markets, far from doing away with the need for control, regulation, and intervention, enormously increased their range. Administrators had to be constantly on the watch to ensure the free working of the system. Thus even those who wished most ardently to free the state from all unnecessary duties, and whose whole philosophy demanded the restriction of state activities, could not but entrust the self-same state with the new powers, organs, and instruments required for the establishment of laissez-faire.

Polanyi-Levitt and Seccareccia (2016) have also pointed out the relevance of Polanyi's (1944) analysis for understanding the current neoliberal ideology.

Concerning the ambivalent attitude of the neoliberals towards the state, let us note that Friedman himself changed his mind about the need for a strong state to guarantee competition. Back in 1944, Hayek had agreed to some sort of a guaranteed minimum income for those who are in need. Hayek actually went as far as to suggest that the state can play an important role in ensuring social protection. It may sound inconsistent with the neoliberal project, but here is what Hayek (1944: 125) wrote:

[t]here can be no doubt that some minimum of food, shelter, and clothing, sufficient to preserve health and the capacity to work, can be assured to everybody . . . Nor is there any reason why the state should not assist the individuals in providing for those common hazards of life against which, because of their uncertainty, few individuals can make adequate provision. Where, as in the case of sickness and accident, neither the desire to avoid such calamities nor the efforts to overcome their consequences are as a rule weakened by the provision of assistance, where, in short, we deal with genuinely insurable risks, the case for the state helping to organise a comprehensive system of social insurance is very strong.

Hayek's early ideas were willingly muddled in the vast array of propositions that make up what Mirowski (2013) calls the "neoliberal thought collective", which has been developing under the guidance of the Mont Pelerin Society, created in 1947 by Hayek to bring together into a network philosophers, economists, journalists and private foundations whose goal is to promote free market ideas. Indeed, it was during the 1950s and 1960s that neoliberals started sharpening their ideas and focusing on freedom and the role of markets. With Friedman as their outspoken leader, neoliberal writers tirelessly repeated that the realization of their values can only happen in a 'free' society and through the functioning of free and unfettered markets. Friedman (1962: 191), for instance, insisted that any "program should, while operating through the market, not distort the market or impede its functioning". Programmes that deliver public services such as education, health care or unemployment benefits must be dismantled; and the delivery of these services must be entrusted to private corporations. Neoliberalism wants every aspect of human relations to be governed by the market, including work and nature (see Polanyi, 1944). Where markets do not exist, they must be created (see Harvey, 2005). This is where neoliberals have been active and this is where they have had a lot of success. They have created markets for just about everything.[7] How do they do it?

This is neoliberalism in practice and the logic is in fact quite simple. Since the overriding objective is to empower that individual (not just any individual but the one) who is already 'well-endowed' to make more money (see Baker, 2006) and since such a task can only be accomplished through transactions with other members of the society, then it is obvious that commodities (of whatever nature, goods or services) must be created. And commodities require markets. This is where neoliberals deploy most of their efforts. In addition to engineering consent among the population by cultivating a market culture through the intensive use of shocking and provocative marketing images and messages, they also make a shrewd use of political power and institutions. This work is carried out by an army of "ideological entrepreneurs" who are very well organized in a worldwide network of think tanks that "helped turn neoliberal thought into a neoliberal political program" (Stedman Jones, 2012: 184). The heavy reliance on the use of various institutions has also been noted by Desai (1994), Bougrine (2012) and Mirowski (2013), among others. Mirowski (2013, 2014) provides a good account of the proliferation of these think tanks worldwide and how they work hard to get a hold of the centre of policymaking.

For instance, the strategy followed by neoliberals in privatizing public services is surprisingly similar from Chile to Mexico, from Britain to Egypt and from Morocco to South Africa: they first get hold of political power, either through elections or through a military coup d'état – since the end justifies the means, the government then legislates and legitimizes cuts to the public funding of these services; thus making their provision problematic (in terms of availability and quality) to recipients while at the same time encouraging the creation of private, competing enterprises by offering sizeable subsidies. When public corporations and sectors offering public services are choked off and start crumbling, the state proceeds to sell them to private interests, usually in dubious deals and at fire-sale prices, with little or no objection from the general public who has now been largely appeased. This was true in education, health care, water, electricity, telephone and postal services and so on. The irony is that privatization in Morocco, for instance, was handled by a 'socialist' minister and in South Africa it occurred under the presidency of the late Nelson Mandela and his fellow ex-communists.[8] But irony became wicked in Greece where, as noted by Galbraith (2016):

> In the case of the Port of Piraeus, in line for sale to the state-owned Chinese firm Cosco, one had the interesting postmodern twist of a left-wing government in a capitalist country imposing labor standards on a right-wing company from a communist country.

Furthermore, in order to generalize the business-like atmosphere, policymakers from around the world, infatuated as they are with neoliberalism, adopted what became known as 'new public management'. This mode of 'good' or 'best-practice' governance of public institutions uses the profit-seeking corporate model as a reference. Public sector employees are no longer 'public servants' working for the common good of the society. Instead, they are told to behave as self-motivated managers working to deliver goods and services to their 'customers' in the most efficient way. 'Customers' now include patients seeking health care in a hospital and students seeking knowledge and learning in a university (see Weeks, 2014: 88–9). Government entities and public corporations would now behave like private enterprises and must be subjected to the usual criteria of cost-benefit analyses, performance-based evaluation and so on to gauge their competitiveness (see Steger and Roy, 2010). Using a trick called decentralization or devolution, neoliberal policymakers remove entities that deliver public services from the responsibility of central governments and put them under the financial responsibility of lower-tier or local governments – a strategic move that would facilitate their closure or sale to private investors when they become uncompetitive or insolvent since now they become dependent on local taxes (essentially property taxes) and user fees.

The introduction of markets or their liberalization did not rely on democratic means only. The use of force, shock and awe, is part of the 'shock treatment', which was conceived by Milton Friedman and his 'Chicago Boys'[9] in the early

1970s for Chile under the dictatorship of Pinochet. Later on, throughout the 1980s and 1990s, countries accustomed to despotic regimes in Africa and Latin America and those of the disintegrating Soviet bloc all provided fertile grounds for experimenting with different degrees of 'shocks' and forms of neoliberalism (Campbell, 2013). In Eastern Europe and ex-Soviet republics, markets were introduced overnight to help hastily build a savage type of capitalism with fast-track privatization and where all the rights hitherto achieved by workers in Western Europe were rejected and denied to the new working class in these countries: it was Jeffrey Sachs' 'shock therapy'; an updated version of Friedman's shock policy.

The worst and most brutal version of shock therapy was applied to Iraq after its occupation in 2003, with overnight mass privatization and massive layoffs from the public sector, including the dismantling of the entire national army. War and destruction proved to be very profitable not only to the military-industrial complex but also to the firms involved in the 'reconstruction' – a scenario reminiscent of that described by Daniel Guérin (1945: 288) in his book *Fascism and Big Business* in which he showed that "the real nature of the fascist state" was nothing more than a "military and police dictatorship in the service of big business". More recently, Asimakopoulos (2014) and Pauwels (2013) gave a somewhat detailed account of the US corporations that effectively supported and supplied Hitler's Nazi regime and the fascists in Spain and Italy not only with equipment and ammunitions but also with services and commodities that are vital for a war. In this respect, several authors (e.g. Amin, 2004; Chossudovsky, 2005; Duncan and Coyne, 2013) have emphasized the recourse to military spending and the need for a 'permanent war economy' to solve domestic problems of unemployment and economic decline – a policy referred to as 'military Keynesianism', but truly loved by neoliberals who would now wear the hats of neo-cons.

In Africa, neoliberal policies were put in place under the banner of expanding further the 'structural adjustment programmes' in order to build the so-called macroeconomic fundamentals; as set out by the ideologues of the IMF and the World Bank. This policy package has been part of the IMF's conditionality since the 1980s and has become the all-time and everywhere favourite 'advice' given by its so-called experts; without any concern for the devastating effects on the local populations. The net effects of these programmes have been a drastic increase in poverty in the whole continent (World Bank, 2016). In South America, Stokes (2004: 45–52) reported on what she called "neoliberalism by surprise" during the early 1990s when presidential candidates campaigned and won using an 'anti-neoliberal', 'anti-shock' platform but once in power they turned into staunch neoliberals: they removed subsidies to the basic foodstuffs, increased prices, laid off public sector employees, privatized public corporations and so on. In the case of Fujimori of Peru, the switch occurred ten days before he took office – of course after meeting with international bankers and neoliberal advisers.

The immediate consequence of privatization has been an increase in unemployment because of the layoffs that typically precede the sale of public corporations. Here, the parallels between the neoliberal state and the primitive state become all too evident: while the primitive chiefs created artificial scarcity simply by *withholding* resources and thus forcing some members of the community into deprivation and poverty, the modern rulers create artificial scarcity by *denying* access to resources through legal and sophisticated means; and unemployment is one of these. The creation of poverty and deprivation through unemployment has long been recognized by scholars of various persuasions. The transfer of owner-ship/property of the collective good to some individuals reinforces the position of a class whose role and function in society is reminiscent of the primitive inter-mediaries (the headmen) who stood in charge of the distribution on behalf of the chief, with one fundamental difference: the primitive intermediaries were armed with sticks while the modern intermediaries are armed with *property rights* and empowered by the legal and institutional setting.

As mentioned earlier, even though neoliberals emphasize free markets and publicly scorn the state, implicitly they admire strong and coercive government and in their most pragmatic programmes they combine both market and state to achieve their goals. They rely on government in using its power to ensure the submission of the masses and thus guaranteeing the acceptance of the neolib-eral ideals as part of a worldwide project.[10] They understand that the power to implement neoliberal policies resides with institutions like parliaments, ministe-rial positions, local and international NGOs or international institutions like the IMF, the World Bank, the World Trade Organization, the United Nations and its various bodies. For instance, in her analysis of "the activities of individuals and organizations associated with the Mont Pelerin Society (MPS)", Bair (2009: 348) gives a vivid account of the well-coordinated attack by the think tank Heritage Foundation against the UN Center on Transnational Corporations (UNCTC) and its work on economic independence and sovereignty, ultimately leading to the dismantling of the UNCTC. That is why the main concern for neoliberals since the creation of the MPS has been how to get a hold of these key institutions.

This 'long march' through institutions happened only twice during the twentieth century. The first time it was by the fascists and the Nazis – as docu-mented in detail by Guérin (1945). The second time it was by the neoliberals since the 1970s. As a result, in much of the world today, in politics and in econom-ics, neoliberalism has become by far the dominant view and the 'common sense' approach to policymaking and social organization among conservatives and socialists alike (Parguez, 1993; Bougrine, 2000: 2). Unable to question it or think that there might be alternatives to it, they see neoliberalism as the 'natural way of doing things'. It is worth noting, however, that while fascism enjoyed some popular support because some institutions that provided welfare to the working class were preserved and even developed, under neoliberalism these were down-sized or eliminated, causing discontent, anxiety and revolt among the masses. Popular anti-neoliberal protests are nowadays a common occurrence in practically every country where such policies are implemented (Plehwe *et al.*, 2006; Silva, 2009; Amin, 2012a, 2012b). There is also mounting evidence that "the tide is turning" against neoliberalism; such as in South America (Silva, 2009; Ponniah and Eastwood, 2011) and other parts of the world (Westra, 2010). These reactions are certainly counter-movements attempting to protect society and nature from the devastating effects of neoliberalism, just as was expected by Karl Polanyi (see Jessop, 2007; Polanyi-Levitt and Seccareccia, 2016).

Since neoliberals put so much emphasis on individualism and on the optimality of free markets' outcome, let us see how individuals have actually fared during the neoliberal era since the 1980s. We can do this by looking at market incomes and how these have changed over time, before any corrective measures through taxation or transfers. The World Top Income Database recently made public gives information on the shares of income for the richest 10 per cent and 1 per cent of the population over a relatively long period for several countries. Figure 1.1 shows that shares of the top 1 per cent of population in total income have increased between 1980 and 2012 in all 18 OECD countries in their sample, including the Nordic countries where income distribution is known to have been more equitable in the past. These increases have been particularly large in the United States where the top 1 per cent more than doubled its share of income, which increased from 10 per cent in 1981 to 22.5 per cent in 2012. A similar pattern is observed in Canada, the United Kingdom and Germany. The trend line indicates that income inequality is much greater in the countries to the right, meaning that the gap between the richest individuals and the rest of the population in these countries has become much wider and that the very rich are indeed getting richer. The World Top Income Database indicates that this is also true for the richest top 10 per cent of the population whose share of total income in the United States has increased from 32 per cent in 1980 to 46 per cent in 2010. In Canada, Japan and the United Kingdom the richest 10 per cent of the population increased their shares of total income to over 40 per cent by 2010. Even though the share going to the top 10 per cent increased in all the other countries, it still remained hovering around 30 per cent of total income – thus making the United States the country with the highest income inequality.

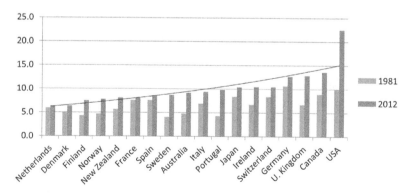

Figure 1.1 Shares of the top 1% of the population in pre-tax income, 1981–2012.

Source: Author's calculations based on The World Top Income Database. Available online http://topincomes.parisschoolofeconomics.eu/#Database.

Note: All incomes are before taxes and transfers. Incomes do not include capital gains, except for Canada, Germany, Japan, Spain, Sweden and the USA.

Table 1.1 Changes in wealth distribution in Canada

	1999		2012	
	Total net worth in billions	Net worth in percentage	Total net worth in billions	Net worth in percentage
Lowest 20%	−4.16	−0.1	−10.83	−0.1
Second quintile	102.04	2.3	180.3	2.2
Third quintile	343.42	8.4	728.65	9.0
Fourth quintile	785.53	20.2	1,735.01	21.5
Fifth quintile	2,676.20	69.2	5,440.45	67.4

Source: Statistics Canada (2014).

Note: Amounts are in constant 2012 Canadian dollars.

These trends in income distribution have important implications for wealth and poverty. For example, a study by Statistics Canada (see Morissette *et al.*, 2002) indicates that while the richest 10 per cent of the population in Canada increased their share of total wealth from 51.8 per cent in 1984 to 55.7 per cent in 1999, the lowest 10 per cent of the population saw their share drop from a negative 0.5 per cent to a negative 0.6 per cent, meaning that they got deeper into debt. In fact, the increase in indebtedness affected the entire lowest 20 per cent of the population since their total debt jumped from $4.16 billion in 1999 to almost $11 billion in 2012, an increase of 160 per cent; with their share remaining a negative 0.1 per cent of the total wealth versus a huge 67.4 per cent for the richest 20 per cent of the population (see Table 1.1).

Unequal distribution of wealth and its concentration in the hands of a small minority of the population is now a stylized fact in most industrialized countries, as documented by Piketty (2014). Critics of the current economic model, including Stiglitz (2011, 2013, 2016) came to the conclusion that neoliberalism is "the economics of the 1%". For instance, as shown in Figure 1.2, the top 1 per cent of the population in the United States had seen its share decline somewhat during the 30 'glorious years' when the Welfare State was attempting to create a more egalitarian society, but since the 1980s this share has steadily increased to return to almost 42 per cent of the total net wealth in 2012. The share of the top 10 per cent of the population follows a similar pattern, reaching almost 80 per cent of total net wealth – levels not seen since the eclipse of the 'roaring 1920s'. What is important to note about this concentration of wealth is that it is not entirely earned. Piketty and Zucman (2015) estimate that, in 2010, inherited wealth represented between 60–70 per cent of total wealth in France and more or less similar shares in other industrialized countries.

Given these hefty rewards for the rich, it is no wonder that they generally support neoliberal policies. This also explains the historically stubborn alliance between the economically dominant class and the state. It is for this reason that we say that markets are created, planned and manipulated by the neoliberal state in order to produce expected outcomes and give determined results in favour of

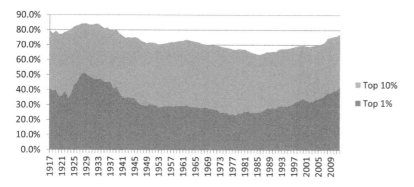

Figure 1.2 Shares of the top 10% and top 1% of the total net household wealth in the USA.

Source: Based on the data set on wealth in the USA, kindly made available online by Emmanuel Saez and Gabriel Zucman (2014): http://gabriel-zucman.eu/uswealth/.

the elite. Now, whether neoliberalism dares speak its name or not is not all that important – what matters is the results and the 'proof is in the pudding' (see Mirowski, 2014).

The increase in indebtedness of the lowest 20 per cent of the population and the fall in their relative share in total wealth in Canada and other industrialized countries translated into an increase in poverty among low-income citizens. There is a serious lack of consistent and comparable data on rates of poverty, but the OECD publishes what it calls "poverty rates expressed as ratios of the number of people whose income falls below the poverty line; taken as half the median household income of the total population". The OECD database contains information on poverty rates before and after taxes and transfers, that is, what we can call poverty as a result of the workings of 'unfettered markets' and the 'corrected outcome' after state intervention. Using this definition, the OECD published tables[11] which indicate that poverty rates have increased in all countries for which data are available since the 1980s, and that in 2012 at least a quarter of the population (and as much as one third in some countries such as France, Finland, Germany, Italy, etc.) live below the poverty line and would therefore need government help and assistance.

This brings us to a point where we can actually gauge the size and importance of government intervention and even make an assessment of the role played by the state in reducing poverty. This can be done by comparing two countries such as, for instance, Canada and Finland, which are known to have somewhat 'generous' social programmes and a relatively solid social safety net. Figure 1.3 indicates that poverty rates before government intervention have been increasing in both countries since the 1980s, stabilizing at around 25 per cent of the population for Canada and 33 per cent for Finland. However, state intervention was much more important in the latter where poverty rates were successfully brought down to nearly 5 per cent, whereas in Canada the rates remained around 11 per cent on average for the period.

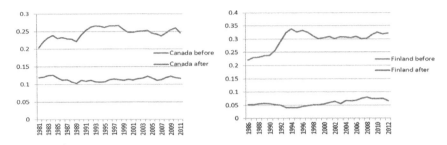

Figure 1.3 Poverty rates before and after government intervention: the role of the state in reducing poverty, Canada vs. Finland.

Source: Author's calculations using OECD database.

Now, there is nothing that prevents Canada from also bringing poverty rates to 5 per cent, neither is there anything preventing Finland from bringing those rates to zero and therefore eliminating poverty altogether. Obviously, this last observation applies to all other countries. Government policies can eliminate poverty and there is no reason why we should be targeting rates such as 5 per cent or 6 per cent instead of zero. The elimination of poverty is possible and it should be done. Refusing to adopt and implement policies to eliminate poverty can only be explained by the lack of will, which ultimately rests on the fact that policymakers today remain prisoners of the neoliberal market principles, particularly those relating to public finance – a topic to which we will return in the following chapters. But as Chomsky (2014: 43) so emphatically stated: "To some extent, we can create the future rather than merely observing the flow of events. Given the stakes, it would be *criminal* to let real opportunities pass unexplored".

Conclusion

The chapter examined the role of the state and the market in shaping the organization of human relationships in the context of production and distribution of resources. The study of the emergence and evolution of these two institutions indicates that the state apparatus has been historically used as an instrument by the economically dominant social class to protect and further its own interests. It was shown that the social relations built around the activities of production and exchange of resources have been gradually framed and integrated into the institution called 'the market'. Ever since the rise of the primitive state, the central issue has been the guarantee of individuals' social protection in the form of access to resources. Under the neoliberal state, the manipulation of the market has taken a particularly violent form to ensure an outcome that is largely in favour of the dominant class, with wealth being concentrated in the hands of a minority of the population. This gross inequality in the distribution of wealth and the associated high levels of poverty stand out as the main characteristic of modern society and call into question the ethics and even the efficiency of the system on which it is based.

Notes

1 The practice of mutual assistance through free labour is still found today (2015) in tribal communities of North Africa such as in Morocco, whereby members of usually geographically close tribes help each other during the seasons of planting and harvesting (a practice called *twiza*). Exchange of goods occurs in a market place still on a weekly basis, even though these transactions are monetized nowadays.

2 Such evidence flies in the face of those who claim that innate human behaviour is based on the principle of least effort. See, for instance, George Zipf (1949).

3 A popular Mexican adage says "Quien parte y comparte, se queda con la mayor parte", meaning that "He who divides and distributes, keeps the biggest share (for himself)".

4 Archaeological evidence from Peru and Mesoamerica indicates that high-status housing and elite residences were burned and/or destroyed by the low status population on several occasions (see, Haas, 1981: 91–5).

5 Hayek often talked about the need for a strategy. The creation of the Mont Pelerin Society (MPS) was an effective means of garnering ideological and financial support for the neoliberal cause.

6 For example, Friedman (1962: 177) writes that "the humanitarian and egalitarian sentiment which helped produce the steeply graduated individual income tax has also produced a host of other measures directed at promoting the 'welfare' of particular groups. The most important single set of measures is the bundle misleadingly labeled 'social security'. Others are public housing, minimum wage laws, farm price supports, medical care for particular groups, special aid programs, and so on".

7 Connell (2010: 23) commented that, on this account, "we can certainly say that neoliberals have had astonishing success in creating markets for things whose commodification was once unimaginable: drinking water, body parts, and social welfare among them".

8 See the study by McDonald and Smith (2004) on the relentless privatization in post-apartheid South Africa. See also the recent book by Saul and Bond (2014) where they report on the Marikana massacre. On 16 August 2012, the news media around the world reported on what became known as the Marikana massacre in which the South African police intervened in a labour dispute between the workers and the owners of the Marikana platinum mine (the British Lonmin, Inc., based in London). The miners, who were on strike, demanded a wage increase but the tragedy ended with the police firing on the strikers, killing 34 miners, wounding dozens and arresting over 200 mineworkers, after which the company offered an increase of about 75 euros per month. While the company gave an ultimatum to the workers to return to work, the South African President Jacob Zuma could only declare a week of national mourning for those who were killed. See, www.theguardian.com/world/2014/aug/15/-sp-south-africa-platinum-mining-massacre-strike. Similar tragedies are quite common all over the African continent in countries such as Mauritania, the Congo, Nigeria and so on.

9 See, *Two Lucky People: Memoirs*, by Milton and Rose Friedman (1998: 398). Chossudovsky (2003: xxi) recounts that at the time of the military coup in Chile, he was a visiting professor at the Catholic University and that barely a week after the coup, several of his 'Chicago Boys' colleagues from the Economics Department were appointed to key positions in the military government.

10 The use of state violence to achieve neoliberal goals is very prominent in the developing countries of Asia and Africa. For instance, in her book *Capitalism: A Ghost Story*, Roy (2014) reports that privatization in India is accompanied by appalling levels of different types of corporate and state violence against the poor and the vulnerable in society. In the case of Ukraine, Chossudovsky (2014: 1–2) noted that the implementation of the neoliberal agenda was carried out by neo-Nazi groups which have close ties with international institutions. He wrote that "To reach its unspoken goals, the IMF-World Bank – often in consultation with the US Treasury and the State Department – will exert control over key appointments including the Minister of Finance, the Central Bank governor as well as senior officials in charge of the country's privatization program. These key appointments will require the (unofficial) approval of the 'Washington Consensus' prior to the conduct of negotiations pertaining to a multibillion IMF bailout agreement".

11 The statistical tables are available online from: http://stats.oecd.org/index.aspx?r=451988.

References

Amin, S. (2004) *The Liberal Virus: Permanent War and the Americanization of the World* (New York: Monthly Review Press).

Amin, S. (2012a) *The People's Spring: The Future of the Arab Revolution* (Dakar, Senegal: Pambazuka Press).

Amin, S. (2012b) *The Arab Revolutions: A Year After*, Pambazuka News Online, available at www.pambazuka.net/en/category/features/80745, accessed 20 March 2016.

Asimakopoulos, J. (2014) *Social Structures of Democracy: On the Political Economy of Equality* (Leiden, The Netherlands: Brill)

Bair, J. (2009) "Taking Aim at the New International Economic Order" in Mirowski, P. and D. Plehwe (eds), *The Road From Mont Pèlerin: The Making of the Neoliberal Thought Collective* (Cambridge, MA: Harvard University Press).

Baker, D. (2006) *The Conservative Nanny State: How the Wealthy Use the Government to Stay Rich and Get Richer* (Washington, DC: Center for Economic and Policy Research).

Bentham, J. (1797) "Tracts on Poor Laws and Pauper Management" in *The Works of Jeremy Bentham*, Part XVI (Edinburgh, UK: Printed by William Tait, Prince's Street).

Bougrine, H. (ed.) (2000) *The Economics of Public Spending: Debts, Deficits and Economic Performance* (Cheltenham, UK: Edward Elgar).

Bougrine, H. (2012) "Fiscal Austerity, the Great Recession and the Rise of New Dictatorships", *Review of Keynesian Economics*, Volume 1, No. 1, pp. 109–25.

Campbell, H. (2013) *Global NATO and the Catastrophic Failure in Libya* (New York: Monthly Review Press).

Carneiro, R. L. (1981) "The Chiefdom: Precursor of the State" in Jones, G. D. and R. R. Kautz (eds), *The Transition to Statehood in the New World* (Cambridge, UK: Cambridge University Press, pp. 37–79).

Chomsky, N. (2014) *Masters of Mankind: Essays and Lectures 1969–2013* (Chicago, IL: Haymarket Books).

Chossudovsky, M. (2003) *The Globalization of Poverty and the New World Order* (Pincourt, Quebec: Global Research).

Chossudovsky, M. (2005) *America's "War on Terrorism"*, (Pincourt, Quebec: Global Research).

Chossudovsky, M. (2014) *Regime Change in Ukraine and the IMF's Bitter "Economic Medicine"*, Pincourt, Quebec: Global Research, available online at: www.globalresearch.ca/regime-change-in-ukraine-and-the-imfs-bitter-economic-medicine/5374877, accessed 20 March 2016.

Connell, R. (2010) "Understanding Neoliberalism" in Braedley, S. and M. Luxton (eds), *Neoliberalism and Everyday Life* (Montreal, Canada: McGill-Queen's University Press).

Culver, J. C. and J. Hyde (2000), *American Dreamer: A life of Henry A. Wallace* (New York: W. W. Norton and Co.).

Dalton, G. (1961) "Economic Theory and Primitive Society", *American Anthropologist*, Vol. 63, No. 1, pp. 1–25.

Desai, R. (1994) "Second-Hand Dealers in Ideas: Think-Tanks and Thatcherite Hegemony", *New Left review*, Vol. I, No. 230, pp. 27–64.

Duncan, T. K. and C. J. Coyne (2013) "The Origins of the Permanent War Economy", *The Independent Review*, Vol. 18, No. 2, pp. 219–40.

Engels, F. ([1884]) (1972) *The Origin of the Family, Private Property and the State* (New York: Pathfinder Press).

Friedman, M. (1994) "Introduction to the Fiftieth Anniversary Edition" in Hayek, F. A. (1994 [1944]) *The Road to Serfdom* (Chicago, IL: University of Chicago Press).

Friedman, M. (2002 [1962]) *Capitalism and Freedom* (Chicago, IL: University of Chicago Press).

Friedman, M. and R. Friedman (1980) *Free to Choose* (New York: Harcourt Brace Jovanovich).

Friedman, M. and R. Friedman (1998) *Two Lucky People: Memoirs* (Chicago, IL: University of Chicago Press).

Galbraith, J. K. (2016) *Welcome to the Poisoned Chalice: The Destruction of Greece and the Future of Europe* (New Haven, CT: Yale University Press).

Godelier, M. (1974) *Un domaine contesté: l'anthropologie économique* (Paris: Mouton).

Guérin, D. (1965 [1945]) *Fascisme et grand capital* (Paris: Maspero).

Haas, J. (1981) "Class Conflict and the State in the New World" in Jones, G. D. and R. R. Kautz (eds), *The Transition to Statehood in the New World* (Cambridge, UK: Cambridge University Press, pp. 80–102).

Harvey, D. (2005) *A Brief History of Neoliberalism* (Oxford, UK: Oxford University Press).

Hayek, F. A. (1994 [1944]) *The Road to Serfdom* (Chicago, IL: University of Chicago Press).

Herman, E. S. and N. Chomsky (1988) *Manufacturing Consent: The Political Economy of the Mass Media* (New York: Pantheon Books).

Jessop, B. (2007) "Knowledge as a Fictitious Commodity: Insights and Limits of a Polanyian Analysis", pp. 115–33, in Bugra, A. and K. Agartan (eds), *Reading Karl Polanyi for the Twenty-First Century: Market Economy as a Political Project* (New York: Palgrave Macmillan).

Kotz, D. R. (2015) *The Rise and Fall of Neoliberal Capitalism* (Cambridge, MA: Harvard University Press).

Malinowski, B. (1939) "Anthropology as the Basis of Social Science" in Cattel, R. B., Cohen, J. and R. Travers (eds), *Human Affairs* (London: Macmillan).

McDonald, D. A. and L. Smith (2004) "Privatizing Cape Town: From *Apartheid* to Neo-Liberalism in the Mother City", *Urban Studies*, Vol. 41, No. 8, pp. 461–84.

Mirowski, P. (2013) *Never Let a Serious Crisis Go to Waste* (New York: Verso).

Mirowski, P. (2014) *The Political Movement that Dared Not Speak its own Name: The Neoliberal Thought Collective Under Erasure*, Institute for New Economic Thinking, Working Paper No. 23.

Monbiot, G. (2016) "Neoliberalism – the Ideology at the Root of All Our Problems", *The Guardian*, online: www.theguardian.com/books/2016/apr/15/neoliberalism-ideology-problem-george-monbiot, accessed 15 April 2016.

Morissette, R., X. Zhang and M. Drolet (2002) *The Evolution of Wealth Inequality in Canada, 1984–1999* (Ottawa: Statistics Canada).

Nozick, R. (1999 [1974]) *Anarchy, State and Utopia* (Oxford, UK: Blackwell Publishers Ltd.).

Ostry, J. D., P. Loungani and D. Furceri (2016) "Neoliberalism: Oversold?", *Finance & Development*, Vol. 52, No. 2 (Washington, DC: International Monetary Fund).

Parguez, A. (1993) "L'austérité Budgétaire en France" in Paquette, P. and M. Seccareccia (eds), *Les piéges de l'austérité* (Montreal, Canada: Les Presses de l'Université de Montréal, pp. 83–103).

Pauwels, J. (2013) *Big Business avec Hitler* (Brussels: Aden).

Piketty, T. (2014) *Capital in the Twenty- First Century* (Cambridge, MA: Harvard University Press).

Piketty, T. and G. Zucman (2015) "Wealth and Inheritance in the Long Run" in Atkinson, A. B. and F. Bourguignon (eds), *Handbook of Income Distribution*, vol. 2 (North-Holland: ScienceDirect, pp. 1303–68).

Plant, R. (2009) *The Neoliberal State* (Oxford, UK: Oxford University Press).

Plehwe, D., Walpen, B. and G. Neunhöffer (eds) (2006) *Neoliberal Hegemony: A Global Critique* (New York: Routledge).

Polanyi-Levitt, K. and M. Seccareccia (2016) "Thoughts on Mirowski and Neoliberalism from a Polanyian Perspective", *Symposium on Neoliberalism*, INET: https://ineteconomics.org/ideas-papers/research-papers/thoughts-on-mirowski-and-neoliberalism-from-a-polanyian-perspective, accessed 25 May 2016.

Polanyi, K. (1944) *The Great Transformation: The Political and Economic Origins of Our Time* (Boston, MA: Beacon Press).

Ponniah, T. and J. Eastwood (eds) (2011) *The Revolution in Venezuela: Social and Political Change Under Chávez* (Cambridge, MA: Harvard University Press).

Roy, A. (2014) *Capitalism: A Ghost Story* (Chicago, IL: Haymarket Books).

Saez, E. and M. Zucman (2014) *Wealth Inequality in the United States Since 1913: Evidence from Capitalized Income Tax Data*, NBER Working Paper 20625, available online: www.nber.org/papers/w20625, accessed 20 March 2016.

Sahlins, M. D. (1958) *Social Stratification in Polynesia* (Seattle, WA: University of Washington Press).

Sahlins, M. D. (1972) *Stone Age Economics* (Chicago, IL and New York: Aldine Atherton Inc.).

Saul, J. S. and P. Bond (2014) *South Africa – The Present as History: From Mrs Ples to Mandela and Marikana* (Rochester, NY: Boydell & Brewer Inc.).

Service, E. R. (1962) *Primitive Social Organization* (New York: Random House).

Service, E. R. (1975) *Origins of the State and Civilization: The Process of Cultural Evolution* (New York: W. W. Norton & Co.).

Silva, E. (2009) *Challenging Neoliberalism in Latin America* (Cambridge, UK: Cambridge University Press).

Smith, A. (1981 [1776]) *An Inquiry Into the Nature and Causes of the Wealth of Nations*, in Campbell, R. H. and A. S. Skinner (eds) (*Glasgow Edition of the Works and Correspondence of Adam Smith*, Vol. II, Liberty Press).

Smith, J. (2016) *Imperialism in the Twenty-First Century: Globalization, Super-Exploitation, and Capitalism's Final Crisis* (New York: Monthly Review Press).

Statistics Canada (2014), *Survey of Financial Security, 2012* (Ottawa: Statistics Canada, available online: www.statcan.gc.ca/daily-quotidien/140225/t140225b003-eng.htm, accessed 15 June 2016).

Stedman Jones, D. (2012) *Masters of the Universe: Hayek, Friedman, and the Birth of Neoliberal Politics* (Princeton, NJ: Princeton University Press).

Steger, M. B. and R. K. Roy (2010) *Neoliberalism: A Very Short Introduction* (Oxford, UK: Oxford University Press).

Stiglitz, J. E. (2011) "Of the 1%, by the 1%, for the 1%" *Vanity Fair*, available online: www.vanityfair.com/society/features/2011/05/top-one-percent-201105#/gotopage2, accessed 20 March 2016.

Stiglitz, J. E. (2013) *The Price of Inequality: How Today's Divided Society Endangers Our Future* (New York: W. W. Norton & Co.).

Stiglitz, J. E. (2016) *Rewriting the Rules of the American Economy: An Agenda for Growth and Shared Prosperity* (New York: W. W. Norton & Co.).

Stokes, S. C. (2004) *Mandates and Democracy: Neoliberalism by Surprise in Latin America* (Cambridge, UK: Cambridge University Press).

Thurnwald, R. (1969 [1932])) *Economics in Primitive Communities* (London: Oxford University Press).

Weeks, J. F. (2014) *Economics of the 1%: How Mainstream Economics Serves the Rich, Obscures Reality and Distorts Policy* (New York: Anthem Press).

Westra, R. (2010) *Confronting Global Neoliberalism: Third World Resistance and Development Strategies* (Atlanta, GA: Clarity Press).

World Bank (2016) *Poverty in a Rising Africa: Africa Poverty Report*, authored by Beegle, K., L. Christiaensen, A. Dabalen, and I. Gaddis (Washington, DC: The World Bank).

Zipf, G. (1949) *Human Behavior and the Principle of Least Effort* (Cambridge, MA: Addison-Wesley).

2 Democracy in government

The power of policymaking

Virtually all U.S. senators, and most of the representatives in the House, are members of the top 1 percent when they arrive, are kept in office by money from the top 1 percent, and know that if they serve the top 1 percent well they will be rewarded by the top 1 percent when they leave office. By and large, the key executive-branch policymakers on trade and economic policy also come from the top 1 percent.

Joseph E. Stiglitz (2011)

Introduction

Tanzi (2011: 1) quoted the renowned Russian philosopher Nikolai A. Berdyaev as having said that "The government exists not for turning life on earth into a paradise but for preventing it from turning into a complete hell". The use of metaphors of paradise and hell is obviously due to Berdyaev's deep belief in Christianity, but it seems somewhat incongruous that such a celebrated philosopher and apparently a committed Christian would settle for an outcome that is hellish, albeit less than a 'complete hell'. The relationship between government's actions and how they affect life on earth is subsumed today under the heading of 'economic and social policies'. Life on earth can be less than a 'complete hell' when humans suffer the ills of poverty and deprivation as a result of these policies. Berdyaev's suggestions would imply that, if all the government can do is prevent life on earth 'from turning into a complete hell', then people should just accept that and not expect more.[1] This is problematic particularly when we know that Berdyaev was a prominent writer within the existentialist movement, which considers that human beings create their own existence by choosing the particular meaning they want to give to their lives.

Against this fatalistic attitude, Jean-Paul Sartre, another existentialist philosopher, sounded like he was shouting back directly at Berdyaev when he wrote:

> Get this into your head: if violence were only a thing of the future, if exploitation and oppression never existed on earth, perhaps displays of nonviolence might relieve the conflict. But if the entire regime, even your nonviolent thoughts, is governed by a thousand-year-old oppression, your passiveness serves no other purpose but to put you on the side of the oppressors.[2]

In the *Wretched of the Earth*, Frantz Fanon (1961: 97) reacted by saying that "the unpreparedness of the [intellectual] elite, the lack of practical ties between them and the masses, their apathy and, yes, their cowardice at the crucial moment in the struggle, are the cause of tragic trials and tribulations" adding that "sooner or later a people gets the government it deserves" Fanon (1961: 139).

Just what type of government do the people deserve? Ironically, it was a politician, Thomas Jefferson (1812, vol. 13: 135), who gave the unequivocal answer when he stated that "The only orthodox object of the institution of government is to secure the greatest degree of happiness possible to the general mass of those associated under it" insisting that "the happiness and prosperity of our citizens . . . is the only legitimate object of government and the first duty of governors" (Jefferson, 1811, vol. 13: 41). In the political field, it can be said that the greatest achievement in the twentieth century has been the acceptance of the 'one person, one vote' principle. When each person, free of any influence, exercises their right to vote, there is a certain sense of equality. Universal direct suffrage gives democracy in government but for this to be effective, it should be as easy to remove political representatives from office as electing them to any level of government. Political representatives, in order for them to be worthy of people's confidence, should aim to do precisely the sort of thing that purports to turn 'life on earth into a paradise'.

It should be understood that equality in the political field is only a means to achieve equality in the economic and social spheres, which means that politicians must not only be talented and creative in their thinking about the political process but also, and above all, knowledgeable about matters of 'economic and social policies' – whose overall objective must always be the continuous improvement in the general welfare of the whole population, that is, a life with dignity for everyone and in harmony with nature. Aggregate risks in the form of economic threats such as unemployment and poverty require a permanent and collective action. Government is the only agency equipped to deal with the effects of such hazards over time and to ensure that social protection is provided to all citizens. For this reason, the government can become 'the great agency for achieving happiness', to borrow Polanyi's (1944: 139) expression, but it is the responsibility of the people to make sure they do indeed get the government 'they deserve'. In the following two sections, the chapter explores ways in which the state in modern societies can be reformed and used as an instrument to build a society based on social and economic democracy.

Democracy in government

The need for democracy in government is dictated by the fact that power to design the economic system and the type of social organization resides primarily with the state and that such power is crucial for the control and distribution of resources. Wright (2004: 48) noted that "In hunter-gatherer societies . . . if a leader became overbearing, or a minority disliked a majority decision, people could leave. In an uncrowded world without fixed borders or belongings, it was easy to vote with one's feet". Walking away from dictatorial regimes by voting with one's feet is not always an option in modern times. Today, confrontation is the dominant way of resolving conflicts and disagreements. In parliamentary democracies, confrontation takes the form of political struggle among political parties, each aiming to have access to power. But politicians do not rely only on political persuasion and intellectual argumentation. They also depend on the support of economically influential members of society and on the amount of money they can get to finance a successful propaganda campaign. The successful candidate or party always ends up implementing polices and measures that serve the interests of the backers. Economic and social policies, therefore, are not, and cannot be, ideologically neutral. In fact, the entire institutional and legal framework governing the social organization is designed to preserve the interests of the dominant class. This is a characteristic of both aristocracies and parliamentary democracies.

Chapter 1 gave evidence that, since the 1980s, largely as a result of neoliberal policies, there has been a worldwide rise in income and wealth inequalities (see Piketty, 2014; Oxfam, 2015). Those who are hurt by these policies have protested but, on the other side of the fence, those who wield political power were even more defiant. The 'angry crowd' could rant and protest all they want (e.g. Occupy this and that, Arab revolts, Greek, Spanish, French demonstrations and so on), but the state would not budge because it has a mission. When those protests gather momentum and become a threat, the state simply steps in to ban them and declare them illegal: it has the *power* to do so. Drastic punitive measures are routine. For instance, in the wake of the recent anti-austerity protests, the government in Spain passed a law that would fine protesters up to 600,000 euros for block-occupying key public infrastructure such as an airport. In fact, more often than not, the state has even used force and violence to prevent opposition to its agenda. Or whose agenda is it? Is the state some sort of a supra-individual, paternalistic and neutral agency acting for the best interests of all members of society? Does the elected politician sitting in parliament or on the executive represent and defend *equally* the interests of all voters?

There are many who are quick to dismiss these questions as ill-intentioned, out of fashion or even naïve. But serious scholars who have put modern democracies to close scrutiny have noted a pervasive collusive behaviour between the state and the dominant class. If we restrict our study to the current period, which we identified earlier as the neoliberal era of capitalism, then we can say that all the available evidence indicates that elected politicians in today's parliamentary democracies show a clear bias by adopting economic and social policies that primarily serve the interests of the dominant class and that the state is far from acting as a neutral agency. The relationship between the political class and the economically dominant class is so intricate that the two are often one and the same. Let us not talk about Africa and other parts of the world where corruption and cronyism are rampant. This is how the US economist and Nobel Prize Laureate Joseph Stiglitz (2011) described the situation in his own country:

The Supreme Court, in its recent *Citizens United* case, has enshrined the right of corporations to buy government, by removing limitations on campaign spending. The personal and the political are today in perfect alignment. Virtually all U.S. senators, and most of the representatives in the House, are members of the top 1 percent when they arrive, are kept in office by money from the top 1 percent, and know that if they serve the top 1 percent well they will be rewarded by the top 1 percent when they leave office. By and large, the key executive-branch policymakers on trade and economic policy also come from the top 1 percent. When pharmaceutical companies receive a trillion-dollar gift – through legislation prohibiting the government, the largest buyer of drugs, from bargaining over price – it should not come as cause for wonder. It should not make jaws drop that a tax bill cannot emerge from Congress unless big tax cuts are put in place for the wealthy. Given the power of the top 1 percent, this is the way you would *expect* the system to work.

Control of the political process is crucial to maintaining the type of economic system that benefits the dominant class and its business associates. As Roberts (2014) remarked:

> [i]n more recent years, the private interest groups seem to have taken control of the government. Wall Street, Military Security Complex, Agribusiness, the extractive industries – *their campaign donations elect the House, the Senate, the President, and they then write most of the bills that Congress passes and the President signs,* so it's a form of state capitalism in which the capitalists seem to have the upper hand (emphasis added).

After all the praise and the smooth talk about the latest elections of the Congress, Paul Krugman (2014), another Nobel Laureate, retorted that "the Masters of the Universe [the bankers] . . . bought themselves a Congress". Galbraith (2006) had already called the US political system a "corporate democracy" and referred to government as a "predatory state" Galbraith (2008). The situation tends to be quite similar in other Western democracies, regardless of which political party accedes to power. Stiglitz (2013: 361) concluded that:

> [i]f we are to preserve a system of one person one vote – rather than one dollar one vote – reforms in our political system will be required; but we are unlikely to achieve a fair and responsive political system within an economic system that is characterized by the degree of inequality that marks ours.

In their empirical study, *Testing Theories of American Politics*, Gilens and Page (2014: 572, 575) used a data set of 1,779 policy issues to estimate the influence of four sets of actors over the US policy making. The four actors identified by the authors are: the Average Citizen or "median voter", Economic Elites, Mass-based Groups and Business-oriented Interest Groups or industries. The authors concluded that:

The estimated impact of average citizens' preferences drops precipitously, to a non-significant, near-zero level. Clearly the median citizen or "median voter" at the heart of theories of Majoritarian Electoral Democracy does not do well when put up against economic elites and organized interest groups . . . Not only do ordinary citizens not have uniquely substantial power over policy decisions; they have little or no independent influence on policy at all. By contrast, economic elites are estimated to have a quite substantial, highly significant, independent impact on policy.

In other countries, we note in passing that under the common 'first-past-the-post' electoral system, a political party often ends up governing the country with less than 40 per cent of the total votes in countries like Canada and the United Kingdom. In the case of the United States, Burnham and Ferguson (2014) report that the turnout in the 2014 US Congressional elections was around 36 per cent of the potential electorate that had legal rights to cast a ballot and that in some states the turnout was as low as 26 per cent – rates similar to those recorded in the late eighteenth century when voting was exclusive to propertied white men. This situation has prompted Chomsky (2014) to call the US political system "an oligarchy, not a democracy".

If we now consider the unfolding drama in Greece and in other peripheral European countries where the influence of the economic elites on policymaking is clearly being demonstrated through its dictated austerity programmes, then the verdict is that parliamentary democracy has failed the masses or say 'the average citizen' – and the question now is how can we reform the political system so as to achieve economic and social democracy? For any reform to have a meaningful effect, it should go to the heart of the *decision-making process* because that is where power resides. The reform must aim at creating a state with the political power to design and implement economic and social policies that permanently seek to eliminate all forms of poverty and inequality.[3]

The history of modern democracies indicates that such a state could not be created by traditional party politics and parliamentary representation. Several political models have been proposed as alternatives (see, among others, Dalton *et al.*, 2001; Emerson, 2006), but one that has the potential of achieving the aims stated above is *direct democracy* (see Cockshott and Cottrell, 2005; Fotopoulos, 2005; Asimakopoulos, 2014). This is a model in which the masses will have leverage on the political process, allowing them to have a say and participate directly in the design of economic and social policies that affect their lives. From this perspective, political democracy is necessarily only one component of an *inclusive* democracy that extends to the economic and social spheres – all within the context of respect and care for nature and the environment.

Direct democracy is often associated with universal suffrage to which some countries tend to resort for approval of key pieces of legislation such as constitutions or for voting in presidential elections, but this is a narrow interpretation. We define direct democracy here as a process by which citizens *collectively* make decisions regarding *all matters* that concern their community whether at the local, regional or national level. Obviously, in large societies, there is the problem of how local citizen bodies can be 'represented' at the regional or national levels. This is the area where so many slippery slopes can easily take us down to the representative, liberal democracy or what Castoriades (1991: 221) calls "liberal oligarchy", where representatives tend be chosen repeatedly because of their great talent, ability or knowledge, i.e. their expertise. Once these so-called experts become professional politicians, they become distinguished, socially eminent, notables, and acquire political power over their fellow citizens, thus becoming members of the political elite. We should not be surprised then when these elected 'representatives' end up actually representing themselves and defending the interests of their social class and not the interests of those who voted for them. It is for this reason that Greek philosophers such as Plato, Isocrates and Aristotle preferred to see society governed by those who show the least eagerness for the task and not by those who show excessive ambition. As Hansen (1991: 307) noted, this is an old problem which affected even Athenian democracy:[4]

> The Athenians knew perfectly well that a skillful demagogue could win the citizens to his proposal irrespective of whether it was really in their best interest: competition among political leaders could lead to their bidding against each other with promises to the people and to the people being seduced by their promises . . . The purpose of some Athenian institutions was to counter just such risks. Demagogues were open to all the public prosecutions we have seen: breaking a promise to the people was a crime for which a man could be charged by *eisangelia* or *probole* [roughly equivalent to impeachment and blame].

In order to avoid the formation of elite professional politicians in a regime of direct democracy, it will be necessary to adopt strict rules of representation. Here again the Athenians' solution is illuminating. Hansen (1991: 308) wrote that in Athens:

> All citizens were to take part, if they wished, in running the state, but all were to be amateurs . . . professionalism and democracy were regarded as, at bottom, contradictory. The Athenians ensured the absence of professionalism in their administration by insisting that most magistrates should be picked by lot and could fill a particular magistracy only once and for one year only; and they prevented continuity in the administration by always replacing all members of a board at the same time.

In modern representative or parliamentary democracy, management of public affairs is routinely carried out by what has been aptly called top-down administrative decisions or governing by administrative decree. The vast majority of the population today is not only excluded from the decision-making process, it also suffers the effects of draconian measures taken by the small political elite (see Gilens and Page, 2014). It is therefore crucial that we have a mechanism in place to ensure that direct democracy does not degenerate into representative democracy. Fotopoulos (2005: 202) proposed that:

> [w]here delegation of authority takes place to segments of the citizen body, in order to carry out specific duties (e.g. to serve as members of popular courts, or of regional and confederal councils, etc.), the delegation is assigned, on principle, by lot, on a rotation basis, and it is always recallable by the citizen body. Furthermore, as regards delegates to regional and confederal bodies, the mandates should be specific. This is an effective step towards the abolition of hierarchical relations since such relations today are based, to a significant extent, on the myth of the "experts" who are supposed to be able to control everything, from nature to society.

To emphasize the point further, Fotopoulos (2005: 205) added that:

> The members of these confederal councils are strictly mandated, recallable, and responsible to the assemblies that choose them for the purpose of co-ordinating and administering the policies formulated by the assemblies themselves. Their function is thus purely administrative and practical, not a policy-making one, like the function of representatives in representative "democracy".

It is only in so doing that the citizen bodies, the assemblies and the works councils will ever have the chance of building a state that serves them rather than a state to which they end up being servants. Economic policies will be decided upon by the assemblies and judged by their effects on the total population in a setting that evokes the optimality principle. This is the creative state that every democratic person deserves.

The skeptics and critics who charge that direct democracy is a utopia that can never be achieved are also the ones who want to preserve capitalist representative democracy and advocate it as the *natural* order. There are several experiences of different forms of direct democracy throughout the recent history of mankind. For example, in addition to Athenian democracy of which Hansen (1991: 3) said that it is "the best case of a significant state governed by direct democracy", there are other cases such as in Switzerland where "since the Middle Ages four Swiss cantons and four half-cantons have been governed by assemblies of the people (*Landsgemeinden*), five of which exist to this day" (Hansen, 1991: 2). The International IDEA Handbook (2008) mentions several cases from around the world where some weaker forms of political direct democracy exist. According to Dalton *et al.* (2001: 143), other parts of Europe also have some form of direct democracy and, for instance, in Germany:

> [s]ince 1990, seven states . . . have passed new constitutions with referendum provisions. In fact, the new eastern state constitutions feature an array of direct-participation devices, ranging from state legislative initiatives to the recall of

locally elected mayors. Other reforms are expanding citizen participation in local administrative and planning processes, and several states are incorporating referenda and citizen initiatives in local community affairs. Thus some German analysts claim that there appears to be an irreversible long-term "trend from representative democracy to a widened participatory democracy".

The trend towards direct participatory democracy is indeed an aspiration of the majority of people worldwide. Dalton *et al.* (2001: 144–5), for instance, report that a German election study in 1998 confirmed that "Most Germans lean toward giving the public a greater say in important political decisions" and that according to the Eurobarometer survey (1997) "Among those Europeans who express an opinion, 70 percent are positive about the direct democracy of the Swiss political system". Similarly, Asimakopoulos (2014: 74–5) cites the widespread preferences of workers in many countries to organize in 'works councils', which give them direct participation in the management of their workplaces.

Evidently, all of the above examples of direct participatory democracy are only at the level of the firm, the canton or the province and do not represent the dominant practice in any one country. This has led the critics and skeptics to argue that direct democracy is impossible to implement at the national or federal level, at least for technical and practical reasons such as the large scale of the population. A quick and lucid rebuttal to these claims was given by Hansen (1991: 1) who wrote that:

> [a]sserting that direct democracy no longer exists . . . tends to be followed by the assertion that such democracy *can* no longer exist because of the size of modern societies (which is, actually, to ignore the fact that modern technology has made a return to direct democracy quite feasible – whether desirable or not is another matter).

The difficulties of transforming a capitalist society into an inclusive democracy are numerous. One of those difficulties is what Hirschman (1991) calls the "Rhetoric of Reaction". Indeed, the neoliberals' opposition to and disdain for direct universal suffrage and, in general, for any political system that would give a voice to the masses constitutes a serious obstacle to be overcome. Such opposition obviously stands in the way of extending democracy to the economic sphere since, as noted above, it is economic power and the fear of losing it that motivates the capitalists' opposition to direct democracy in the political sphere.

Economic and social democracy

Most people would easily approve of a change to direct democracy in the political sphere. There is less agreement about the merits of economic democracy. But if limited to the political sphere, direct democracy would be meaningless. In fact, direct democracy as we define it here would not be sustainable and not even attainable if it is not combined with democracy in the economic and social spheres. Nobel Laureate Angus Deaton (2013: 213) noted that "If democracy becomes plutocracy, those who are not rich are effectively disenfranchised . . . The political equality that is required by democracy is always under threat from economic inequality, and the more extreme the economic inequality, the greater the threat to democracy".

That is so because those who have economic power can just sit back and, in various subtle ways, manipulate the outcome of the elections – and therefore choose the type of economic policies to be implemented. Given the importance of political power in shaping the economic outcome, it is surprising and indeed disappointing that those who are leading the fight against 'economic' inequality rarely pay any attention to a reform of the political system. Economic policies are such a powerful instrument that can alleviate poverty and reduce income and wealth inequalities as demonstrated by the experiences of the 'Welfare States' after the Second World War. However, because of the class structure of these societies, the efficacy of these policies has been weakened – particularly with the implementation of neoliberal policies since the 1980s. This outcome should have been expected because the type of policies in place necessarily reflect the orientation and philosophical thinking of the governing political elite. It is for this reason that traditional 'Welfare State' policies can only go so far in improving the living standards of the masses, but they can never eliminate poverty and inequality because that would undermine the economic power of the ruling elite. Taxes and transfers no matter how progressive they are – by definition – can only attenuate income inequalities *ex post* and do not address the primary cause of unequal distribution of wealth.

The central pillar of economic power today is the private ownership of productive resources. The political system, whether a democracy or not, simply legitimizes that ownership by institutionalizing property rights and enforcing them, to the point of sanctification, via its judicial system. Scholars of all persuasions now recognize that private ownership of productive resources is the basis of the existence of social classes and the root cause of unequal distribution of wealth. But property rights over productive resources are not immutable. They are socially established and so can also be changed by the people who make the laws of the land. And this is indeed what societies have done throughout their recent history. Land, for instance, as an important productive resource, has not always been private property. In fact, as recently as the nineteenth and the beginning of the twentieth centuries, in different parts of the world, land was still communal property and individuals had only the right to its use, that is, the right to enjoy whatever products they could get from it by way of farming or fishing and hunting and so on (see, among others, Ike, 1984).

It is important to be aware of the fundamental differences in the meaning that different civilizations give to the idea of ownership and property rights. Throughout Africa and up until today, for instance in Morocco, communal ownership of land is still quite common. For example, Ike (1984: 469) informs us that in Nigeria "The legal position of a member is that of entitlement to a block of land for cultivation" and that "A member is one of the 'many dead, the few living and countless others unborn', who in customary law are the owners of the land". Morgan (1877: 537) was among the early writers to have noted the absence of the idea of property in ancient societies. He wrote that "Lands, as yet hardly a subject of property, were owned by the tribes in common, while tenement houses were owned jointly by their occupants". Wright (2004: 48) added that:

> In hunter-gatherer societies (barring a few special cases) the social structure was more or less egalitarian, with only slight differences in wealth and power between greatest and least . . . Land was either communally owned or thought of as having no owner but the gods. Farmers whose effort and skill made them wealthier had an obligation to share with the needy, to whom they were bound by kinship.

In his excellent but not so popular book, *Economics and Power*, Bartlett (1989: 151–3) presented a lucid and penetrating analysis of the forms of property rights and their evolution during the recent history of Western civilization. His analysis of the outcome of legislative processes instituting, enforcing and defending property rights is particularly relevant to the understanding of the current rise in poverty and destitution on the one hand and the concentration of wealth on the other. For this reason, it is worth quoting him *in extenso*:

> Under feudalism, [in England] serfs had a socially determined and defended right to the use of various lands for crops and grazing. Those rights survived for many generations. With the rise in the value of wool, there were potential gains to be made by converting that land to sheep farming. The serfs, however, did not have exchange rights to the land, only use rights. Their rights could not be purchased, nor could any of the serfs have bought the rights of others . . . To take advantage of these potential profits . . . new forms of rights had to "evolve". In this case rights "evolution" meant burning the homes of the serfs, killing their stock, and on occasion killing them. After decades of this violent "emergence" of the new rights, Parliament ratified the change with the Acts of Enclosure in the eighteenth century.

> The expansion of the territories of the United States during the middle years of the nineteenth century is another example of changing the forms of the rights within a social group . . . The lands of the Great Plains were clearly occupied long prior to European expansion. Rights to the use of that land were also clearly established within the boundaries of the social groups living there. In most cases the form of the rights was communal use rights. Whichever member of the tribe was using a resource was entitled to it until he stopped using it. Then any other could use it at will. There was no concept of exchange rights in resources at all. The relevant society had not defined them as such and certainly would not defend them.

As contact with white society grew, new concepts of rights made their way into the region. Whites wanted the fully exclusionary, fully exchangeable rights in land common to their society, even though this concept made no sense to the current occupants . . . Native Americans, however, perceived those incursions as clear violations of the communal tribal rights systems that defined their society. The path to resolution was clear. Decide which system of rights will prevail via resort to force. A new system of rights "evolved". . . . Hundreds of thousands of Native Americans died, and those remaining were either removed to or contained within specific reservations.

The imposition of transferable property rights was crucial to establishing and generalizing the market system – and hence to the development of capitalism itself. From early on, this meant the mobilization of all supporters of the nascent capitalist class. The definition of tradable property rights became the mission of the "Enlightenment" thinkers, while implementation and enforcement were relegated to the army and the ministry of police. Today, we witness the mobilization of the same forces working in tandem under the neoliberal flag. And so, as far as land is concerned, every parcel of it in urban areas is privately owned and subject to exchange in the midst of a frantic price speculation.[5] Scores of small farmers in Africa and Asia are driven to migrate to the city to serve as cheap labour while their farms are grabbed to form the *latifundia* needed for large-scale production of specific products destined for exports, including genetically modified products (on privatization under neoliberalism in Africa, see, Saul and Bond (2014) and Evers *et al.* (2013); in India, see among others, Roy (2014)). New Acts of Enclosure are being endorsed to close off coast lines to local inhabitants as resort hotels and luxury condominiums are built along the best beaches on the Atlantic and Indian oceans. Private ownership of land and whatever is on its surface has certainly caused misery to all those who were excluded by the Enclosure Acts[6] (from the serfs of eighteenth-century England to the native Americans to the present-day marginalized of Africa and Asia), but private ownership of the riches beneath the surface is the most dramatic by all measures (see Bougrine, 2006, 2014).

Indeed, since the start of the exploitation of oil and other natural resources in Africa and east of the Mediterranean in the beginning of the twentieth century, millions of people have lost not only the source of their livelihood but also their lives, either directly in wars about the ownership and control of these resources or as a result of poverty and diseases that ensued from such exploitation. The pillage of natural resources by transnational corporations (TNCs) and their local allies in the so-called developing countries is well documented (see Rodney, 1972; Maddison, 2006; Vries, 2015) and has prevailed for a long time, dating back to early colonial times. Colonial domination through bloody conquests, pillage and slavery proved to be so rewarding for European powers that it had to remain a guiding principle in their dealings with colonies. Under various guises and justifications, imperial powers have sought to dominate oil, gas and other strategic resources or at least secure access to them by toppling governments, coercing politicians and direct military occupation (e.g. the overthrow of Mossadegh in Iran in 1953, the occupation of Iraq in 2003, the ongoing destruction of Libya, Syria, etc.). Throughout this history, the scenario has been the same: the local ruling class is in a position to sign contracts "legitimizing" the exploitation of oil and other natural resources by TNCs and the latter obligingly reward the local elite while keeping the rest of the population out of sharing in the economic benefits extracted from their own land. As a result, Africa and the region east of the Mediterranean now have the highest rates of poverty and destitution but also some of the wealthiest individuals on earth, some of whom are on the list of the richest 80 persons who own as much as half of the world's population (see Oxfam, 2015).

Ownership of land makes you a lord, a landlord, an influential member in society and gives you credibility and collateral not only when you run for political positions but also when you go to the bank. This allows you access to money and finance and hence opens up a world of opportunities to start new businesses by acquiring raw materials, machinery and equipment, and hiring labour. The story of the Englishman William Knox D'Arcy who started as a speculator in land and ended up being one of the principal founders of the oil and petrochemical industry is archetypical in this regard. The supposed opposition between landlords and capitalists as told by David Ricardo and other classical economists is largely fictitious and indeed lacking lucid analysis and credible justification. The entrepreneur capitalist certainly did not emerge from the serfs or the working poor. Karl Marx and later on Joseph Schumpeter and John Maynard Keynes have all recognized that access to credit (finance) is limited to a privileged class and plays a crucial role in the start-up of entrepreneurial activity (see Bougrine and Seccareccia, 2009). The enforcement of property rights that excludes the poor from ownership of land and other resources also leads to their exclusion from having access to banking and finance – and thus contributes to maintaining them in poverty.

However, since banks discovered the trick of securitization, there has been a new twist to this general rule of exclusion. Banks started encouraging middle-income and even poor households to take loans to buy homes, new cars and appliances and ordinary consumption goods. These loans were repackaged into 'securities' and sold on financial markets as new financial products, which contributed to the phenomenal and fictitious growth of wealth in the financial sector. The shift towards this era of financialization was made easier by the collusion between the bankers, the landlords and the political elite. The so-called subprime crisis of 2007–8 that turned into the Great Recession is the latest manifestation of this flagrant collusion of interests, which we summarize below by the following stylized facts:[7]

(a) Governments repealed key acts of legislation that regulated banking and finance (e.g. The Glass-Steagall Act in the United States) – thus leaving it all to 'market forces'.
(b) The banks lured poor workers to apply for mortgages and get their 'dream homes' on terms they clearly could not afford (a practice that became known as predatory lending).
(c) Meanwhile, the banks and other financial institutions engaged in high speculation by packaging and selling the same mortgages as new financial assets named collateralized debts obligations or CDOs, CDOs squared, and so on.

(d) The same financial institutions entered into bets that said the mortgages will default and purchased insurance against their bets (the infamous credit default swaps or CDSs).
(e) When the mortgages did default, the financial institutions got reward for their bets, the banks foreclosed on the homes and the poor workers simply became . . . homeless.[8]

The dynamics of this class struggle was well understood by Bertolt Brecht (1934) who expressed it cleverly in this poem:

> Rich man, poor man,
> faced each other in a van.
> Said the poor man with a twitch:
> Were I not poor, you wouldn't be rich.

Economic democracy requires the elimination of economic and social inequalities. In his book, *Rewriting the Rules of the American Economy*, Stiglitz (2016: 100) recognized the "need to tackle the rules and institutions that have generated low investment, sluggish growth, and runaway incomes and wealth accumulation at the top and created a steeper hill for the rest to climb". Stiglitz's twofold agenda to fix the economy essentially seeks to (a) tame rent-seeking behaviour, and (b) promote full-employment policies. But at a closer look, it appears that the rules are only being rewritten in order to save capitalism from itself, once again. The chief cause of inequality is private ownership of productive resources, including the sources of money creation, that is, the banks. And for as long as that remains intact, the situation will likely not be different for future generations. Unless the institutional arrangements that make our particular economic, political and cultural system are changed so as to eliminate the private property of all productive resources, the problem of inequality and poverty will not disappear. For wealth to be shared equitably among members of the community, ownership of productive resources must become public, with real production firms being owned and managed by workers, and banks becoming state-owned enterprises – a topic we develop in Chapter 3.

Conclusion

The chapter argued that in a representative democracy the state cannot be equated with a neutral institution that defends equally the interests of all social classes. Using the experiences of Western democracies as examples, we noted that there exists a strong alliance between the state and the economically dominant class, which uses its power and money to determine who gets elected and the type of policies they should implement once in office. This long-standing practice has forced the political system to degenerate into a disguised form of oligarchy where economic and social policies are designed with the objective to serve the interests of the elite. Recognizing the importance of the power of policymaking and how it can shape economic outcomes, the chapter has proposed ways to reform the political process and has offered suggestions about how to achieve economic and social democracy.

Notes

1 Early philosophers of the Enlightenment such as John Locke were more critical of political authority when it contradicted the "Law of nature", precisely because of their deep belief in Christianity. Commenting on Locke's views, Bristow (2011: 9) wrote that according to Locke (1690), "The law of nature 'teaches all mankind . . . that, being all equal and independent, no one ought to harm another in his life, health, liberty, or possessions [and that] [T]he law of nature stands as an eternal rule to all men'. Consequently, when established political power violates that law, the people are justified in overthrowing it".

2 See preface to Fanon (1961: Lviii). Jean-Paul Sartre must have certainly read Victor Hugo's (1883: 179) *L'homme qui rit*, where Hugo wrote that "c'est de l'enfer des pauvres qu'est fait le paradis des riches", that is, "The paradise of the rich is made out of the hell of the poor".

3 It is interesting to note here that, in an empirical study, Galbraith (2012: 108–9) finds communist states have less inequality than other regime types.

4 "Athenian democracy of the fifth and fourth centuries BC is the most famous and perhaps the most nearly perfect example of direct democracy". From the back cover of the book by Hansen (1991).

5 Back in the nineteenth century, Henry George (1879: 161–2) summarized this situation best when he wrote "Take now . . . some hard-headed business man, who has no theories, but knows how to make money. Say to him: 'Here is a little village; in ten years it will be a great city – in ten years the railroad will have taken the place of the stage coach, the electric light of the candle; it will abound with all the machinery and improvements that so enormously multiply the effective power of labor. Will in ten years, interest be any higher?' He will tell you, 'No!' Will the wages of the common labor be any higher . . .?' He will tell you, 'No, the wages of common labor will not be any higher . . .'. 'What, then, will be higher?' 'Rent, the value of land. Go, get yourself a piece of ground, and hold possession'. And if, under such circumstances, you take his advice, you need do nothing more. You may sit down and smoke your pipe; . . . and without doing one stroke of work, without adding one iota of wealth to the community, in ten years you will be rich!".

6 Polanyi (1944: 35) described the situation as follows: "Enclosures have appropriately been called a revolution of the rich against the poor. The lords and nobles were upsetting the social order, breaking down ancient law and custom, sometimes by means of violence, often by pressure and intimidation. They were literally robbing the poor of their share in the common, tearing down the houses which, by the hitherto unbreakable force of custom, the poor had long regarded as theirs and their heirs'. The fabric of society was being disrupted; . . . endangering the defenses of the country . . . harassing its people and turning them from decent husbandmen into a mob of beggars and thieves".

7 Wray (2011) gives a thorough analysis of the fraudulent deals surrounding the subprime crisis and refers to the whole situation as the "mother of all frauds".

8 Amartya Sen, Economics Nobel Laureate in 1998, was also awarded the Charleston-EFG John Maynard Keynes prize for 2015 and on that occasion he commented: "The world in which we live today has been made much more secure by the economic wisdom that Keynes brought to us during the dark days of the Great Depression. When that wisdom is partly or wholly ignored in the making of economic policy, large numbers of people are made to suffer unnecessarily. I am afraid we have seen several depressing examples of that in the recent years, especially in Europe, with a huge human toll". See www.charleston.org.uk/amartya-sen-announced-as-winner-of-charleston-efg-john-maynard-keynes-prize-2015/, accessed 10 February 2015.

References

Asimakopoulos, J. (2014) *Social Structures of Democracy: On the Political Economy of Equality* (Leiden, The Netherlands: Brill).

Bartlett, R. (1989) *Economics and Power: An inquiry Into Human Relations and Markets* (Cambridge, UK: Cambridge University Press.

Bougrine, H. (2006) "Oil: Profits of the Chain Keepers", *International Journal of Political Economy* Vol. 35, No. 2, pp. 35–53.

Bougrine, H. (2014) "A Societal Natural Monopoly for Natural Resources" in Leadbeater, D. (ed.), *Resources, Empire and Labour: Crises and Alternatives* (Halifax, Nova Scotia: Fernwood Publishing, pp. 262–76).

Bougrine, H. and M. Seccareccia (2009) "Financing Development: Removing the External Constraint", *International Journal of Political Economy*, Vol. 38, No. 4, pp. 44–65.

Brecht, B. (1934) *Alfabet*, (Berlin: 10. POS Weißensee).

Bristow, W. (2011) "Enlightenment", *The Stanford Encyclopedia of Philosophy*, edited by Edward N. Zalta, available online: http://plato.stanford.edu/archives/sum2011/entries/enlightenment, accessed 20 March 2016.

Burnham, W. D. and T. Ferguson (2014) "Americans Are Sick to Death of Both Parties: Why Our Politics Is in Worse Shape Than We Thought", in *AlterNet*, 18 December 2014, online www.alternet.org/americans-are-sick-death-both-parties-why-our-politics-worse-shape-we-thought, accessed 20 March 2016.

Castoriades, C. (1991) *Philosophy, Politics, Autonomy: Essays in Political Philosophy* (Oxford, UK: Oxford University Press).

Chomsky, N. (2014) *Masters of Mankind: Essays and Lectures 1969–2013* (Chicago, IL: Haymarket Books).

Cockshott, W. P. and A. Cottrell (2005) "Reflections on Economic Democracy" in *The Capitalist State and Its Economy; Democracy in Socialism, Research in Political Economy*, Vol. 22, pp. 217–58 (Amsterdam: Elsevier).

Dalton, R. J., W. Bürklin and A. Drummond (2001) "Public Opinion and Direct Democracy", *Journal of Democracy*, Vol. 12, No. 4, pp. 141–53.

Deaton, A. (2013) *The Great Escape: Health, Wealth, and the Origins of Inequality* (Princeton, NJ: Princeton University Press).

Emerson, P. (2006) *Designing an All-Inclusive Democracy* (Berlin: Springer-Verlag).

Eurobarometer (1997) *47.1: Images of Switzerland* (March–April).

Evers, S., C. Seagle and F. Keijtenburg (2013) *Africa for Sale?* (Leiden, The Netherlands: Koninklijke Brill NV).

Fanon, F. (1963 [1961]) *The Wretched of the Earth* (New York: Grove Press).

Fotopoulos, T. (2005) *The Multidimensional Crisis and Inclusive Democracy*, Special Issue of *The International Journal of Inclusive Democracy* (August).

Galbraith, J. K. (2006) *Unbearable Cost: Bush, Greenspan and the Economics of Empire* (New York: Palgrave Macmillan).

Galbraith, J. K. (2008) *The Predator State: How Conservatives Abandoned the Free Market and Why Liberals Should Too* (New York: Free Press).

Galbraith, J. K. (2012) *Inequality and Instability: A Study of the World Economy Just Before the Great Crisis* (Oxford, UK: Oxford University Press).

George, H. (2006 [1879]) *Progress and Poverty*, New York: Robert Schalkenbach Foundation, also available online at: http://progressandpoverty.org, accessed 20 March 2016.

Gilens, M. and B. I. Page (2014) "Testing Theories of American Politics: Elites, Interest Groups, and Average Citizens", *Perspectives on Politics*, Vol. 12, No. 3, pp. 564–81.

Hansen, M. H. (1999 [1991]) *The Athenian Democracy in the Age of Demosthenes* (Norman, OK: University of Oklahoma Press).

Hirschman, A. O. (1991) *The Rhetoric of Reaction: Perversity, Futility, Jeopardy* (Cambridge, MA: Harvard University Press).

Hugo, V. (1883) *L'homme qui rit* (Paris: J. Hetzel & Cie).

Ike, D. N. (1984) "The System of Land Rights in Nigerian Agriculture", *American Journal of Economics and Sociology*, Vol. 43, No. 4, pp. 469–80.

International IDEA Handbook (2008) *Direct Democracy* (Stockholm, Sweden: International IDEA).

Jefferson, T. (1811 and 1812) *The Writings of Thomas Jefferson*, Definitive Edition, 1905, Albert E. Bergh (ed.) (Washington, DC: The Thomas Jefferson Memorial Association. Available online: www.constitution.org/tj/jeff.htm, accessed 20 March 2016.

Krugman, P. (2014) "Wall Street's Revenge", *New York Times*, December 16.

Maddison, A. (2006) *The World Economy: A Millennial Perspective* (Paris: OECD Development Center Studies).

Morgan, L. H. (1877) *Ancient Society: Or Researches in the Lines of Human Progress from Savagery through Barbarism to Civilization*, New York: Holt & Co., available online from the *Internet Archive*: https://archive.org/details/ancientsociety00morg, accessed 20 March 2016.

Oxfam (2015) *Wealth: Having it All and Wanting More*, available online: www.oxfam.org/en/research/wealth-having-it-all-and-wanting-more, accessed 20 March 2016.

Piketty, T. (2014) *Capital in the Twenty- First Century* (Cambridge, MA: Harvard University Press).

Polanyi, K. (1944) *The Great Transformation: The Political and Economic Origins of Our Time* (Boston, MA: Beacon Press).

Roberts, P. C. (2014) *Conversation Between Noam Chomsky, Paul Craig Roberts and Rob Kall: The future of Capitalism, Climate Change and Suicidal Russia Policy*, online: http://chomsky.info/interviews/20140928.htm, accessed 20 March 2016.

Rodney, W. (1972) *How Europe Underdeveloped Africa* (London: Bogle-L'Ouverture).

Roy, A. (2014) *Capitalism: A Ghost Story* (Chicago, IL: Haymarket Books).

Saul, J. S. and P. Bond (2014) *South Africa – The Present as History: From Mrs Ples to Mandela and Marikana* (Rochester, NY: Boydell & Brewer Inc.).

Stiglitz, J. E. (2011) "Of the 1%, by the 1%, for the 1%" in *Vanity Fair*, available online: www.vanityfair.com/society/features/2011/05/top-one-percent-201105, accessed 20 March 2016.

Stiglitz, J. E. (2013) *The Price of Inequality: How Today's Divided Society Endangers Our Future* (New York: W. W. Norton & Co.).

Stiglitz, J. E. (2016) *Rewriting the Rules of the American Economy: An Agenda for Growth and Shared Prosperity* (New York: W. W. Norton & Co.).

Tanzi, V. (2011) *Government versus Markets: The Changing Economic Role of the State* (Cambridge, UK: Cambridge University Press).

Vries, P. (2015) *State, Economy and the Great Divergence: Great Britain and China, 1680s–1850s* (New York: Bloomsbury Academic).

Wray, R. (2011) "Anatomy of Mortgage Fraud, Part II: The Mother of All Frauds", available online: www.huffingtonpost.com/l-randall-wray/post_1423_b_795802.html, accessed 20 March 2016.

Wright, D. (2004) *A Short History of Progress* (Toronto: House of Anansi Press, Inc.).

3 Private wealth . . . and public debt

We have eliminated hunger, want, the need for possessions – The acquisition of wealth is no longer the driving force in our lives. We work to better ourselves and the rest of humanity.

(Captain Jean-Luc Picard, *Star Trek* in the twenty-fourth century)

Introduction

In his well-known book, *Democracy in America*, Alexis de Tocqueville (1840: 932–4) argues that revolutions in aristocratic societies are less likely because people get used to their poverty and do not strive to get material well-being "because they despair of gaining it and do not know it well enough to desire it". In democracies, however, he maintains that everyone wants the comforts of a good life and so "the desire to gain well-being occurs to the imagination of the poor, and the fear of losing it to the mind of the rich" so much so that "The love of well-being has become the national and dominant taste". Does this mean that we should expect revolutions to happen more easily in democratic societies? No. Tocqueville gives a thoughtful and subtle explanation to this seemingly disappointing answer. First, he notes that:

Nearly all the revolutions that have changed the face of peoples have been made in order to sanction or to destroy *inequality*. Take away the secondary causes that have produced the great agitations of men, you will almost always arrive at inequality. It is the poor who have wanted to steal the property of the rich, or the rich who have tried to put the poor in chains. So if you can establish a state of society in which each man has something to keep and little to take, you will have done a great deal for the peace of the world (emphasis added).

To clarify his argument, Tocqueville then adds that while aristocracies vest permanent wealth and hence permanent power in an entrenched elite, democratic societies offer equal opportunities for everyone to get rich, which leads him to believe that, in democracies, the poor are in small numbers. Tocqueville (1840: 1135–50) emphasizes that in such societies "the rich . . . do not have privileges that attract attention; their wealth itself, no longer incorporated in and represented by the land, is elusive and as if invisible" and that they:

[e]merge each day from within the crowd, and return to it constantly. So they do not form a separate class that you can easily define and despoil; and since, moreover, the rich are attached by a thousand secret threads to the mass of their fellow citizens, the people can scarcely hope to strike them without hitting themselves.[1]

The implication of Tocqueville's analysis is that in democratic societies, wealth itself becomes democratic since it circulates and spreads among enterprising and ambitious individuals so as to create a middle class, which forms the majority – thus making inequality less of a problem. With the benefit of hindsight, it is now clear that Tocqueville's claims about social mobility and the disappearing inequality were certainly exaggerated and that, in any case, his notion of 'democratic wealth' could not be equated with economic and social justice as we defined it in Chapter 2. Clark (2014, 2015) has shown that "the American dream is an illusion" and that "social mobility barely exists". Galbraith (2000: 69) cynically remarked that "single moms don't move from welfare to Forbes 400", whereas Mahfouz Saber, Egypt's minister of justice, openly scorned the poor and disdainfully declared that "children of garbage collectors cannot grow up to become judges" because "a judge has prestige, so he must come from a respectable milieu; must be respectable financially, morally and so on".[2]

At any rate, inequality today is the most pernicious problem that democratic societies must deal with and is a salient feature of all modern capitalist economies; particularly in the country studied by Tocqueville – namely the United States. It must also be noted that the mobility that transpires from the notion of 'democratic wealth' is not the result of society's deliberate implementation of the democratic ideals, but rather a consequence of the increased liberty and freedom in a market economy. However, empirical evidence on the historical trends and on the current state of income and wealth distribution worldwide (Stiglitz, 2013; Piketty, 2014) indicates that inequality has actually been rising in parallel with the implementation of pro-market, neoliberal policies. Wealth has become so concentrated that only 80 individuals hold as much wealth as half of the entire population on earth, that is, about 3.5 billion people (see Oxfam, 2015).

Market economies, functioning under the institutions of representative democracy, have, therefore, failed to bring our societies closer to that state in which 'all citizens have equal opportunities to acquire wealth' and, most importantly, to escape poverty. The question now really is whether we still want to experiment with the market economy and parliamentary democracy for yet two more centuries, or should we look for alternative modes of organizing our economic system? Phelps (2013) seems to have faith that American-style, laissez-faire capitalism can still give rise to what he calls "mass flourishing", which he defines as the good life that everyone shall get from the benefits of dynamism and innovation. Skidelsky (2010: 335), however, calls for "the rehabilitation of the state as an instrument of the public interest". And Stiglitz (2013) has reached the conclusion that laissez-faire capitalism "endangers our future" by having transformed itself into an oligarchy that serves the interests of the super-rich while condemning the masses into unbearable poverty. The historian Gareth Stedman Jones (2004) gave a history of the idea of "ending poverty" since the eighteenth century and listed the various proposals made towards this end from the role of ministrations by charitable organizations to reforming the Poor Laws to the present Welfare State. But there is one strange omission from the otherwise quite complete list of proposals he reviewed and that is the odd, inhumanly vicious, proposition made by Jeremy Bentham (1797), which we wish to emphasize here because of its seeming resemblance to the current proposals under the neoliberal regime.

In the midst of the debate among philosophers, economists, sociologists and politicians over how to deal with the social problem of poverty by way of reforming society and its economic system, Jeremy Bentham (1797) had the cunning idea of locking the poor in workhouses where they would be forced to perform profitable work for which they would receive food – a programme he referred to as "Pauper Management Improved". The inmates were to be classified according to several criteria but most importantly by 'hands', that is, according to their varying degrees of ability to perform work. The workhouses or factories were inspired by and modelled on his eerie jailhouse, which he proudly named the Panopticon. The workers, or the working hands, were subjected to what he called the *Earn-first* principle, according to which:

> When ability adequate to the task is certain, and laziness apprehended, no meal given, till the task by which it is earned has been *first* performed. Without this, or some severer and less unexceptionable spur, the lazy among them would do nothing.
>
> (Bentham, 1797: 383)

Because history is relevant to the present, we recall here Bentham's 'solution' to the problem of poverty so that we can appropriately analyse some current proposals to deal with unemployment and poverty such as 'workfare' to replace 'welfare' and similar draconian measures inspired by the 'earn-first' principle.

Our proposal in this chapter differs diametrically from Bentham's. The aim is to improve the well-being of all members of society, but we recognize that our economic system is built on a permanent antagonism of interests in which the distribution of wealth is necessarily skewed in favour of the economically dominant class, as we have shown in the previous two chapters. Relying on the market system to redress the problem of inequality and to bring about a convergence in wealth distribution must be recognized for what it is: a chimera. The purpose of this chapter is to show that, contrary to common belief, prosperity and 'democratic wealth' in a capitalist economy depend in a crucial way on greater government intervention. A corollary of this statement is that it is in the private sector's interest – and that of society as a whole – to develop a strong public sector, capable of providing not only law and order but also, and more importantly, social services and public goods that are essential to growth, prosperity and equality. In this way, it is hoped that we "can establish a state of society in which each man has something to keep and little to take" so that we would contribute to doing "a great deal for the peace of the world".

Of assets and liabilities

The ultimate desire of every individual is to enjoy a comfortable life by securing access to such material things as a house, a car and so on, in addition to a bank account with money in it to ensure purchasing power. Ideally, people want to have their own material and financial things. When these things do belong to individuals, we say that they have their own assets. The issue of wealth and prosperity essentially revolves around making sure that everyone has their own assets and that these are expanding over time in order to meet the increased demand and requirements to enjoy life. The acquisition of assets or as we shall call it 'the accumulation of wealth' in a capitalist society is limited by the amount of income one is able to earn. In general, these incomes can be grouped under two broad categories: direct compensation for work (wages and salaries) and compensation from ownership (profits, rent of money, rent of property and capital gains) – with employment income being the main source of earnings for the great majority of the population in any country. The immediate consequence of this is that the poor and the unemployed can never be in a position to build assets. Instead, they may have to borrow, say from a bank, to pay for their housing and other expenses – in which case they are incurring liabilities. The reality today is that even those who are working resort to borrowing in order to be able to build assets and improve their wealth – which explains the rise of households' indebtedness in most industrialized countries (see Seccareccia, 2005). Building on seminal works of Hyman Minsky and Wynne Godley, Keen (2015) argued that the latest crisis that began in 2007–8 – or the Great Recession as others refer to it – was a direct consequence of the dynamics of such private debt.

Financial assets and liabilities are two sides of the same coin. The money available in the bank account held by an individual is an asset to them but a liability to the bank. Similarly, a loan owed to the bank is obviously a liability to the person who borrowed the money but an asset to the bank.

We can learn more about the relationships linking the different sectors of the economy if we now focus on the stock of assets and liabilities held by each sector. Let us focus on the case of a closed economy and divide it into a private and a public sector. The private sector would comprise households, firms and banks while the public sector is generally represented by the government – with the Central Bank often in the background.

An easy way of keeping track of assets and liabilities is to record them using the double-entry bookkeeping system. This work is routine to accountants at the firm level and quite familiar to most households. However, the details can get quite messy as we move to the macroeconomic level. Godley and Lavoie (2007) have proposed a tidy technique based on the use of what they call a "matrix of sectoral balance sheets".

This method makes use of the coherent stock-flow accounting where, according to Godley and Lavoie (2007: 38), "everything comes from somewhere and everything goes somewhere". The stock-flow consistent accounting is indeed a neat way of capturing transactions and their counterparts throughout the entire macroeconomic system. Here, because assets add to the wealth or net worth of their holders, they are entered with a plus sign, while liabilities are entered with a minus sign (see Table 3.1).

Say you buy a government security such as a Treasury bill (denoted by B). This would be an asset for you ($+B_h$) and a liability for its issuer – namely the government ($-B$). Similarly, when you ask for a loan (L) from the bank, if your loan is approved, the bank records the amount as its own asset ($+L$) and in your records as a household it shows as a liability ($-L_h$), thus making you indebted to the bank. But in order to make use of that loan, you need the money to be made available to you. So the bank opens an account for you in which it deposits the amount of the loan by *inscribing* in it a credit to you. The bank deposits held by households ($+M_h$) and firms ($+M_f$) are assets for them but show as a liability on the bank's balance sheet ($-M$). Note by the way that this is the current practice by which private banks create money as shown by Post-Keynesian theorists of endogenous money (Lavoie, 1985; Moore, 1988; Parguez and Seccareccia, 2000; Rochon and Rossi, 2007, 2013; Smithin, 2016a, 2016b).

What is important to realize at this point is that if we add up your liability (what you owe to the bank) and the bank's asset (the claim which the bank has on you), the sum is necessarily equal to zero. And that is true for all households' liabilities to the banks and the corresponding banks' assets. This is also true of liabilities linking firms ($-L_f$) to the banks ($+L$). In fact, it holds for all other sectors of the economy so that, for instance, if we add all the cash (denoted by H) held as assets by households ($+H_h$), firms ($+H_f$) and banks ($+H_b$) to the Central Bank's total liability ($-H$), the horizontal sum of the row 'cash' is necessarily zero. Similarly, if we add up all the T-bills (B) held as assets by households ($+B_h$), firms (B_f), banks (B_b) and by the Central Bank (B_{cb}) to the liabilities issued by the government ($-B$), the sum is again necessarily zero. Monetary (or financial) assets and liabilities necessarily cancel each other out, as further shown by adding the assets and liabilities concerning the rows 'loans' (L) and 'equities' (E).

This rule obviously does not apply to real tangible assets such as houses ($+K_h$), because these belong only to their owners or machinery and equipment ($+K_f$) wholly owned by firms, thus giving us the positive sum of ($+K$) across the row 'tangible capital'. The empty cells in Table 3.1 indicate that we ignore some assets (and their liabilities) either because they are insignificant or irrelevant to the analysis. For example, for 'tangible capital' we could add real estate assets held by banks and all the public infrastructure such as hospitals, schools and so on that can be attributed to government, but these complications do not change the conclusions in any fundamental way.

A well-known general principle in accounting is that a balance sheet must be balanced, meaning that the sum of all the items on the left-hand side of the balance sheet must be equal to the sum of the items on the right-hand side. We mentioned earlier that assets are entered with a plus sign while liabilities are entered with a minus sign. The difference between the total value of assets and the total value of liabilities is called the *net worth*. When the value of assets exceeds the value of liabilities, the net worth is positive, but since it must be added to the liabilities side in order to ensure that the equality or balance is maintained,

Table 3.1 Private sector balance and public sector balance compared

	Households	Production firms	Banks	Government	Central Bank	Σ
Tangible capital	$+K_h$	$+K_f$				$+K$
T-Bills	$+B_h$	$+B_f$	$+B_b$	$-B$	$+B_{cb}$	0
Cash	$+H_h$	$+H_f$	$+H_b$		$-H$	0
Deposits	$+M_h$	$+M_f$	$-M$			0
Loan	$-L_h$	$-L_f$	$+L$			0
Equity	$+E_h$		$-E_b$			0
Net worth	$-NW_h$	$-NW_f$	$-NW_b$	$-NW_g$	0	$-K$
Σ	0	0	0	0	0	0

it is entered with a minus sign. Consequently, the sum of all the elements of each column in Table 3.1 is necessarily zero. Obviously, when liabilities exceed assets, the net worth is negative and the agent or sector is said to be in debt. Such is the case with the government, for instance, which typically has an outstanding debt, known as the *public debt*.

In Table 3.1, the public debt or government's net worth is a negative amount but preceded by a minus sign, $-NW_g$, becomes a positive entry – thus ensuring that the balance sheet is balanced. Therefore, as emphasized by Godley and Lavoie (2007: 27), "These conventions will insure that all the rows and all the columns of the balance sheet matrix sum to zero, thus providing consistency and coherence in our stock accounting".

The most interesting point in this whole discussion lies in the information given by the last row labelled 'net worth' in Table 3.1. The total net worth of the whole economy, which is obtained by adding the net worth of all sectors, is given in the last column as the amount of existing tangible capital (K). If we leave aside, for the moment, tangible capital and focus only on financial assets, it is obvious that the sum of the net worth of all sectors is zero.[3] This is because, as explained earlier, financial assets have a liability side to them. Your cash, money deposits, bonds and stocks, government securities and so on are all liabilities to their issuers. Therefore, the sum of the financial net worth of the private sector: households, firms, banks ($NW_h + NW_f + NW_b$) and that of the government sector (NW_g) is:

$$(NW_h + NW_f + NW_b) + NW_g = 0$$

Or

private sector balance + government sector balance = 0   (3.1)
$$(NW_h + NW_f + NW_b) = -NW_g$$

This is simply stating that the private sector's financial net worth (or private financial wealth) is equal to public debt – a conclusion that is crucial for understanding the effects of government policy. The relevance of this result for our study is that it makes clear the relationship between private financial wealth and public debt, and forces us to recognize that an increase in public debt *logically* leads to an increase in private financial wealth. From a policy perspective, this is very important because it gives the government a powerful instrument in its quest for the creation and expansion of wealth – and ultimately, in the fight against poverty.

In this regard, all payments made by the government sector necessarily flow as a revenue and represent an income for the private sector. Purchases of goods and services from the private sector by the government are a source of income for firms and households and represent an *injection* of money into the private sector. Similarly, when the government collects taxes, private agents lose some of their income and become somewhat poorer, as money is *withdrawn* out of the private sector. Ideally, private agents would wish that the government does not take away all of what it has just paid out to them. But for that to happen, the government must pay them more than what it collects in taxes, that is, it must accept being in a *deficit* position. Obviously, the private sector will be much poorer if forced into a situation such as when the government decides to have a *surplus* by withdrawing more money than it had injected into the economy during a given period.

An obvious question that follows from the discussion on government spending is: where does the government get the money it spends? A moment of reflection leads us to exclude the possibility of taxes as a source of revenue for the government since private agents must first receive the money before being in a position to pay it back to the government in the form of taxes – that is, the government must first spend, then collect taxes. The same remark also applies to the government borrowing from the private sector (via the sale of bonds): government spending must precede any withdrawal of liquidity from the private sector. That leaves us with only one source of funding and that is through the creation of money by banks and primarily Central Banks. This is the practice of financing government spending, and it has long been recognized by Post-Keynesians but also by central bankers. As stated earlier, since the process of money creation has long been controversial and deliberately shrouded in mystery, it is worth reading carefully what these central bankers say.

> When banks extend loans to their customers, they create money by crediting their customers' accounts . . . The way in which the Bank of England expands the money supply is to purchase government gilts from the non-bank private sector and credit the bank accounts of people from whom the gilts are purchased. Please note that we are not giving money away.
>
> (Mervyn King,[4] Governor of the Bank of England (2003–13))

> "Is that tax money that the Fed is spending?" Chairman Bernanke: "It's not tax money. The banks have accounts with the Fed, much the same way that you have an account in a commercial bank. So, to lend to a bank, we simply use the computer to mark up the size of the account that they have with the Fed".
>
> (Ben S. Bernanke,[5] Chairman of the US Federal Reserve
> (2006–14) in an interview on the CBS TV programme
> *60 Minutes*, answering a question by Scott Pelley)

Question: But there is no question about it that banks create that medium of exchange? Mr. Towers: That is right. That is what they are for. *Question*: And they issue that form of medium of exchange when they purchase securities or make loans? Mr. Towers: That is the banking business, just in the same way that a steel plant makes steel. Each and every time a bank makes a loan (or purchases securities) new bank credit is created – new deposits – brand new money. Broadly speaking, all new money comes out of a bank in the form of loans. *Question*: When $1,000,000 worth of bonds is presented (by the government) to the bank, a million dollars of new money or the equivalent is created? Mr. Towers: Yes. *Question*: It is a fact that a million dollars of new money is created? Mr. Towers: That is right.

> (Graham Towers,[6] Governor of the Bank of Canada (1934–54)
> answering questions from the *Standing Committee of the
> House of Commons on Banking and Commerce*)

Question: How did you get the money to buy those $2,000,000,000 of Government securities [and advance that money to the government]? Mr. Eccles: We created it. *Question*: Out of what? Mr. Eccles: Out of the right to issue credit, money. *Question*: And there is nothing behind it, is there, except the Government's credit? Mr. Eccles: We have the Government bonds. *Question*: That's right, the Government's credit. Mr. Eccles: That is what your money system is.

> (Marriner S. Eccles,[7] Chairman of the US Federal Reserve Board
> (1934–48) answering questions from the members of the *Committee on
> Banking and Currency of the House of Representatives* who wanted
> to know how the government pays for its expenditures)

Now, as Samuelson (1966: 583) put it "If all this causes headaches for those nostalgic for the old time parables of neoclassical writing, we must remind ourselves that scholars are not born to live an easy existence. We must respect, and appraise, the facts of life".

Traditionally, governments relied on their own banks, i.e. Central Banks, for such money creation whenever they needed financing. The practice and procedures tend to vary from one country to another, but it always boils down to the same thing: the government gets a loan or a line of credit from its Central Bank. As explained above, the loan to the government is recorded as an asset on the Central Bank's balance sheet and as a liability on the government's own balance sheet. And by this process the Central Bank advances money to the government simply by putting a credit in its account. Having now secured a positive amount of money in its account – a credit to it by the Central Bank – the government can start making payments to its employees and other suppliers of goods and services by transferring to them some of those credits. All these expenditures lead to a flow of liquidity (money) from the public sector into the private sector thus adding to the latter's liquid holdings (or monetary assets). Indeed, as private agents receive their payments, these are deposited in their bank accounts – either through direct deposits or via cheques and represent an increase in their deposits, which as explained earlier are assets to their depositors and liabilities to the banks (Mosler, 2010; Wray, 2015).

Note that in this manner, the sovereign national government can pay for any expenditure – whether it is related to building a new hospital, a school or a highway, or to the hiring of teachers, nurses, engineers or street sweepers – simply by crediting their bank accounts (at commercial banks) and debiting its own account at the Central Bank. This analysis invalidates the widely popular claim that the government often has scarce funds and faces a binding budget constraint. The process may in fact involve several successive steps, which can be summarized as follows: the cheques or e-deposits that increased the private agents' deposits are held by the banks as claims on the government and thus are recorded as an equal increase in their assets. Banks' claims on the government in this form are called 'reserves'. Banks can claim these reserves by presenting the cheques or e-deposits to the Central Bank, which keeps accounts for both the government and commercial banks. In a setting where the Central Bank is the banking arm of the government, the Central Bank executes the operation simply by *crediting* commercial banks' accounts (that is, by adding to their reserves[8]) and *debiting* the government's account by an equal amount. Government spending results in a net injection of liquidity (money) into the private sector; the government is now running a *deficit*, but the private sector has a *surplus*. We conclude that government spending increases the private sector's incomes and, therefore, that the accumulated deficits – the public debt – add to the private sector's financial wealth, as shown by Equation (3.1).

It should be noted, however, that with the rise of monetarism and the associated ideas of 'fiscal responsibility' and 'sound finance', neoliberal policies have succeeded in imposing severe restrictions on how Central Banks could participate in financing governments' expenditures and in some cases making it illegal for Central Banks to advance funds to their own governments – hence, severely hampering the role of public policy in fighting poverty and other economic and social problems. Governments, such as those in the European Monetary Union, are now forced to rely on taxes and loans from private lenders, namely banks. A solution to this obstacle is the public ownership of all banks, including commercial banks, which would then act as *State Development Banks*, as we argue in the following section.

When the government remains indebted to the Central Bank and when the latter is publicly owned and is therefore the government's banking arm, the issue of a government's debt to its own bank becomes largely a technical issue – one to which we will return with more details in the next section. However, we can already point out at this stage that any taxes collected by the government are deposited in its own account at the Central Bank as credits and would, therefore, serve to lower the amount of the debt (loan). If the government is eager to pay down its debt to the Central Bank, it can withdraw more money from the private sector by various ways and use the proceeds in the same way as taxes. All these withdrawals lead to a decrease in liquidity in the private sector and, from an accounting perspective, they are recorded in exactly the opposite manner of recording government spending.

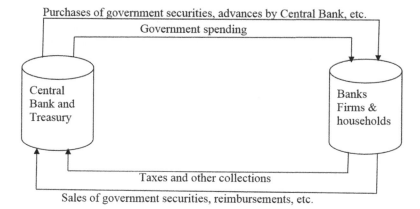

Figure 3.1 The flow of funds between private and public sectors.

The interactions described above can conveniently be summarized by the following diagram (see Figure 3.1), developed by the monetary circuit theory to capture the flow of funds between the various agents in the national economy (see Bougrine and Seccareccia, 2002; Parguez, 2002).

One further observation is worth making in this respect. The sustained injections, for example through government spending, necessarily result in an increase in banks' reserves and therefore in the amount of liquidity in the banking system. The increased liquidity can have two consequences: (1) cause the rate of interest to fall, as inter-bank lending becomes cheaper, and (2) lead to inflation. The latter effect, which is the only one emphasized by neoclassical economists, is in fact highly unlikely for as long as the economy is below full employment, and anyway as Lerner (1943) showed, this is easily resolved through taxation. The first effect is more of a short-run nature and tends to manifest itself almost immediately. The inter-bank lending rate is also sensitive to a decrease in liquidity and tends to go up as banks' reserves fall. It is for this reason that Central Banks nowadays rely heavily on the technique of increasing or decreasing reserves in order to manipulate the inter-bank rate and bring it close to the Central Bank's chosen target. Government spending and taxing – injections and withdrawals of liquidity – are important policy tools that help the government and its Central Bank achieve the desired target rate of interest and the 'balancing' between the two is done with this objective in mind – not for the concerns of avoiding a deficit or attempting to achieve a surplus in the public budget, as neoclassical economists would like us to believe.

Public policy and the creation of wealth

It must have become clear by now from our discussion that the net worth of a sector such as firms or households can be greatly affected by what goes on in the government sector, that is, by the type of economic policies implemented by the government, particularly as regards spending and taxing – or what we call fiscal policy. It is important to point out here that our accounting result in Equation (3.1) is not a hypothesis or a theory, but rather an identity that is empirically true and is strongly supported by evidence from the actual experiences of several countries (see, among others, Bougrine, 2010 for Canada; Wray, 2011 for the United States). However, that result focused on the closed economy case and ignored transactions with the rest of the world. In terms of data and empirical evidence, this meant that the sum of the two balances of the domestic private and government sectors did not always add up to zero because some funds would have flown into or out of the national economy. Therefore, a more realistic mapping of the flow of funds between the different sectors of the economy must certainly include lending to, and borrowing from, the foreign sector. So, the accounting equation for an open economy is:

Domestic private balance + Domestic government balance +
Foreign sector balance = 0   (3.2)

In Figure 3.2, we use data from the Canadian Income and Expenditures Accounts, provided by Statistics Canada, to further demonstrate the validity of our statements. The new and updated series contain quarterly data from 1981 to 2014 on the net lending or borrowing by the consolidated government sector in Canada (the public sector), the net lending or borrowing by the domestic private sector (represented by households and corporations) and the net lending or borrowing by the foreign sector. We have expressed all data as a percentage of GDP in order to scale down the values. As can be seen from Figure 3.2, over the entire period, whenever the public sector is running a deficit (is 'in the red'), the private sector as a whole, that is, the sum of domestic and foreign balances, is running a surplus, and vice versa. Therefore, the public budget really does reflect – almost like a mirror – the private sector's net accumulation of savings. For instance, a surplus in the public budget is achieved by reducing government spending and/or increasing taxes, but this directly translates into a reduction of incomes received by those (firms and households) who supply goods and services to the government thus forcing the private sector, sometimes including the foreign sector, to be in deficit. This is indeed what happened in Canada from the late 1990s to the beginning of the 2007–8 global crisis, as shown in Figure 3.2. The slow performance of the economy and even negative growth during this period have forced many governments around the world to become more pragmatic about deficit spending. Indeed, it was only after these governments reversed their austerity policies that national economies begun sluggishly to climb out of recession – with the private sector's balance slowly becoming positive from 2008 onwards, as can be seen in Figure 3.2.

The importance of a public deficit and its impact on the private sector's performance can be clarified further by returning to national income accounting

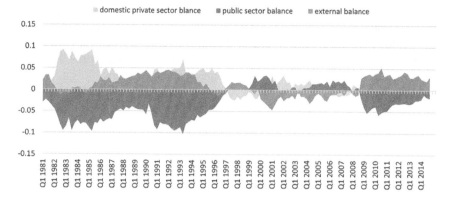

Figure 3.2 Sectoral balances in Canada, 1981–2014, quarterly data.

Source: Author's calculations based on Statistics Canada, Cansim Series Nos. 380-0063, 380-0071 and 380-0082.

once again. The basic national income identity states that disposable income (*Y*) is equal to the sum of total spending by households (*C*), firms (*I*), government (*G* – *T*) and the foreign sector, which can be approximated by (*X* – *M*):

$$Y = C + I + (G - T) + (X - M) \tag{3.3}$$

Which can be re-written as:

$$Y - C - I = (S - I) = (G - T) + (X - M) \tag{3.3'}$$

where *S* stands for private sector's total saving, *I* for investment, *G* for government spending, *T* for taxes, *X* for exports and *M* for imports. Equation (3.3') restates the by-now familiar idea that private net saving is equivalent to government deficit plus the balance of payments. It also implies that, for a given position of the balance of payments, any attempt to balance the public budget and/or achieve a surplus will necessarily result in a reduction of the private sector's savings, and hence of its wealth. Moreover, since a public surplus means, by definition, that the government is withdrawing more resources from the private economy than it is injecting into it, (*G* – *T* < 0), government surpluses necessarily lower aggregate demand, which results in lower sales and lower profits for private firms – and ultimately leads to prolonged recessions and economic crises (see Bougrine, 2004; Mosler, 2010).

To emphasize the direct relationship between firms' profits and public deficits, we can decompose private sector's total savings (*S*) into households' savings *(S*$_h$*)* and firms' savings or, more precisely, their profits (*P*), and rearrange Equation (3.3') to obtain the familiar Kaleckian profit equation:

$$P = (I - S_h) + (G - T) + (X - M) \tag{3.4}$$

Equation (3.4) clearly indicates that firms' profits are positively affected by investment, government spending and exports (see Bougrine, 2000; Halevi and Kriesler, 2000; Lavoie, 2000). It is also clear that households' savings, taxes and imports lower business profits because these act as leakages since they withdraw funds away from the domestic income spending flow. In other words, long-run firms' profits can be sustained by a combination of three factors:

1   low or negative households' savings (indebtedness);
2   a public budget deficit; and/or
3   an improvement in the balance of payments.

Since budget deficits are clearly a source of profits for firms, we find it ironic that free-market pundits should be advocating a policy based on balanced budgets and/ or surpluses. Given the centrality of profit in a market economy and the related importance of firms in the real production sector, we think it imperative to explore further the role and limitations of each of the three factors mentioned above, as well as the relationship between them.

As Bougrine (2004: 35) observed, improving the balance of payments is a possibility but has its limitations:

(a) It can be achieved if a country uses the traditional trade measures (tariffs, quotas and so on), but these measures are no longer permitted by the World Trade Organization rules.
(b) In a globalized world, it is indeed difficult to exercise control over capital flows with any degree of effectiveness. The situation is particularly problematic for poor developing countries either because they lack the institutions that would allow them to do that or because they are vulnerable to threats from international lenders.
(c) A country cannot improve its balance of payments without negatively affecting its trading partners. So, if the possibility of improving the balance of payments is feasible for one country, it cannot be feasible for all.

Similarly, Godley (2000: 4) argued that the negative effect of a budget surplus can be offset by an increase in private indebtedness but:

An increase in private debt relative to income can go on for a long time, but it cannot go on forever because the decisive constraint on borrowing may come not from the extent to which net worth is being mortgaged, but from the extent to which payments of interest and repayments of principal . . . can be met out of conventional income.

The constraint will indeed become binding since households' income will continuously be eroded by long-term budget surpluses. Furthermore, once households decide to stop borrowing and start saving or reducing their debt, aggregate demand, and consequently production, must fall, thus leading to a recession unless the government reverses the surplus policy and starts increasing its net spending. Therefore, a policy of long-term budget surpluses is not viable because it would force households into unsustainable debt. This is indeed the present situation of households in many OECD countries, particularly in Canada and the United States (see Seccareccia, 2005) where households' indebtedness (and asset price inflation) have become the new engine of demand growth – a model referred to by Seccareccia (2005) as a state of "affluenza" and by Palley (2013) as "America's exhausted paradigm".

Therefore, the only sustainable policy instrument that remains for improving the private sector's wealth is the public deficit. This leads us to examine more closely the controversial issue of the efficacy of public deficits in creating wealth and resolving problems of poverty – which can be done by assessing the differential effects of various types of government spending. As suggested above, the implementation of a socially responsible fiscal policy would require that public spending benefit directly the poor and the unemployed and at the same time target key productive sectors of the economy and not the bailing out of financial institutions. In addition to investment in public infrastructure, which is crucial to the start-up, growth and development of private businesses, the state should also focus on "investments in technology and human capital that foster growth" (Mazzucato, 2014: 34). These investments are what actually makes the difference today between the most industrialized countries and those euphemistically referred to as 'developing' or 'emerging' economies.

Funding R&D is particularly important for innovation and progress. In her recent work, Mazzucato (2014) has shown that the state is actually behind the core inventions of modern-day technology and their applications, including the internet, pharmaceutical-biotechnology, nanotechnology and more recently green technology. Investment in innovation is costly and risky and for this reason private investors do not dare to venture beyond the beaten track. As Mazzucato (2014: 23) explains:

> [i]t is naïve to expect venture capital to lead in the early and most risky stage of any new economic sector today (such as clean technology). In biotechnology, nanotechnology and the Internet, venture capital arrived 15–20 years *after* the most important investments were made by public sector funds.

That is why the state must take the lead and act as a:

> [p]roactive, *entrepreneurial* State, one able to take risks and create a highly networked system of actors that harness the best of the private sector for the national good over a medium- to long-term time horizon. It is the state acting as lead investor and catalyst which sparks the network to act and spread knowledge.
> (Mazzucato, 2014: 21, emphasis in original)

There is another reason why public deficit spending should be channelled towards innovation: new inventions are obviously a great source of wealth creation and from which we tend to reap benefits for quite a long time. Innovations affect various firms and sectors throughout the economy and have the *potential* to spread the benefits to more people in society – thus contributing to the creation of a more democratic wealth. However, as Mazzucato (2014: 182) has argued, if under the current economic model the costs of innovation are largely collective and socialized, the rewards and benefits tend to accrue to private owners of corporations who have the power to lobby and influence government decisions. Such a skewed distribution of the gains from innovation has been widely decried as a "dysfunctional system of socialized risks and privatized rewards" (see, Salvemini, 1936; Chomsky, 1999; Feige, 2008).[9]

The issue of maldistribution of the gains from innovation is obviously only one aspect of the wider problem of unequal distribution of wealth and income, which finds its root cause in the private ownership of productive resources. To mitigate the negative effects of such a distorted distribution of risk and reward from innovation and to make growth "not only smart but also inclusive", Mazzucato (2014: 185–91) proposed that:

(a) The government should earn a direct return from its risky investments through royalties. Such returns would be paid into a national 'innovation fund' and would serve to fund future innovations and/or cover the losses that arise in high-risk areas.
(b) The government should earn an income by retaining equity in the companies it funds and by making loans and grants to businesses contingent on receiving a share of the profits made.
(c) The government should earn income directly by financing investment in innovation and new technological projects through state-owned investment banks.

The government should certainly levy taxes and must obviously recoup the money advanced to subsidize successful projects through the means mentioned above, but it should be underlined that the government's ability to pursue its search for new ideas and to sustain its investments in risky innovative projects *does not depend* on these funds – as it transpires from Mazzucato's assumption. While I agree with the general principle of fairness that motivates Mazzucato's arguments, I am inclined to add that her proposal does not address the bigger and thorny issue of income and wealth inequality discussed earlier, since the proposal is limited to how the state would deal with companies involved in the innovation business. The share of labour in the fruits of growth is limited to job creation, while capital continues to reap the high profits. But, as (Mazzucato, 2014: 190) herself says, this is capitalism "pure and plain". And so, in the end, risks remain socialized and rewards remain privatized. There is of course the implicit assumption that the government would also use the above proceeds to pay for social programmes that benefit the workers and their communities.

But it is not through progressive taxation and increased social spending on programmes targeting the poor – though these are important and necessary – that we can achieve the higher goal of economic and social democracy. To ensure that it is not 'capitalism as usual', we need social institutions that seek to eliminate all forms of economic and social inequalities – hence our proposal, which calls for: (1) communal and workers' ownership of productive resources, and (2) public ownership of banks. This is similar to Mazzucato's proposal except that it goes a step farther in the sense that it makes all banks 'State Development Banks' and includes workers and communities as shareholders in the businesses operating in their own environment. In this setting, the democratic state would have more leverage allowing it to continue being an aggressive risk-taker by investing in exciting innovative projects. This is the creative, entrepreneurial state and it is not utopia.

Historical evidence indicates that public banks have indeed been playing a crucial role in the development of many industrialized countries in Europe ever since the Second World War, including, among others, France and Germany (see Mattey, 2010). As Bougrine and Seccareccia (2013: 153) noted, "In most developed countries, public banks have traditionally been a major source of funding for small businesses, infrastructure development, housing construction and other investments for social purposes". The importance of public banks in the democratic society comes from the fact that they play a social and economic function based on public interest: they must provide the needed finance and eliminate the problem of artificial scarcity of money for the greater public interest, which is – and ought to be – the creation of wealth and prosperity for the whole society. The system of public banks is a means by which the democratic society can achieve the collective control over the creation of money and the equitable distribution of financing among its members.

Up until the 1970s and just prior to the wave of neoliberal privatizations, Canada, for example, had a strong public sector – with its iconic, world-famous 'crown corporations' (state enterprises) operating in virtually all sectors of the economy from mining (oil, gas) to transportation (air, railways), media and communications, banking and so on. The state financed high-risk innovation projects and invested in areas as varied as aerospace engineering (Avro Canada Jetliner, Canadarm), energy generation (the Candu reactor), internet/telecommunications (CANARIE, the world's first national optical internet research and education network for the transfer of very large data files), agriculture and the arts (The National Arts Centre Orchestra and its support for other performing arts). The number of government (federal and provincial) organizations devoted exclusively to scientific research, not counting universities which are *all publicly owned*, is still quite impressive by most standards. The fact remains, however, that the wealth generated through these and other activities does not trickle down evenly to all social classes. Indeed, as shown in Chapter 1, wealth in Canada remains largely concentrated in the hands of the richest 20 per cent of the population.

Conclusion

Poverty and the related question of unequal distribution of wealth have always been at the centre of the debate on social issues. Government interventions to alleviate poverty are often met with fierce opposition on the grounds that public funds are limited by what the government can collect from taxes and that policymakers should not venture beyond these limits. The prevailing wisdom is that taxes are the only legitimate source of government revenue – the *primary and principal* source of government finance – and that borrowing and money creation must be avoided because supposedly they lead to higher interest rates and inflation. Public deficits and public debt are seen as a threat to the economy and society. The chapter has shown that this view is based on a serious and dangerous misunderstanding of money, taxes and public finance. In particular, it was shown that deficits are a source of income for the private sector and that a sovereign national government faces no such budgetary constraints since financing is routinely secured through its Central Bank. Using empirical evidence, the chapter offered an alternative interpretation by which public deficits are in fact equivalent to surpluses in the private sector, and public debt is an important source of growth for the private wealth.

Notes

1 Tocqueville (1840: 1141) did, however, point out that "If America ever experiences great revolutions, they will be brought about by the presence of Blacks on the soil of the United States: that is to say that it will be not equality of conditions, but on the contrary inequality of conditions that gives birth to them".

2 Following these comments, which stirred controversy and indignation, Mahfouz Saber was forced to resign on 11 May 2015. It's ironic that the present government claims to have been brought to power by the popular uprising of 2011 whose stated objectives are democracy and social justice. See http://stream.aljazeera.com/story/201505111230-0024744, accessed 20 March 2016.

3 As pointed out by Godley and Lavoie (2007: 28–30) and by Lavoie in a private exchange, this result will not hold if firms, for instance, evaluate their issued liabilities at historical cost, i.e. "at the price paid *at the time that the assets and liabilities were purchased*", whereas households evaluate their corresponding claims (assets) at ongoing market prices.

4 Speech by Mervyn King, Speech number 613 on 23 October 2012 (p. 3), online: www.bankofengland.co.uk/archive/Pages/digitalcontent/historicpubs/speeches.aspx, accessed 20 March 2016.

5 Quoted in Mosler (2010: 15).

6 In the *Proceedings of the Standing Committee of the House of Commons on Banking and Commerce*, Ottawa: Edmond Cloutier, 1945, p. 1051.

7 In the *Hearing before the Committee on Banking and Currency House of Representatives*, Eightieth Congress, Washington, DC: United States Government Printing Office, 1947, p. 52.

8 Commercial banks can convert some of their reserves into cash represented by banknotes to satisfy their clients' demand for such type of money holding, which is often needed for smaller transactions or in situations where the payments system is not fully developed.

9 As explained earlier in Chapters 1 and 2, the position of the state as a subservient agent and an ally to the economically dominant class is a feature of most types of economic and social organizations. Already in the 1930s, historian Gaetano Salvemini (1936: 416) criticized the Fascist economy by noting that "In fascist Italy the State pays for the blunders of private enterprise . . . Profit is private and individual. Loss is public and social".

References

Bentham, J. (1841 [1797]) "Tracts on Poor Laws and Pauper Management" in *The Works of Jeremy Bentham*, Part XVI (Edinburgh, UK: Printed by William Tait, Prince's Street).

Bougrine, H. (2000) "Fiscal Policy and the Current Crisis: Are Budget Deficits a Cause, a Consequence or a Remedy?" in H. Bougrine (ed.), *The Economics of Public Spending: Debts, Deficits and Economic Performance* (Cheltenham, UK: Edward Elgar, pp. 6–29).

Bougrine, H. (2004) "Public Debt and Private Wealth" in L. Randall Wray and M. Forstater (eds), *Contemporary Post-Keynesian Analysis* (Cheltenham, UK: Edward Elgar, pp. 24–43).

Bougrine, H. (2010) "The Stabilizing Role of Government Spending" in Bougrine, H. and M. Seccareccia (eds), *Macroeconomic Analysis: Competing Views* (Toronto: Emond Montgomery Publications).

Bougrine, H. and M. Seccareccia (2002) "Money, Taxes, Public Spending, and the State Within a Circuitist Perspective", *International Journal of Political Economy*, Vol. 32, No. 3, pp. 58–79.

Bougrine, H. and M. Seccareccia (2013) "Rethinking Banking Institutions in Contemporary Economies: Are There Alternatives to the Status Quo?" in Rochon, L. P. and M. Seccareccia (eds), *Monetary Economies of Production Banking and Financial Circuits and the Role of the State* (Cheltenham, UK: Edward Elgar).

Chomsky, N. (1999) *Profit over People – Neoliberalism and Global Order* (New York: Seven Stories Press).

Clark, G. (2014) "The American Dream is an Illusion", *Foreign Affairs*, (August 26).

Clark, G. (2015) "Social Mobility Barely Exists But Let's Not Give Up on Equality", *The Guardian*, (February 4).

Feige, D. (2008) "Socializing Risks, Privatizing Profits", *The Huffington Post*, online: www.huffingtonpost.com/david-feige/socializing-risk-privatiz_b_129281.html, accessed 20 March 2016.

Galbraith, J. K. (2000) "The Burden of Wealth", *Public Interest*, Vol. 141, pp. 68–74.

Godley, W. (2000) "Drowning in Debt", *Policy Note*, No. 2000/6, Jerome Levy Economics Institute, available online: www.levyinstitute.org/publications/drowning-in-debt, accessed 20 March 2016.

Godley, W. and M. Lavoie (2007) *Monetary Economics: An Integrated Approach to Credit, Money, Income, Production and Wealth* (New York: Palgrave Macmillan).

Halevi, J., and P. Kriesler (2000) "On the Limitations of Fiscal Policy: A Radical Kaleckian View" in Bougrine, H. (ed.), *The Economics of Public Spending: Debts, Deficits and Economic Performance* (Cheltenham, UK: Edward Elgar, pp. 135–49).

Keen, S. (2015) "Post Keynesian Theories of Crisis", *American Journal of Economics and Sociology*, Vol. 74, No. 2, pp. 298–324.

Lavoie, M. (1985) "Credit and Money: The Dynamic Circuit, Overdraft Economics, and Post Keynesian economics" in Jarsulic, M. (ed.), *Money and Macro Policy* (Boston, Dordrecht, Lancaster: Boston-Dordrecht-Lancaster).

Lavoie, M. (2000) "Government Deficits in Simple Kaleckian Models" in Bougrine, H. (ed.), *The Economics of Public Spending: Debts, Deficits and Economic Performance* (Cheltenham, UK: Edward Elgar, pp. 122–34).

Lerner, A. P. (1943) "Functional Finance and the Federal Debt", *Social Research*, Vol. 10, pp. 38–51.

Mattey, A. (2010) "Do Public Banks Have a Competitive Advantage?", *European Journal of Finance*, Vol. 16, No. 1, pp. 45–55.

Mazzucato, M. (2014) *The Entrepreneurial State: Debunking Public vs. Private Sector Myths* (New York: Anthem Press).

Moore, B. (1988) *Horizontalists and Verticalists: The Macroeconomics of Credit Money* (Cambridge: Cambridge University Press).

Mosler, W. (2010) *The Seven Deadly Innocent Frauds of Economic Policy* (St Croix, VI: Valance Co., Inc.).

Oxfam (2015) *Wealth: Having it All and Wanting More*, available online: www.oxfam.org/en/research/wealth-having-it-all-and-wanting-more, accessed 20 March 2016.

Palley, T. I. (2013) "America's Exhausted Paradigm: Macroeconomic Causes of the Financial Crisis and Great Recession" in Cynamon, B. Z., Fazzari, S. and M. Setterfield (eds), *After the Great Recession: The Struggle for Economic Recovery and Growth* (Cambridge, UK: Cambridge University Press, pp. 31–60).

Parguez, A. (2002) "A Monetary Theory of Public Finance", *International Journal of Political Economy*, Vol. 32, No. 3, pp. 80–97.

Parguez, A. and M. Seccareccia (2000) "The Credit Theory of Money: The Monetary Circuit Approach" in Smithin, J. (ed.), *What is Money?* (London and New York: Routledge, pp. 101–23).

Phelps, E. S. (2013) *Mass Flourishing: How Grassroots Innovation Created Jobs, Challenge, and Change* (Princeton, NJ: Princeton University Press).

Piketty, T. (2014) *Capital in the Twenty First Century* (Cambridge, MA: Harvard University Press).

Rochon, L. P. and S. Rossi (2007) "Central Banking and Post-Keynesian Economics", *Review of Political Economy*, Vol. 19, No. 4, pp. 539–54.

Rochon, L. P. and S. Rossi (2013) "Endogenous Money: The Evolutionary versus Revolutionary Views", *Review of Keynesian Economics*, Vol. 1, No. 2, pp. 210–29.

Salvemini, G. (1936) *Under the Axe of Fascism* (London: Victor Gollacz).

Samuelson, P. A. (1966) 'A Summing Up', *Quarterly Journal of Economics*, Vol. 80, No. 4, pp. 568–83.

Seccareccia, M. (2005) "Growing Household Indebtedness and the Plummeting Saving Rate in Canada: An Explanatory Note", *The Economic and Labour Relations Review*, Vol. 16, pp. 133–51.

Skidelsky, R. (2010) "The Crisis of Capitalism: Keynes Versus Marx", *The Indian Journal of Industrial Relations*, Vol. 45, No. 3, pp. 321–35.

Smithin, J. (2016a) "Endogenous Money, Fiscal Policy, Interest Rates and the Exchange Rate Regime: A Comment on Palley, Tymoigne and Wray", *Review of Political Economy*, Vol. 28, No. 1, pp. 64–78.

Smithin, J. (2016b) "Some Puzzles about Money, Finance and the Monetary Circuit", *Cambridge Journal of Economics, (forthcoming):* doi: 10.1093/cje/bew010.

Stedman Jones, G. (2004) *An End to Poverty? A Historical Debate* (New York: Columbia University Press).

Stiglitz, J. E. (2013) *The Price of Inequality: How Today's Divided Society Endangers Our Future* (New York: W. W. Norton & Co.).

Tocqueville, A. de. (2009 [1840]) *Democracy in America*, Vol. 4, edited by E. Nolla; translated from the French by J. T. Schleifer (Indianapolis, IN: Liberty Fund).

Wray, R. (2011) "Recent USA Sectoral Balances: Goldilocks, the Global Crash, and the Perfect Fiscal Storm", *New Economic Perspectives*, online: http://neweconomicperspectives.org/2011/06/recent-usa-sectoral-balances-goldilocks.html, accessed 20 March 2016.

Wray, R. (2015) *Modern Money Theory: A Primer on Macroeconomics for Sovereign Monetary Systems* (New York: Palgrave Macmillan).

4   Full employment versus scarcity

> The Conservative belief that there is some law of nature which prevents men from being employed, that it is 'rash' to employ men, and that it is financially 'sound' to maintain a tenth of the population in idleness for an indefinite period, is crazily improbable – the sort of thing which no man could believe who had not had his head fuddled with nonsense for years and years . . .

> Our main task, therefore, will be to confirm the reader's instinct that what *seems* sensible *is* sensible, and what *seems* nonsense *is* nonsense. We shall try to show him that the conclusion, that if new forms of employment are offered more men will be employed, is as obvious as it sounds and contains no hidden snags; that to set unemployed men to work on useful tasks does what it appears to do, namely, increases the national wealth; and that the notion, that we shall, for intricate reasons, ruin ourselves financially if we use this means to increase our well-being, is what it looks like – a bogy.

> (Keynes, 1972: 90–2)

Introduction

One of the key concepts in neoclassical economics is "scarcity". It is used to explain price determination in the goods and services markets, the high levels of interest rates, the value of money and the allocation of all resources – tacitly explaining away the problem of unequal distribution of wealth and income. The notion of scarcity permeates neoclassical modelling so much that most introductory textbooks define the field of economics as "the study of the allocation of *scarce* resources among *unlimited* wants" – thus reducing humanity's 'economic problem' to one of "scarcity". In short, scarcity is the basis of the entire neoclassical system of thought. The problem, however, is that the existence of scarcity is always assumed but never proved. Whether we are dealing with the trivial issue of satisfying the appetite of a gluttonous man or with a more fundamental question such as the need for financing for the construction of a school or a hospital, neoclassical economists are quick to put forth the argument of a binding constraint of scarcity – either of food or of money. The scarcity of money, as it turns out, is the overarching argument used to justify all the ills in society. It justifies hunger and malnutrition, homelessness, illiteracy and all other manifestations of poverty.

At the microeconomic level, it is understandable and even tautological to say that a person is poor because they do not have a lot of money – and that, for objective reasons, they cannot get more of it no matter how hard they try. Workers just cannot stretch their wages to make them grow higher (unless they get a pay raise) and the poorer ones cannot even stretch their wages enough to make them last until the next payday. Many of the working poor end up falling further into poverty as they resort to payday loans, rent-to-own and so on for which they pay usury interest rates and higher prices through installments and fees. In her book, *The Cost of Being Poor*, Barnes (2005) summarizes some of the additional economic and noneconomic costs faced by the poor. From our perspective, this is the problem of unequal distribution of income and wealth, which we dealt with in the previous three Chapters.

At the macroeconomic level, however, the notion of scarcity of money is much more problematic for several reasons, the most important of which is the fundamental difference between the national government and private citizens, be they firms or households, as regards access to money. While households and firms are recipients and end-users of that which we call money, the national government, through its Central Bank, is its issuer, its *creator*. Although orthodox theories of money and public finance insist that national governments, just like households, are subject to a budget constraint, the facts and experiences of modern Central Banks tell us otherwise. It is nowadays widely acknowledged among Central Banks' practitioners (see Bank of England, 2014) and pragmatic policymakers that money is indeed a 'creature of the state' (see Lerner, 1943) and that there is no physical limit as to how much of it can be created. Budgetary constraints on government spending are arbitrary and self-imposed.

Two decades ago, Krugman (1996) wrote an article in which he showed why it is important to distinguish between a country and a company. Even though his main concern was with the effect of international imbalances in trade on domestic employment, he ended up bringing in the role of the Federal Reserve (the US Central Bank) as the *creator of money*. Krugman (1996: 41, emphasis added) recognized that the Fed can create as much money as it wants and use it to stimulate the economy and create more jobs, but suggested that it should not do so because:

> [t]he result would be unacceptable and accelerating inflation. In other words, the constraint on the number of jobs in the United States is not the U.S. economy's ability to generate demand . . . but the level of *unemployment* that the Fed thinks the economy needs in order to keep *inflation* under control.

The admission that unemployment is (only) *needed* in order to keep inflation under control smacks of callousness towards those who suffer deprivation and poverty as a result of not being able to get a job.

Arguing that unemployment is the price society should accept to pay in order to *keep* money scarce and avoid inflation is famously summarized in the economics literature by the Phillips curve, which was developed in the 1950s but continues to dominate current policymaking and is still the main justification and guiding principle for austerity policies (see, Feldstein, 2015). It must be noted here that, to his credit, Krugman has changed his opinion about fighting unemployment and has now become an anti-austerity activist (see, among others, Krugman, 2012). Indeed, Krugman (2012: xi) introduced his book, *End This Depression Now*, by stating that it "attempts to break the hold of that destructive conventional wisdom and to make the case for the expansionary, job-creating policies we should have been following all along", emphasizing that "Now is the time for the government to spend more, not less, until the private sector is ready to carry the economy forward again – yet job-destroying austerity policies have instead become the rule". Recently, Krugman (2015a) has even argued that (public spending financed by) government debt is actually a good thing and that "austerity policies didn't just impose short-term losses of jobs and output, but they also crippled long-run growth" (Krugman, 2015b).

Conservative economists not only endorse widespread poverty but, more importantly, they seek to perpetuate it by advocating policies that are based on flawed reasoning and sheer demagogy – whose ultimate objective is the subjugation of labour and its submission to a perpetual state of *artificial* scarcity of jobs, homes, education and health services. And, for this purpose, fiscal austerity proves to be a useful means because it forces the middle and low-income groups to shoulder additional costs in order to have access to these services as they become privatized. In the context of rising unemployment and stagnant or falling real wages, the rational reaction of the working poor is to resort to borrowing – thus fulfilling the expectations of those who are behind the design of these policies, namely the financiers.

Yet, it is perfectly feasible to achieve a state of full employment without causing inflation to rise. Put simply, the government can devise expansionary fiscal and monetary policies to stimulate economic growth and pursue them until a job is created for everyone who is willing and able to work. Since every new worker adds to the production and supply of goods and services, theoretically at least, there is no reason why their additional demand for goods and services would lead to price inflation. If, as claimed by conservative economists (see, Feldstein, 2015), the money used to finance full-employment programmes leads to the extraordinary situation where "too much money is chasing too few goods", then, in practice, the government has at its disposal a centuries-old, tested and proven, method for effectively withdrawing the extra liquidity – and that is taxation. This leads us to conclude that unemployment, not inflation, is "our number one economic problem"[1] and that governments have – not only the moral but also – the legal obligation to resolve it. And lest we forget, let us note here that high unemployment and *deflation*, without government intervention, were the recipe for the damages of the Great Depression of the 1930s. In this chapter, I argue that full employment must be a priority on the agenda of policymakers but for it to be successful, it must be part of a wider strategy that seeks to eliminate the crushing burden of artificial scarcity by guaranteeing a share in economic growth and prosperity for all members of society through access to decent housing, good education, health care and other social protection programmes that counter the immiserating effects of austerity.

Austerity and the creation of artificial scarcity

In primitive societies, as we have seen in Chapter 1, the endeavour to achieve material well-being was a collective task. Communities organized themselves in a way to maximize the welfare of the whole community. Social values encouraged the ability to gather and/or produce more goods and services for the community. Members took pride in doing this because protecting their community against the calamities of nature meant their own individual protection. Together they were stronger, and they knew it instinctively. This behaviour was guaranteed – and reinforced – through the practice of reciprocity and strict redistribution. As we have already noted, in egalitarian and non-stratified primitive societies, the recip-rocal gift-giving and the equal redistribution of resources among the members of the community are their two most outstanding characteristics. Economic scarcity was not an individual problem. Like natural catastrophes, it was faced collec-tively and solved through sharing and equal redistribution. As Carneiro (1981: 60) noted, redistribution in egalitarian communities meant "the complete and equi-table reassignment of a village's harvest back to its producers by a chief who is merely a temporary and benign custodian of it".

Economic scarcity became an individual problem when redistribution ceased to be equal. And redistribution ceased to be equal the moment those who were in charge of it accumulated the power to keep a bigger share by diverting more resources for themselves and for their allies – thus depriving other members of the community who became victims to an artificial scarcity. As self-interest became dominant, society became 'graded and stratified' and access to food and other resources became very much a zero-sum game. The tragic turning point in human history occurred when the function of distribution was snatched by "powerful families of influential men . . . the ruling aristocracy, or . . . the administrative bureaucracy" (see Thurnwald, 1932: 106), for it was then that these 'distributors' secured their direct control over the distribution of land, water rights, and other goods and services essential for survival, which then gave them the power "to dispossess the means of subsistence from those persons who failed to contribute labor demanded of them, who failed to produce suffi-cient resources, or who secretly accumulated resources" (Haas, 1981: 98). This is what Haas (1981: 96) calls the distributors' "power to govern by reward and punishment through providing and withholding the economic goods and services they control". There is overwhelming evidence that the primitive state used bru-tal force to uphold decisions made by these distributors who enjoyed increasing power by *withholding* resources from their fellow citizens – that is, by creating an artificial scarcity to make them hungry, homeless, cold and so on in order to force them into submission and obedience.

Today, the neoliberal state uses austerity to achieve the same objective. Unlike primitive societies which may have relied on henchmen to enforce exclusion, in parliamentary democracies we prefer to do it through the market.[2] Here is how it works: in primitive economies, transactions and exchange were mostly in kind[3] so that privation or access to goods and services took a direct, physical form. Modern economies are monetary economies, and access to goods and services means that one must be endowed with money, a lack of which keeps you out. There is no quarrel about how money is earned in our capitalist societies. All the different sources of income are actually specifically listed on any tax form in most countries. In general, these incomes can be grouped under two broad categories: direct compensation for work (wages and salaries) and compensation from ownership (profits, rent of money, rent of property and capital gains).[4] Employment income is the main source of earnings for the great majority of the population in any country, but while property rights laws guarantee the bond between owners and their property (protection of ownership and the flow of income derived thereof), there is no guarantee for the right to a job. You lose your job and you are out of luck. In most developing countries, there are no social security or unemployment benefits programmes. Austerity is the state's official policy that openly seeks to keep government spending low even if it means dismantling those 'safety net' programmes when they do exist. So, if, for instance, in the G-7 countries unemployment means relative poverty, in developing countries it means destitution. By maintaining unemployment persistently high and forcing real wages to stagnate or fall in most industrial countries (see ILO, 2014), austerity has succeeded in making artificial scarcity a fact of everyday life. Given the striking resemblance of the objectives and the management techniques of class relations, we are tempted to say that the neoliberal state appears to be the modern reincarnation of the primitive state – a primitive state 2.0

The core of the problem discussed above reduces to this simple fact: while every member of society feels that they deserve to enjoy the benefits of increased wealth, the ruling elite want to exclude the lower classes. But people naturally reject poverty and have an innate desire to enjoy a comfortable life. Throughout the known history of humankind, there has always been opposition to a skewed distribution of wealth simply because poverty makes people feel oppressed, disobedient and at times difficult to govern and ready for revolt, particularly when they see the wealth and the lavish lifestyle of the dominant class[5] (see Haas, 1981). Spurred by these contradictions, the extremists would claim that a life of deprivation is not even worth living. Therefore, not only will they question the unequal distribution of wealth but they will also try – by whatever means available – to change the status quo. Class struggle, as Marx (1867) argued, is a dynamic force of change in all class societies.

Even though ancient philosophers talked about life on earth as only a transitory state, many still wanted it to be a good life; an opportunity to perform "good deeds" and achieve "prosperity on earth". By praising moderation and 'the wealth of the soul', religious thought did not seek to consecrate poverty either. In fact, the sacred books of the major monotheistic religions explicitly condemn those who through avarice, artificial scarcity and exploitation cause poverty to their 'brothers in faith', often insist on the respect of God's canons of justice and fairness and warn the transgressors of punishment. The view that God is perhaps on the side of the poor (because God does not like injustice) is represented and defended by the Liberation Theology movement, which calls for action against the *institutionalized sin* of poverty and social injustice[6] (Gutiérrez, 1971; Gutiérrez and Muller, 2015). The movement started in the 1950s in Latin America, but quickly gained worldwide support among the oppressed.

It was the same feeling of oppression of poverty and injustice that gave impetus to the rise of a more radical rejection, such as by Paulo Freire (1968), of the whole system of economic, social and political domination of the elite in Latin America. In his book, *Pedagogy of the Oppressed*, Freire (1968: 44) denounced the "injustice, exploitation, oppression, and the violence of the oppressors" but was also struck by the lack of consciousness and the "culture of silence" from which the dispossessed suffered; and so he sat out on an educational mission on the field to achieve *Conscientização* – a deepening of the awareness and consciousness of the masses; with the objective of achieving liberation and freedom. These sentiments were echoed in Africa and Asia by peoples seeking independence from the yoke of colonial powers and their vassals. During this long struggle, Paulo Freire remained defiant until his last days, always dreaming of a world "that is less ugly, more beautiful, less discriminatory, more democratic, less dehumanizing, and more humane" Quoted in Macedo (2000: 25).

Under neoliberalism, however, colonial exploitation returned with an even uglier face in the first two decades of the twenty-first century as access to resources justified military invasion and the savage destruction of entire countries and their millennia-old civilizations such as Iraq, Syria, Libya and others. Such destruction, as anticipated, resulted in the biggest wave on record of displaced persons,[7] who instinctively seem to follow the trail of their stolen wealth – leading them to the centres of imperial powers in Western Europe and North America. Thousands of people died *en route* to their destination either because of starvation or by drowning in the Mediterranean Sea, which turned into a mass grave.

The struggle for democracy and economic justice has been long and arduous, and it would be utterly wrong to frame it in terms of a mystical battle between good and evil as this would only blur the lines, diffuse the tensions and prolong the status quo.[8] Economic scarcity exists because a minority of oligarchs and millionaires has the power and the means to impose it. And it does so in order to ensure and to preserve its economic domination over those who are disenfranchised. This reality must be understood in its historical context if we want to change it and propose concrete alternatives. What, then, are the tools used by this minority, under the current circumstances, to maintain its domination?

By far the most effective method to perpetuate domination is that by which the elite succeeds in convincing the rest of the population in adopting the elite's ideology and view of the world and in bringing them to defend it as if it were their own. There is nothing more ironic than to see the poor and the workers rally behind the politician who promises them to eliminate government deficits and to force the government to abide by the rules of "fiscal rectitude" and "sound finance" – meaning a strict implementation of the principles of austerity. Yet, as the latest Canadian elections show, political parties from the left and from the right use this rhetoric to garner popular support; and it works. This is certainly due to the lack of understanding of the full implications of austerity, which clearly aims at dismantling the social programmes that were built after the Second World War by the 'Welfare State' in an effort to avoid a return of the disastrous effects of the Great Depression.

One would expect that any policy measure based on austerity should, therefore, be rejected by the majority of the population. Unfortunately, with the exception of a few dissident voices in academia and some isolated popular revolts (e.g. Greece (2014–15), Spain (2015), Argentina (2001–2)), austerity is widely applauded by policymakers around the world, by professional economists and, ironically, by many of those who are hurt most by it, i.e. the masses. As Galbraith (2016) shows, popular rebellion in Europe and elsewhere is being skilfully crushed by the powerful elite. The success of the minority in imposing its neoliberal agenda revolves around the clever use of three instruments: (1) imposing a generalized atmosphere of economic insecurity (unemployment, illiteracy, ignorance and fear) to discipline workers and the general public through austerity measures, (2) writing the curriculum to ensure cultural conditioning and the spread of its ideology through the education system and (3) engaging in the falsification of history for the purpose of misleading and deception through an army of '*intellectuels faussaires*'[9] who sell the idea that the market does it best (see Bougrine, 2012). Hudson (2015: 180) refers to these ideas as neoliberal 'junk economics' that are "crafted to disable society's defense mechanisms".

The necessity of full employment

Martin Feldstein (2015) thinks that the US economy is already at full employment. To justify his claim, Feldstein (2015) wrote:

> Accelerating wage growth implies that the economy is now at a point at which increases in demand created by easier monetary policy or expansionary fiscal policy would not achieve a sustained rise in output and employment. Instead, this demand would be channeled into higher wages and price . . . [adding that] . . . since the beginning of this year, hourly earnings are up 3.3%, and in May alone rose at a 3.8% rate – a clear sign of full employment.

So what's there to worry about?

When several of the recipients of the *Orwell Award*[10] complained about the increasing use of *doublespeak* – words and phrases, which are intentionally designed to obscure the meaning of plain language, they probably were not thinking of "full employment". Yet, the concept of "full employment" as used above refers to an economy in which there are officially 15 million persons who are willing to work but cannot find a job plus an additional 6 million people who are working part-time but would like to find a full-time job.[11] The use of the concept of "full employment" in this sense is so prevalent among economists that in order to accurately describe reality, one is tempted to add another adjective: 'true' full employment cannot exist when there are so many unemployed people[12] (see Pollin, 2012: 12, for anecdotes). That is, only when everyone who is willing and able to work would have found a job can we really speak of full employment (see Wray, 1998a). But because one cannot hide the sun with a sieve, some sort of an explanation is needed to justify the existence of these millions of unemployed people. The typical explanation, also reproduced by Feldstein (2015), is that these are unemployed either by choice or because of the barriers to job creation, erected by the government, such as minimum wage laws, payroll taxes and the availability of social programmes.

In his special message to the Congress on the occasion of presenting what turned out to be his only *Manpower Report of the President*, John F. Kennedy (1963: 249) warned of the high social and economic costs of unemployment. He wrote:

> The costs of prolonged unemployment are high. The individual and society both suffer – the individual through cuts in income, depletion or elimination of savings, hardship for family, erosion of unused skills, and sickness of spirit which may be lastingly harmful – and society through unrealized output, reduced demand, and the social costs of poverty.

Using recent data, Schneider *et al.* (2016) have shown that unemployment creates an atmosphere of uncertainty and anxiety, which negatively affects intimate relationships. One would think that when society is aware of the costs of unemployment, it would seek and use all the means available to eliminate it.[13] This point is shared by Davidson (2010) who likened economic threats to foreign threats of wars and called on the government to fight both with equal tenacity. But when scholars ignore the existence of unemployment or dismiss it, then we have to start wondering. For instance, this year's Nobel Laureate in economics (2015), Angus Deaton, mentioned the word 'unemployment' *only once* in his recent book on *Health, Wealth and the Origins of Inequality*. Deaton (2013: 176) who won the prize for his work on "consumption, poverty and welfare" mentions 'unemployment' only in passing in the following sentence, saying that "it [wealth] increases when people save and decreases when they 'dissave', spending more than they earn, for example in retirement or during a temporary period of unemployment!" It is indeed odd that in a book which is supposed to deal with the 'origins of inequality', unemployment plays no role in the analysis. Obviously, there is much more at stake than the interests of the unemployed or the common social good. In a class society, as Henry (2008: 16) put it, "If the interests of some are to prevail, the interests of others must be suppressed". And so, unemployment is there but it is considered as the 'normal' result of the implementation of efficiency principles at the firm level. However, for society, unemployment is a net waste, a dead loss and an outrageous expression of *systemic inefficiency* whereas "Full employment serves efficiency directly by avoiding the waste of potential output by unemployed workers" (Lerner, 1946: 169).

Unemployment has been and remains a chronic and salient characteristic of capitalism. In Marxist analysis, unemployment plays an important function in the system: it prevents wages from rising and keeps labour unions in check. Unemployment is a means by which to ensure a docile and 'cheap' labour force.

For this reason, even the most progressive economic policies would never aim to eliminate it because, as recognized by Kalecki (1943), in their essence these are designed to serve the interests and preserve the domination of the capitalist class. Unemployment levels may go up and down with the business cycle, but unemployment must not disappear. Several Keynesian economists subscribe to this view; arguing that lowering unemployment below a certain threshold will lead to inflation (Palley, 2015a, 2015b) and few are prepared to defend a programme that seeks to achieve 'true' full employment, because, as pointed out by de Brunhoff (2005: 216), they "fear that low unemployment might undermine wage moderation". After reviewing the successful experience of Sweden with high employment in a capitalist economy, Pollin (2012: 33, emphasis added) suggested that the Swedish model could be made to work elsewhere, but warned that the labour movement "should take it upon itself to design a workable full employment program today, recognizing in that program the *importance of inflation control as full employment is approached*".

It should not be surprising, then, that ever since the Great Depression, with the exception of a few initiatives of direct job creation by governments (e.g. the New Deal in the US), the typical policy has always been limited to attempting to reduce unemployment but never to eliminate it – thus vindicating Keynes' (1936: 373) statement that "The outstanding faults of the economic society in which we live are its failure to provide for full employment and its arbitrary and inequitable distribution of wealth and incomes". Kalecki (1943: 331), by contrast, gave the most insightful analysis of full employment in capitalism when he noted that:

> If capitalism can adjust itself to full employment a fundamental reform will have been incorporated in it. If not, it will show itself an outmoded system which must be *scrapped*. But perhaps the fight for full employment may lead to fascism? Perhaps capitalism will adjust itself to full employment in *this* way? This seems extremely unlikely. Fascism sprang up in Germany against a background of tremendous unemployment and maintained itself in power through securing full employment while capitalist democracy failed to do so. The fight of the progressive forces for full employment is at the same time a way of *preventing* the recurrence of fascism.[14]
>
> (Kalecki, 1943: 331, emphasis in original)

Capitalism did not adjust to full employment thus far. And 'capitalist democracy' has failed dramatically not only in Greece (Varoufakis, 2015; Galbraith, 2016) but also in the rest of Europe and in other industrial countries (Stiglitz, 2015; Galbraith, 2016). Stagnation, with all that it entails, has become the 'new normal'. Anchoring unemployment to inflation is an obstinate way of pushing capitalism to its limits for the realization of maximum self-interest, but the pundits should understand that it is not a good idea. The pursuit of an austerity policy for so long has all but exhausted the amount of the surplus that can be extracted from labour in the real production economy. The new stylized facts are that long-term unemployment has been increasing and the job mix shifting more towards part-time work – thus resulting in a fall of the share of labour in national income since the 1980s in most OECD countries (see OECD, 2012, 2015; Giovannoni, 2014; ILO, 2014). In this context, Green and Sand (2015) documented a polarization of Canadian and US labour markets since the early 1980s with a faster growth in employment in both high and low-paying occupations than those in the middle, which further increased inequality in income distribution.

During the same period, we notice a growing recourse to financialization as yet another method of increasing, albeit fictitiously, the wealth of the dominant financial oligarchy (see Bougrine and Rochon, 2015). The transformation of capitalism into a finance-dominated economy has increased the system's vulnerability and aroused among the masses feelings of militantism for alternatives and against economic and social injustice. Capitalism as we know it seems to be evolving towards a crossroads and may well risk being 'scrapped'. And thus shall the punishment befall the wrongdoers. However, the person who is suffering the hardship of daily deprivation does not care about the predicted or promised fateful demise of capitalism that is so prevalent in leftist academic rhetoric. Deprivation makes a person impatient. 'An empty stomach is a heavy burden' as the Arab adage goes. Human beings also feel the need to be healthy, the need to flourish and to express themselves through various forms of art and science. It is the natural urge for the realization of ourselves as persons. But such aspirations can only be fulfilled in a society that bans unemployment and poverty by eliminating inequality in the distribution of wealth, which is the root cause of artificial scarcity and forced deprivation.

So what is to be done? Lenin (1902: 33–4) recognized that trade unions' work was "an important lever in the [workers'] economic struggle", but he severely criticized the Social Democrats for too narrowly focusing on these activities arguing that they:

> [m]erely dealt with the relations between the workers *in a given trade* and their employers, and all they achieved was that the sellers of labour power learned to sell their "commodity" on better terms and to fight the purchasers over a purely commercial deal.

More than a century later, Lenin's criticism remains valid. Today, even the most radical policy proposals by Keynesian economists do not seek more than an improvement in the terms under which workers sell their 'commodity'. To be sure, the pernicious question of unequal distribution of wealth and income is not rejected in these proposals and remains a fundamental characteristic of what Davidson (2015: 136–44) calls "a civilized capitalist economic system".

Building an egalitarian society is certainly a project that may take a long time to materialize, but the following steps towards that end can be implemented immediately and their results will show within the mandate of an elected government: (a) the implementation of a full-employment policy by guaranteeing a job to everyone who is willing and able to work and (b) the elimination of social scarcity and deprivation by guaranteeing universal access to a *social minimum*[15] that includes education and health and so on. It is not particularly difficult to accomplish these objectives as they can be part of the mandate of a government that allies itself with the working class and the masses. However, the overarching objective of a full-employment strategy should be an alteration of the income and wealth distribution in favour of the working class, because otherwise it would have simply increased the enrolment of workers into the wage relationship while keeping intact the current pattern of distribution – that is, it may only increase the number of the working poor. In this respect, Seccareccia (2004) has demonstrated the futility and the danger of attempting to achieve a low-wage type of full employment since in this scenario there remains a massive disguised unemployment that would actually drive the economy into deflation and widen the inequality gap. The obvious implication is that the project of an egalitarian society requires the implementation and achievement of a high-wage form of full employment. As pointed out by Seccareccia (2004), such an objective is consistent with the original proposal by Keynes (1936) and is supported by other Post-Keynesians for whom full employment and redistribution of wealth and income cannot be dissociated.

In what follows, I propose an action plan that can bring us closer to such a noble goal (see other proposals by Forstater, 2004; Darity, 2010). It has been suggested elsewhere that, to increase its effectiveness, the strategy of full employment must be based on two pillars (see Bougrine, 2006).

(a) In the private sector, the state shall actively promote the creation of community and/or worker owned enterprises in the production of goods and services,
(b) The state itself shall maintain a wide web of public enterprises whose primary focus will be the provision and management of public goods and social services but will also operate in all other industries and sectors, including banking and finance – thus ensuring a process of socialization of investment.

The proliferation throughout the economy of community and worker owned and managed enterprises is crucial to the achievement of a permanent and sustainable full employment for several reasons. The first and most obvious is that it breaks away from the capitalist logic which is built on profit maximization for the private owners or shareholders; an objective that is almost always achieved at the expense of workers either through the wage/pay scheme, conditions under which work is performed, the intensive use of labour-saving technology and so on – issues which are at the centre of the class struggle between workers and capitalists. Worker owned and managed enterprises will produce useful and healthy goods and services for their local, regional and national communities and do not have to abide by the efficiency principles of the private capitalist firm. For instance, they can choose the technology that best suits their interests in terms of employment levels, health and environmental effects and so on; as it is done in negotiations between labour unions, managers and the state in some northern countries like Sweden and Denmark (see Jamison, 1991). Schutz (2011: 192–5), after giving a list of such existing workers' owned and managed enterprises and discussing their merits, argued that the real obstacle to their proliferation is obviously the legal or institutional framework. Similarly, Wolff (2012) gives useful details as to how such enterprises can be made successful and viable.

The other important reason is that by directly managing their own enterprises, workers eliminate the sclerotic hierarchy that is typical of the private capitalist corporation and upon which is built the unequal distribution of income and earnings. Jossa (2015) considers that what he calls labour-managed firms represent a move towards an alternative mode of production, since in capitalism firms are owned and managed by capitalists. The immediate implication of this change is the elimination of the high salaries and perks paid to CEOs and top managers and the appropriation of profits – important sums that can be added to the total surplus to be distributed equitably among those who produce it; namely the workers. The idea of course is not to always distribute the totality of the surplus among workers. Funds will be retained for the expansion of the enterprise and the improvement or development of other activities such as re/training, entertainment, relations with suppliers and consumers and so on (see Wolff, 2012). In a related context, Schneider and Susman (2010: 1) show that cooperative enterprises such as the Mondragon have played an important role in the creation of secure and high-skilled jobs, in the promotion of local education and research and development and, therefore, proved to be "a countervailing power to the forces of capitalist uneven development".

What is important for us here is to understand that worker owned and managed enterprises have the clear potential, and the advantage, of creating more jobs and absorbing more unemployed workers than do the privately-owned capitalist corporations. What is even more important is that these workers are no longer selling their labour power, their 'commodity' as Lenin put it, to others and will therefore escape that oppressive feeling of dependency and subjugation (see Jossa, 2015). By owning and managing their enterprises, workers will be able to appropriate and enjoy the fruits of their own work; much like the farmer can make dinner with home-grown vegetables. But ownership by workers should not contradict the public character of these productive resources, which in any case can always be declared by law to fall within the public domain.

The viability of the worker's owned and managed enterprises will be at risk if not vigorously supported and defended by the state – hence the importance of the second pillar of our strategy, the public sector. The activity of public enterprises shall not be limited to the provision of public infrastructure and social services. There is nothing that should prevent them from also engaging in the production of consumer and capital goods. Public enterprises are essential for the success of a full-employment agenda, not because they are not motivated by profit but because they can easily be directed to areas and sectors where unemployment is high (see Schutz, 2011: 190–2). Workers need the skills and education required to perform their jobs (e.g. design, production, sales and marketing, management). Workers and their families need to be healthy, they need to have decent housing, access to outdoor facilities and parks, theatres and arts. They need to have all these things as a *social minimum*, the provision of which is best guaranteed through public enterprises. The Welfare State did provide some of these resources in some countries, particularly during the period following the Second World War. However, with the resurgence of neoliberal ideas, which then came to dominate policymaking since the late 1980s, even the limited contribution by the Welfare State to the social minimum has been severely curtailed by the

implementation of the principles of 'sound finance' and 'rationalization' of government spending – which justified the privatization of the provision of these
resources, wage freeze in the public sector, removal of subsidies and massive
layoffs of public sector employees. The immediate consequence, now a stylized
fact, has been the increase in poverty rates and impoverishment of workers who
cannot afford the market-set higher prices to access these resources.

Since the end of the Second World War, advanced industrialized countries have
experimented with both the interventionist and free-market strategies. And if we
are to judge policies by their effects, then the choice of strategy does not really
need much debate and justification. Capitalism flourished and had its 'glorious
years' when the interventionist strategy reached its apogee. Devastating recessions
and crises became recurrent when the state retreated and when regulations were
dismantled and market forces became unfettered. Market-oriented policies have
produced a lot of human misery and that can and should be stopped. There is an
urgent need to institutionalize intelligent social and economic policies to eradicate
all forms of poverty and privation. In this context, the state has the ultimate moral
and legal responsibility to design an economic system that ensures the equitable
distribution of resources for the well-being of all citizens and to scrap a system that
serves the interests of a dominant social class at the expense of the others.

The idea of the state as an employer of first resort (EFR) may sound peculiar at
first, but after a serious reflection, it makes sense. Others have argued that the state
should instead act as an employer of last resort (ELR) – hiring workers only when
they fail to find jobs in the private sector (e.g. Mitchell and Wray, 2005; Wray,
2010). But such a strategy does nothing to change the class structure of capitalism
with its unequal distribution and uneven development, which is the main source
of permanent and often rising unemployment. Seccareccia (2013) argued that
ELR workers would continue to play essentially the same role as the existing pool
of unemployed workers and that the strategy does not alter the power relationship
in the 'labour market', which means that employment levels would still continue
to depend on the 'state of confidence' of the capitalist. By contrast, the state as an
EFR can direct its enterprises into employment-generating sectors and activities
thereby easily creating skilled, socially useful and productive jobs that pay good
wages and contribute to the sustainable growth and development of the economy.

Such a strategy of full employment is vehemently opposed by conservative
economists and policymakers on the grounds that: (i) the government cannot afford
all these expenditures and, (ii) if the government did venture beyond the limits of
'sound finance', it will cause a budget deficit that would ruin the economy through
inflation and higher interest rates. Sardoni (2016), however, has shown that full
employment in a growing economy is compatible with deficit spending so long as
public expenditures target the increase of the productive efficiency of the economy.
Other studies have demonstrated that the arguments of sound finance are simply
wrong and fail miserably to understand real-world events (see, among others,
Lerner, 1949; Smithin, 1999, 2016; Davidson, 2015;) arguing that sovereign governments using their own currency face no financing constraints (see, Wray, 1998b;
Bougrine and Seccareccia, 2002; Smithin, 2003–4; Mosler, 2010). Several central
bankers have agreed that this is indeed the case (see Chapter 3 for details).

If it can be done so easily, then why do we see so much unemployment and poverty around us? The short answer is that the level of employment in our capitalist economies depends in a crucial way on the will of the capitalists – that is, on the state of their confidence and their expectations of profitable investments or what Keynes called "animal spirits". Most economists, particularly Keynesian-inspired scholars, recognize this simple fact (see Davidson, 2015: 54). That is why all economic policies seeking to achieve higher levels of employment are in essence nothing more than an attempt to cajole the capitalists and entice them into making those investment decisions – such as through tax cuts, lower interest rates and so forth. This happens only because in capitalist democracies the state is not only an ally but a *de facto* representative of the dominant class.[16] This is the source of what Kalecki (1943) called the political obstacles to full employment. If, instead, the role of the state were to serve the public interest, and particularly interests of the workers, then full-employment policies would be a priority.

Kalecki (1943: 326) expected that any policy that seeks to achieve and maintain full employment would be opposed on principle by the tripartite alliance between the 'captains of industry', the rentiers and the political class because in a state of permanent full employment "The social position of the boss would be undermined and the self-assurance and class consciousness of the working class would grow". From a strictly economic point of view, sales and, therefore, profits will be higher if there is a higher demand for goods and services; which is what occurs when there is a high-wage full employment. The higher cost of wages would be included in sales prices and is, therefore, unlikely to affect profits negatively, but as Kalecki (1943: 326) maintains:

> "discipline" in the factories and "political stability" are more appreciated by the business leaders than profits. Their class instinct tells them that lasting full employment is unsound from their point of view and that unemployment must be an integral part of the "normal" capitalist system.

This leads us to the conclusion that opposition to full-employment policies is not for purely budgetary reasons. Rather, it is the social position and the long-term interests of the dominant class that dictate such opposition and that is why Kalecki (1943: 330) expected that:

> [a] powerful block is likely to be formed between big business and the *rentier* interests, and they would probably find more than one economist to declare that the situation was manifestly unsound. The pressure of all these forces, and in particular of big business – as a rule influential in Government departments – would most probably induce the Government to return to the orthodox policy of cutting down the budget deficit.

And return it did. Austerity and the principles of the so-called 'sound finance' are nowadays the dominant view in policymaking; even though back in the 1940s, Lerner (1949: 302) and those trained in the *functional finance* approach had complained that these principles are more "appropriate to a grocery store", and not to a sovereign government of a country.

Indeed, as Lerner (1943, 1946) had been arguing, the sovereign national government can create money to buy whatever it needs, including labour services, to give away to people as welfare payments or to lend to private citizens simply by crediting the accounts of the intended recipients when the goal is to increase the total aggregate spending for the purpose of maintaining full employment and preventing deflation. If, on the other hand, the goal is to lower the total spending in the economy, perhaps in order to prevent inflation, then the government can destroy money by withdrawing it through taxing, borrowing (selling government bonds) or by selling other items which are in its possession. That is why Lerner (1949: 307) insisted that "The purpose of taxation is never to raise money but to leave less in the hands of the taxpayer" – thus proving that the basic principle of 'sound finance' is fundamentally flawed.

Conclusion

Economic scarcity became an individual problem when the function of distribution of resources among members of society was snatched by an alliance of 'powerful families of influential men . . . the ruling aristocracy, or . . . the administrative bureaucracy' who used their social position to divert more resources for themselves. Ever since, the notion of scarcity has become the guiding principle in the management of economic and social affairs. In modern capitalist societies, scarcity is used to justify the existence of unemployment, illiteracy, homelessness and all forms of poverty. The chapter showed that such scarcity is artificially constructed and that a state of full employment and a more equitable distribution of wealth are perfectly possible if we set aside the flawed conceptions of 'sound finance' and replace them with a 'functional finance' that seeks to create conditions of a 'mass flourishing'. As Engels ([1884], 1972: 165) put it, "what is good for the ruling class should be good for the whole of the society with which the ruling class identifies itself". Why not?

Notes

1 In his *Manpower Report of the President*, John F. Kennedy (1963: 245) insisted that "Unemployment is our number one economic problem. It wastes the lives of men and women, depriving both them and the Nation".
2 The market institution is so impersonal and whatever it dictates is presented as a natural outcome. It is also more difficult to revolt against a system than against a person. Still, the use of force and violence by the state to supress dissent and opposition is also common in modern democracies.
3 This has nothing to do with the apocryphal story of generalized barter since economic transactions in these societies were merely expressions of social obligations in the form of mutual exchange of gifts, with no expectation of any personal gain. In his pioneering work on primitive economies, anthropologist Thurnwald (1932: xiii) noted that "the characteristic feature of primitive economics is the absence of any desire to make profits from production or exchange . . . Generous gifts, however, are unquestionably received with gratitude, although such prodigality has generally to be returned with corresponding lavishness".

4 Figures 1.1 and 1.2 in Chapter 1 show who gets what and gave evidence of rising inequality in the distribution of income and wealth in several countries.

5 Veblen's (1899) suggestions of emulative behaviour may not materialize unless there is a minimum of purchasing power. Indeed, Veblen (1899) regarded the exclusion of the lower classes as a means of guaranteeing the power and maintaining the social status of what he called the "leisure class", for it is through this power relationship that wealth is truly valorized. Preventing the lower classes from having access to increased consumption and wealth and keeping the latter concentrated in the hands of the leisure class is crucial to the process of valorising wealth.

6 The idea that wealth must be shared equitably was also defended by classical economists such as Adam Smith (1776: 61) who considered the unequal distribution of wealth to be "the great and most universal cause of the corruption of our moral sentiments". He argued that because workers are the main factor of production, they should have their fair share: "[n]o society can surely be flourishing and happy, of which the far greater part of the members are poor and miserable. It is but equity, besides, that they who feed, cloath and lodge the whole body of the people, should have a share of the produce of their own labor as to be themselves tolerably well fed, cloathed and lodged" (Smith, 1776: 96).

7 According to the United Nations Refugee Agency, UNHCR, there were 60 million forcibly displaced persons by the end of 2014, but the number must be much higher in 2015. See UNHCR data online: www.unhcr.org/556725e69.html.

8 In Quirrell's words to Harry: "There is no good and evil, there is only power and those too weak to seek it", J. K. Rowling (1998: 291), *Harry Potter and the Sorcerer's Stone*.

9 The expression is used by Boniface (2011) to describe those intellectuals who engage in the spread of 'false truths'.

10 Noam Chomsky, Edward S. Herman and Juliet Schor are among the recipients of the award.

11 See the database from US Bureau of Labor Statistics, online: www.bls.gov/cps/lfcharacteristics.htm, accessed 20 March 2016.

12 This doublespeak has annoyed many economists, including Nobel Laureate William Vickery (1994) who felt compelled to return to the definition given earlier by William Beveridge according to whom full employment meant "that there were at least as many job vacancies as there were unemployed people seeking work". Vickery thus redefined the concept as "chock-full employment" – a situation in which a person "can find work at a living wage within 48 hours" (1994: 40).

13 For instance, Field (2012) concluded that, for more than a century, US macroeconomic data indicate that there is a stable relationship between unemployment and productivity whereby a fall in the unemployment rate of 1 percentage point is associated with a 0.9 percentage point increase in productivity growth per year – with every percentage point increase in the unemployment rate doing the reverse.

14 Guérin (1945: 320) noted that "[fascism] certainly bends the masses under its yoke but it likewise wrings from them a measure of support".

15 Stuart White (2008: 1) in *The Stanford Encyclopedia of Philosophy*, edited by Edward N. Zalta, defines 'social minimum' as "that bundle of resources which suffices in the circumstances of a given society to enable someone to lead a minimally decent life. We define a 'social minimum policy regime' as a set of policies and institutions that serve to secure reasonable access to this social minimum for all members of the society", available online: http://plato.stanford.edu/entries/social-minimum/, accessed 20 March 2016.

16 As Kalecki (1943: 325) put it "This gives to the capitalists a powerful indirect control over Government policy: everything which may shake the state of confidence must be carefully avoided because it would cause an economic crisis. But once the Government learns the trick of increasing employment by its own purchases, this powerful controlling device loses its effectiveness".

References

Bank of England (2014) "Money in the Modern Economy: An Introduction" and "Money Creation in the Modern Economy", *Quarterly Bulletin*, Vol. 54, No. 1, pp. 4–27, available online: www.bankofengland.co.uk/publications/Documents/quarterlybulletin/2014/qb14q1.pdf, accessed 3 May 2016.

Barnes, S. L. (2005) *The Cost of Being Poor: A Comparative Study of Life in Poor Urban Neighborhoods in Gary, Indiana* (Albany, NY: State University of New York Press).

Boniface, P. (2011) *Les Intellectuels Faussaires: Le Triomphe Médiatique des Experts en Mensonge* (Paris: Éditions JC Gawsewitch).

Bougrine, H. (2006) "Un programme d'action pour l'élimination du chômage et de la pauvreté au Maroc" in *Revue Critique Économique*, No. 17, pp. 25–40.

Bougrine, H. (2012) "Fiscal Austerity, the Great Recession and the Rise of New Dictatorships", *Review of Keynesian Economics*, Vol. 1, No. 1, pp. 109–25.

Bougrine, H. and M. Seccareccia (2002) "Money, Taxes, Public Spending, and the State Within a Circuitist Perspective", *International Journal of Political Economy*, Vol. 32, No. 3, pp. 58–79.

Bougrine, H. and L. P. Rochon (2015) "Transformations of Entrepreneurial Capitalism, Crises and the Need for a Radical Change in Economic Policy", *Review of Keynesian Economics*, Vol. 3, No. 2, pp. 181–93.

Carneiro, R. L. (1981) "The Chiefdom: Precursor of the State" in Jones, G. D. and R. R. Kautz (eds), *The Transition to Statehood in the New World* (Cambridge, UK: Cambridge University Press, pp. 37–79).

Darity, W. (2010) "A Direct Route to Full Employment", *Review of Black Political Economy*, Vol. 37, pp. 179–81.

Davidson, P. (2010) "Making Dollars and Sense of the U.S. Government Debt", *Journal of Post Keynesian Economics*, Vol. 32, No. 4, pp. 661–5.

Davidson, P. (2015) *Post Keynesian Theory and Policy: A Realistic Analysis of the Market Oriented Capitalist Economy* (Cheltenham, UK: Edward Elgar).

Deaton, A. (2013) *The Great Escape: Health, Wealth, and the Origins of Inequality* (Princeton: Princeton University Press).

De Brunhoff, S. (2005) "Marx's Contribution to the Search for a Theory of Money", in Moseley, F. (ed.), *Marx's Theory of Money: Modern Appraisals* (New York: Palgrave Macmillan).

Engels, F. (1972 [1884]) *The Origin of the Family, Private Property and the State* (New York: Pathfinder Press).

Feldstein, M. (2015) "What is Full Employment?", *Project Syndicate*, available online: www.project-syndicate.org/commentary/what-is-full-employment-by-martin-feldstein-2015-06, accessed 20 March 2016.

Field, A. J. (2012) *A Great Leap Forward: 1930s Depression and U.S. Economic Growth* (New Haven, CT: Yale University Press).

Forstater, M. (2004) "Green Jobs: Addressing the Critical Issues Surrounding the Environment, Workplace and Employment", *International Journal of. Environment, Workplace and Employment*, Vol. 1, No. 1, pp. 53–61.

Freire, P. (2000 [1968]) *Pedagogy of the Oppressed*, 30th Anniversary edition (New York: The Continuum International Publishing Group, Inc.).

Galbraith, J. K. (2016) *Welcome to the Poisoned Chalice: The Destruction of Greece and the Future of Europe* (New Haven, CT: Yale University Press).

Giovannoni, O. (2014) *What Do We Know About the Labor Share and the Profit Share? Part III: Measures and Structural Factors*, Working paper No. 805, Annandale-on-Hudson, NY: Levy Economics Institute of Bard College, online: www.levyinstitute. org, accessed 20 May 2016.

Green, D. A. and B. M. Sand (2015) "Has the Canadian Labour Market Polarized?", *Canadian Journal of Economics*, Vol. 48, No. 2, pp. 612–46.

Guérin, D. (1965 [1945]) *Fascisme et grand capital* (Paris: Maspero).

Gutiérrez, G. (1975 [1971]) *Teología de Liberación: Perspectivas*, 7ᵐᵃ edición (Salamanca, Spain: Ediciones Sígueme).

Gutiérrez, G. and G. L. Muller (2015) *On the Side of the Poor: The Theology of Liberation* (New York: Orbis Books).

Haas, J. (1981) "Class Conflict and the State in the New World" in Jones, G. D. and R. R. Kautz (eds), *The Transition to Statehood in the New World* (Cambridge, UK: Cambridge University Press, pp. 80–102).

Henry, J. F. (2008) "The Theory of the State: The Position of Marx and Engels", *Forum for Social Economics*, Vol. 37, No. 1, pp. 13–25.

Hudson, M. (2015) *Killing the Host: How Financial Parasites and Debt Bondage Destroy the Global Economy* (Petrolia, CA: Counterpunch Books).

ILO (2014) *Global Wage Report 2014/2015: Wages and Income Inequality* (Geneva: International Labour Office).

Jamison, A. (1991) "National Styles in Technology Policy: Comparing the Swedish and Danish State Programmes in Microelectronics/Information Technology" in Hilpert, U. (ed.), *State Policies and Techno-Industrial Innovation* (London and New York: Routledge, pp. 305–27).

Jossa, B. (2015) "Historical Materialism and Democratic Firm Management", *Review of Political Economy*, Vol. 27, No. 4, pp. 645–65.

Kalecki, M. (1943) "The Political Aspects of Full Employment", *The Political Quarterly*, Vol. 14, No. 4, pp. 322–30.

Kennedy, J. F. (1964 [1963]) *Public Papers of the Presidents of the United States: John F. Kennedy: Containing the Public Messages, Speeches, and Statements of the President, January 1 to November 22, 1963*, 1st edition (Washington, DC: U.S. Government Printing Office).

Keynes, J. M. (1936) *The General Theory of Employment, Interest and Money* (London: Macmillan).

Keynes, J. M. (1972) *The Collected Writings of John Maynard Keynes, Volume IX, Essays in Persuasion*, edited by Donald Moggridge (London and Basingstoke, UK: Macmillan).

Krugman, P. (1996) "A Country is Not a Company", *Harvard Business Review*, (January/February), online: https://hbr.org/1996/01/a-country-is-not-a-company, accessed 20 May 2016.

Krugman, P. (2012) *End This Depression Now* (New York: W. W. Norton & Co.).

Krugman, P. (2015a) "Debt is Good", *New York Times*, (21 August), online: www.nytimes. com/2015/08/21/opinion/paul-krugman-debt-is-good-for-the-economy.html?_r=1, accessed 20 May 2016.

Krugman, P. (2015b) "Austerity's Grim Legacy", *New York Times*, (6 November), online: www.nytimes.com/2015/11/06/opinion/austeritys-grim-legacy.html?smid=fb-share, accessed 20 May 2016.

Lenin, V. I. (1929 [1902]) *What is to be Done? Burning Questions of Our Movement* (New York: International Publishers).

Lerner, A. P. (1943) "Functional Finance and the Federal Debt", *Social Research*, Vol. 10, No. 1, pp. 38–51.

Lerner, A. P. (1946) "An Integrated Full Employment Policy", in Lerner, A. P. and F. D. Graham (eds), *Planning and Paying for Full Employment* (Princeton, NJ: Princeton University Press, pp. 163–220).

Lerner, A. P. (1949 [1944]) *The Economics of Control: Principles of Welfare Economics* (New York: Macmillan).

Macedo, D. (2000) "Introduction" to Freire, P. (2000 [1968]) *Pedagogy of the Oppressed*, 30th Anniversary edition (New York: The Continuum International Publishing Group, Inc., pp. 11–26).

Marx, K. (1968 [1867]) *Capital* (Moscow: Progress Publishers).

Mitchell, W. and L. R. Wray (2005) "In Defence of Employer of Last Resort: A Response to Malcolm Sawyer", *Journal of Economic Issues,* Vol. 39, No. 1, pp. 235–44.

Mosler, W. (2010) *The Seven Deadly Innocent Frauds of Economic Policy* (St Croix, VI: Valance Co., Inc.).

OECD (2012) *OECD Employment Outlook 2012* (Paris: OECD Publishing).

OECD (2015) *OECD Employment Outlook 2015* (Paris: OECD Publishing).

Palley, T. I. (2015a) "Money, Fiscal Policy, and Interest Rates: A Critique of Modern Monetary Theory", *Review of Political Economy*, Vol. 27, No. 1, pp. 1–23.

Palley, T. I. (2015b) "The Critics of Modern Money Theory (MMT) are Right", *Review of Political Economy*, Vol. 27, No. 1, pp. 45–61.

Pollin, R. (2012) *Back to Full Employment* (Cambridge, MA: The MIT Press).

Rowling, J. K. (1998) *Harry Potter and the Sorcerer's Stone* (New York: Scholastic Press).

Sardoni, C. (2016) "A Note on the Sustainability of Full Employment in the Presence of Budget Deficits", *Review of Political Economy*, Vol. 28, No. 1, pp. 79–89.

Schneider, D., K. Harknett and S. McLanahan (2016) "Intimate Partner Violence in the Great Recession", *Demography*, Vol. 53, pp. 471–505.

Schneider, G. and P. Susman (2010) "Uneven Development and Grounded Comparative Institutional Advantage: Lessons from Sweden and Mondragon", *Forum for Social Economics*, Vol. 39, pp. 1–11.

Schutz, E. A. (2011) *Inequality and Power: The Economics of Class* (New York: Routledge).

Seccareccia, M. (2004) "What Type of Full Employment? A Critical Evaluation of 'Government as the Employer of Last Resort' Policy Proposal", *Investigación Económica*, Vol. 63, No. 247, pp. 15–43.

Seccareccia, M. (2013) "Budgetary Deficits and Overhanging Public Debt: Obstacles or Instruments to Full Employment? A Kaleckian/Institutionalist Perspective", *Journal of Economic Issues*, Vol. XLVII, No. 2, pp. 437–43.

Smith, A. (1976 [1776]) *An Inquiry into the Nature and Causes of the Wealth of Nations* (Oxford, UK: Oxford University Press).

Smithin, J. (1999) "Money and National Sovereignty in the Global Economy", *Eastern Economic Journal*, Vol. 25, No. 1, pp. 49–61.

Smithin, J. (2003–4) "Can We Afford to Pay for Social Programs?", *Studies in Political Economy*, Vol. 71/72, pp. 163–76.

Smithin, J. (2016) "Endogenous Money, Fiscal Policy, Interest Rates and the Exchange Rate Regime: A Comment on Palley, Tymoigne and Wray", *Review of Political Economy*, Vol. 28, No. 1, pp. 64–78.

Stiglitz, J. E. (2015) "Europe's Attack on Greek Democracy", *Project Syndicate*, online: www.project-syndicate.org/commentary/greece-referendum-troika-eurozone-by-joseph-e--stiglitz-2015–06, accessed 20 May 2016.

Thurnwald, R. (1969 [1932]) *Economics in Primitive communities* (London: Oxford University Press).

Varoufakis, Y. (2015) "How Europe Crushed Greece", *The New York Times*, online: www.nytimes.com/2015/09/09/opinion/yanis-varoufakis-how-europe-crushed-greece.html?_r=1, accessed 20 May 2016.

Veblen, T. (1899) *The Theory of the Leisure Class* (New York: Macmillan).

Vickery, W. (1994) "Why Not Chock-Full Employment", *Atlantic Economic Journal*, Vol. 25, No. 1, pp. 39–45.

Wolff, R. (2012) *Democracy at Work: A Cure for Capitalism* (Chicago, IL: Haymarket Books).

Wray, R. (1998a) "Zero Unemployment and Stable Prices", *Journal of Economic Issues*, Vol. 32, No. 2, pp. 539–45.

Wray, R. (1998b) *Understanding Modern Money* (Cheltenham, UK: Edward Elgar).

Wray, R. (2010) "The Social and Economic Importance of Full Employment" in Bougrine, H. and S. Seccareccia (eds.), *Macroeconomic Analysis: Issues, Questions and Competing Views* (Toronto: Emond Montgomery).

5 Innovation, ownership and progress

Live long and prosper

(Mr. Spock, *Star Trek*)

Introduction

Following early contributions by Schumpeter (1943), it is now accepted as a fact that innovation has a positive effect on economic progress, which relies on the continuous production, use and diffusion of new ideas. The main question that concerns us in this chapter is to find out what drives innovation itself and how the latter can be successfully used to achieve progress. In studying the process of generating innovation, some have emphasized the importance of financing requirements and the return to financiers and entrepreneurs on their risky investments, while others give more weight to the role of incentives to potential inventors and thus call for a more effective system of intellectual property rights. Others, however, object to private intellectual property rights, arguing that they limit the spread of ideas and stifle innovation by encouraging monopolistic behaviour (see Polanvyi, 1944; Baker, 2005; Nicholas, 2011). But beyond the pecuniary rewards to those involved in innovation, there is a more fundamental question: from where do these innovators get their new ideas? Or, how does innovation come about?

Innovation is certainly not manna from heaven, neither can it occur in a vacuum. Innovation relies on, and must benefit from, the progress of knowledge in general and the development of theoretical science in particular. Some scholars such as McCloskey (2010: 371) tend, however, to downplay this point because they consider that "It is not Science that was the key to the door to modernity but the wider agreement to permit and honor innovation, opening one's eyes to novelty, having a go" and that science is "more a result of economic growth than a cause".

This is a major controversy in the history of progress and development. Is science a cause or a result of economic progress? This is not a question of semantics, for it has real implications for developing countries: how can they get development if science is not the key? What was the driving force behind industrialization and development of Britain and other European countries? Wasn't the industrial revolution driven by science? The debate concerns what has become known as the 'Great Divergence' in which economic historians try to explain why the industrial revolution occurred first in Britain and not in other countries such as China, for instance. The two sides of the debate are: (1) those who emphasize the role of the bourgeoisie, its private initiative and the spread of its values of liberty and dignity and (2) those who insist on the crucial role of the state and its institutional apparatus from the banking to the legal systems to the army in paving the way for, and supporting, the rise of the bourgeoisie.

In the next section, the chapter reviews and compares the ideas of both sides of the debate and attempts to draw conclusions regarding what can be a best practice towards nurturing innovation. The third section looks more closely at the system of patents and evaluates its implications for progress and development in modern capitalist societies, particularly for poor countries. Concluding remarks are given in the last section.

Humanity's great leap forward: innovation and the role of the state

Virtually all historians agree that, particularly after the industrial revolution, humanity has made a great leap forward in its quest to overcome the hardships of life imposed by the cruelty of Mother Nature. This great success is largely attributed to the improvement of one thing: Knowledge. Indeed, the entire history of humanity could be summarized by the evolution of its learning – learning how to do things *better* and how to make *more* things available to satisfy its needs. The relatively fast accumulation of such knowledge is in fact what distinguishes humans from other creatures. Much of this knowledge has certainly been acquired through learning-by-doing, but this process cannot be dissociated from thinking and theorizing – that is, from the development of our scientific and philosophical understanding of things and of the circumstances surrounding our existence on earth. There are, however, some scholars who claim that technological development, including the industrial revolution, is attributable only to the ideas of practical men and not to theoretical science.

McCloskey (2010), for instance, argues that industrial technology can develop independently from science and, therefore, insists on separating technology from science. This is somewhat surprising because technology is necessarily the embodiment of ideas – scientific ideas, which spring from thinking and theorizing about the shape and the structure of the tools to be made, the objects to be built, and that is theoretical science. Theorizing is not only done by the scholar in the laboratory but also by the craftsman in the workshop. This is why in fact technological breakthroughs during the industrial revolution have been based on operational concepts developed by, and derived from, modern science that relied on trial and error – thus combining practical and theoretical training (see De Santillana, 1964; Hall, 1964). Separating technology from science, however, serves a purpose. It allows McCloskey, for instance, to argue that industrial development is driven by innovation, and that is clearly true; but more importantly it legitimizes the question of why did this innovation not occur earlier and why does it not happen everywhere? McCloskey's plain answer is that the real driver lies in liberal economic principles or what she calls the 'bourgeois dignity and liberty' – which is the theme of her book.

McCloskey (2010) doubts that science had much to do with the industrial revolution and denies that innovation needs science. For her, technology and its industrial applications are the great gift of the bourgeoisie to society. But for the bourgeoisie to make its gift, it must gain respect, i.e. its dignity and liberty must prevail. To substantiate her argument, McCloskey (2010: 358) looks at the "inspiriting discoveries of a Newtonian clockwork universe, and the great mathematization in Europe of earthly and celestial mechanics in the eighteenth century" and notices that they "had practically no direct industrial applications until the late nineteenth century at the earliest" – that is, until the bourgeois values had flourished in Western Europe. McCloskey extends her argument to other parts of the world and states that:

> [o]ne problem that has to be faced by advocates of science as a cause . . . is that Chinese, and at one point Islamic, science and technology, separately and together, and their humanistic scholarship, were until very lately superior to Western science and enlightenment in most ways, and yet resulted in no industrial revolution.

Similarly:

> Greece's invention of most of the arts and sciences (with borrowings from eastern sources), and its partial freedom to doubt the gods, had not revolutionized the Greek economy or enriched its poor. Ancient Greek society despised physical work as slavish and womanly . . . and above all looked down on the bourgeoisie.
>
> (McCloskey, 2010: 363)

The idea that bourgeois values of dignity and liberty are *the* essential determinants of innovation imposes a unique path to development on all societies and considers Western-style capitalism as the only successful way to achieve industrialization and progress. These arguments rest on a particular reading of history, which was popularized, among others, by Pollard (1968: 29–30) in his book on *The Idea of Progress* in which he claimed that "much of the science of the Renaissance itself arose, not in secluded laboratories, but in the workshops of artisans and craftsmen", and that progress was the work of:

> [t]he merchants and traders and manufacturers, the owners of mines and mills and of banks, and their technicians and managers and doctors and clerks . . . [who] had little regard for the privileges of birth or for divine rights, but required instead rewards for merit, freedom of contact, protection of property and defencelessness of labour, and in the end they won, for their economy was the more efficient.

Hall (1964: 21–2), however, noted that the so-called tinkerers were in fact professionals such as "university teachers, professors of mathematics, anatomy, and medicine" and practitioners such as "physicians, surveyors, mariners, apothecaries, surgeons, and other tradesmen", who had acquired scientific knowledge and occupied positions within the scientific hierarchy: "some had won them through academic study, others through private education and research, others again by apprenticeship and pursuit of an occupation closely related to scientific inquiry". And so "in this way, head and hand were linked for the benefit of science" (Marsak, 1964: 2). Here, it must be noted that most obviously, in the Stone Age, even the best of tinkerers could not have come up with the most tedious gadget that is widely available today. They simply did not have the theoretical capability to imagine it or the scientific knowledge to design and make it. Yet, as Wright (2004: 26) remarked "a late-Palaeolithic child snatched from a campfire and raised among us now would have an even chance at earning a degree in astrophysics or computer science".

James Watt did not just dream up the steam engine. His grandfather was a teacher of mathematics and his father was an architect and a shipbuilder, and from an early age he was making models of machines in his father's workshop (see Mantoux, 1928: 318). James Watt was a trained scientist and he only improved the steam engine which had already been invented by Thomas Newcomen in 1712 (McCormick, 1998) who, in turn, as noted by Spier (2010: 175), had only "improved on the design of an already existing 'fire engine' (which was a primitive steam engine)". In any case, as Asimakou (2009: 61) observed, "innovation is never one man's ideas; ideas are socially constructed and redefined over a long period of time". Like James Watt, others who contributed to technological innovations during the industrial revolution had also learned their science while pursuing their trade and not by just sitting on the benches and listening to academic lectures at universities. But this should not be seen in any way as a decoupling of technology from science.

Innovation, in technology as in other fields, is a dynamic process, and historically it has moved in tandem with the development of science and knowledge. For instance, in the United States, even though the steam engine was invented in 1712, it took 100 years to launch the first commercially successful steamboat in 1807 by Robert Fulton (McCormick, 1998). This, however, does not make innovation linear neither does it impose necessary successive stages of development. Countries can leapfrog and technology – and the knowledge embodied in it – could obviously be stolen, copied or "taken off the shelf", as McCloskey says. However, the simplistic assumption of taking technology off the shelf ignores two major barriers faced by poor countries: the limitations imposed by the laws on patents and intellectual property rights and access to international financing – topics which we will deal with in Chapter 6.

Indeed, this is what the Europeans have done. McCloskey (2010: 104–5) noted that:

> From the seventeenth century on the Europeans in a rising wave of creativity stole, copied, adopted, improved, extended, reverse-engineered, and above all applied what they had learned from the Chinese, and from anybody else they chanced to meet on their fanatical and profitable peregrinations.

In his study of the great divergence between Britain and China during the period 1680s–1850s, Vries (2015: 361) paid particular attention to the role played by the state and concluded that:

> As an increasing number of scholars realizes, quite close links existed between intercontinental trade, exchange and empire on the one hand and the rise of "science", or, if that is too big a word, the accumulation of useful and reliable knowledge on the other. Although (semi-)private initiatives certainly played a big role, the importance of the state in this respect can hardly be overlooked. Private persons as well as governments were extremely interested in collecting information of whatever kind.[1]

In his historical study, *The World Economy: A Millennial Perspective*, Maddison (2006: 23–5) gave data going back to the year 1000 and recalled important historical facts to show that prior to its industrial rise, Britain had benefited greatly from its commercial hegemony which it had secured through armed conflicts, restrictive Navigation Acts, the practice of beggar-your-neighbour policy and what he called "free trade imperialism", which it imposed on its colonies. Mantoux (1928: 271) who studied in great detail the rise of manufacturing in Britain in his classic, *The Industrial Revolution*, noted that "The beginnings of machine industry belong to the history of the textile trades, but its final triumph throughout the world was made possible only by the development of the metal industries". Mantoux (1928: 280) added that:

> The British metal trade was in a poor state, and, if some of the secondary industries still had comparative vitality, this was maintained only by the import of Swedish and Russian ores. As she could not be self-sufficient, England thought that she could at least obtain all her raw or semi-manufactured material from her dependencies, whilst maintaining against them a strict monopoly in manufactured products. To encourage the production of pig or bar iron in those dependencies, whilst on the other hand forbidding all competition with industries of Sheffield and Birmingham, was the policy adopted from 1696 by the home government.

Government intervention and support to the 'national' industry have been an essential part of industrialization in Britain since the early days of capitalism. Indeed, already in those days, government involvement extended to support even research and innovation. Sobel (1995: 6) wrote that during the Age of Exploration, "As more and more sailing vessels set out to conquer or explore new territories, to wage war, or to ferry gold and commodities between foreign lands, the wealth of nations floated upon the oceans". But at that time, nobody knew how to determine the longitude of a ship at sea. As a consequence, many ships sank and thousands of lives were lost. One of these tragic accidents occurred on 22 October 1707 at the Scilly Isles where "four homebound British warships ran aground and nearly two thousand men lost their lives". This represented also a loss of honour for Britain, which depended on "mastery of the seas for security and trade" (see Spencer, 2012). To solve the longitude problem, Sobel (1995: 8) recalls that:

The governments of the great maritime nations – including Spain, the Netherlands, and certain city-states of Italy – periodically roiled the fervor by offering jackpot purses for a workable method. The British Parliament, in its famed Longitude Act of 1714, set the highest bounty of all, naming a prize equal to a king's ransom (several million dollars in today's currency) for a "Practicable and Useful" means of determining longitude.

John Harrison, the lone genius as Sobel called him, responded to the advertisement and eventually was able to find a solution and, as noted by Spencer (2012: 40), "The Longitude Act resulted in the invention of the marine chronometer, which solved the problem the Act sought to address. But the Act *itself* was also an important invention: the well-defined, goal-oriented, open innovation challenge". In fact, what was more important is that this invention was, as were many more, the result of active support and encouragement by the government (the Queen, the Parliament and the Admiralty). In other words, dignity and liberty of the bourgeoisie had nothing to do with it. There was an urgent public need to find a solution to a challenging problem, and public institutions – not the bourgeoisie – took the initiative to sponsor and finance the search for that solution, the benefits of which were to be reaped by the whole society. The inventor was paid a lump sum from public funds and was not supposed to retain any lasting intellectual property rights over his discovery. The idea of ownership of knowledge and ideas was introduced later with the rise of free-market ideology in the early 1800s.

The reward promised by the Longitude Act of 1714 for an innovative solution through a prize to be paid from public funds was not new neither was it unique in its era, but it instituted a process that has become a tradition since the beginning of the eighteenth century. Aware of the importance of technological progress and its effect on economic development in their countries, governments regularly invited scientists and curious minds to participate in innovative projects to solve particular problems or to push the frontiers of scientific knowledge. From France under Napoleon Bonaparte to the United States under the Administration of George Washington, governments publicly funded scientific research and technological development. Table 5.1 gives some of the best known examples of public prizes and funding offered in a number of countries to encourage research and innovation in various fields. The modern equivalent of the Longitude Act is the support by governments, through their various agencies, for Research and Development (R&D) that is so widely prevalent, particularly in the most industrially advanced countries.

Already by the end of the nineteenth century, state-funding to science and technology was seen by governments as a necessity to ensure not only economic growth and progress in their own countries but also to preserve self-sufficiency, sovereignty and national security – a matter of national pride. Consequently, most governments of Western Europe and North America had already adopted a *Science Policy* and established Research Councils and Ministries of Science and Technology to promote scientific R&D of (industrial) technology. Public funding to basic research was a boon for the bourgeoisie who viewed it simply

Table 5.1 Public prizes offered for innovation

Year	Public funding or Prize for	Offered by
1598	Longitude (attempt by Galileo)	Government of Spain (King Philip III)
1666	Longitude (research in Astronomy)	Government of France (King Louis XIV)
1714	Longitude	British government (The Longitude Act)
1794	Interchangeable parts (e.g. guns)	US government (G. Washington)
1795	Food preservation	Government of France (Napoleon Bonaparte)
1810	Sugar beet	Government of France (Napoleon Bonaparte)
1810	Flax spinning	Government of France (Napoleon Bonaparte)
1887	Medicine	French Royal Academy of Sciences
1919	England to Australia flight	Australian government
1800s–1900s	Agricultural innovation	Royal Agricultural society of England
1800s–1900s	Technological innovation	Japanese prefectures and local governments
1950s	Nuclear power	US government (Dwight Eisenhower)
1960s	Microchips	US government (John F. Kennedy)
1970s	Biomedical research	US government (Richard Nixon)

Source: Based on data from Sobel (1995), Nicholas (2011) and the Breakthrough Institute (2010).

as 'priming the pump' since the major benefits were expected to be reaped when practical applications would emerge at the end of the innovation 'pipeline' in the form of 'inventions' that are then *patented*. In a study of the Science Policy in Canada, Clowater (2012: 110) noted that:

> Since the private sector could be expected to under-invest in basic science, it was the responsibility of the federal government to provide this invest-ment, now recognized as a public good. Because fundamental breakthroughs could neither be foreseen nor, it seemed, their course steered by policy, the state's role is to provide funds "on faith" to scientists, in order to prime the pipeline that would generate social and economic returns from discoveries. The special responsibility for priming, however, did not preclude the neces-sity for heavy government funding and policy-steering at other stages of the linear innovation process, whether through procurement, direct stimulus to industrial R&D, or "Big Science" projects of national importance beyond the scope of the private sector.

This interventionist approach to science and technology went uncontested for more than two centuries. During much of the twentieth century, promoting science has become a central tenet of government policy as the state, both in industrially advanced and in the newly industrialized countries (NICs), became much more aggressive and started playing the role of the leader in innovation by undertaking high-risk investment in innovative projects. As pointed out by Link and Link (2009: 19), the reason for such a desired government involvement is obvious since:

The opportunity at hand with respect to technology policy is the provision of a public or quasi-public good – the technology infrastructure itself – that leverages the ability of firms and other actors in a national innovation system to participate efficiently in the innovation process . . . and thereby to contribute to technology-based economic growth.

Science policy is sometimes opposed by neoliberal economists and conservative policymakers who believe in the supremacy of the market and attribute the great inventions to bourgeois values. For instance, in the introduction to her book, McCloskey (2010: xv), after thanking Google, wrote:

I cannot thank the Internet itself, because it is a spontaneous order arising from innovative and bourgeois people, and has no nameable entrepreneur or bureaucrat to thank. Yet come to think of it, the electronic words fashioned inside the virtual halls of Gutenberg, Google, and Wiki . . . also depend largely on spontaneous orders and bourgeois creativity – which is the point of this book.

Yet, as Mazzucato (2014) has demonstrated, the state has done more than just provide technology infrastructure to leverage the ability of private firms; it has gone one step further by investing in path-breaking types of innovation such as those leading to the internet, Google, iPhone or the development of new pharmaceutical drugs and green technology. So when it comes to the great discoveries, it is the government that really deserves the praise not the bourgeoisie. Through her perceptive reading of the history of innovation, Mazzucato (2014) has forcefully documented the leading role of the state in the development and commercialization of these and many other innovations that were identified as crucial and picked as winners in the most industrially advanced countries.

In his review of Mazzucato's book, *The Entrepreneurial State*, Madrick (2014) referred to Milton Friedman's well-known anti-government mantra and commented that "We could perhaps forgive Friedman's ill-informed remarks as a burst of ideological enthusiasm if so many economists and business executives didn't accept this myth as largely true". The danger from this myth, however, is real and its consequences are disastrous when policymakers formulate their policies on that basis. Not only does it derail or delay progress in industrially advanced countries but it literally kills it *ab ovo* in those countries that desperately need to break out of the cycle of poverty and dependence. Policymakers in these countries, unfortunately, do accept the myth as true because it is sold to them in the form of policy advice by the so-called experts from powerful international organizations. Unless poor and 'emerging' countries adopt policy-oriented development strategies where the state plays the leading role, such as in Korea and other NICs, they will continue to buy and rely on outdated technology and thus remain as laggards while others are singing to them the praises of free markets and capitalism.

The commodification of knowledge and the prospects of progress

The essence of human development and progress resides in the pursuit of scientific knowledge and its spread to the wider population in ways that improve our understanding of ourselves and of ongoing phenomena in society and in nature. Even though, over time, scientific knowledge tends to trickle down to the people, in one form or the other, so as to play its expected emancipatory and liberating role, its production remains the act of certain privileged groups in society.[2] There is also the issue of who decides on the criteria to be used in evaluating the correctness of the interpretations offered by what we call 'scientific' knowledge. As Potter (1962: 6) noted "Science is knowledge but it is not wisdom. Wisdom is the knowledge of how to use science and how to balance it with other knowledge". Indeed, without wisdom, science can go astray and inventions or innovations may turn awry. The philosophy of science can be a source of wisdom in the sense that it tends to invite us to judge all propositions – in genetics as in economics – by their effects on us as human beings and on our environment. Yet, even though scientific knowledge is expected to be the means by which humanity achieves an improvement in its economic, cultural and intellectual well-being, including how individuals relate to each other and to their environment, a number of (scientific) knowledge-based innovations since the beginning of the industrial revolution has had a lasting damage on the social and natural milieus and their constituents (Leiss, 1994). Hence, development as a higher purpose of life requires not only that everyone gets the right to enjoy the fruits of innovation but *a fortiori* the right to be protected from its harmful effects.

Indeed, even a cursory reading of the recent history of innovation leads us to the recognition that not all innovations are or have been beneficial to humanity; and yet they have been legitimized and adopted for use in our modern, industrial societies. Examples of these range from the introduction of toxic chemicals into agricultural production, to nuclear bombs and other weapons of mass destruction. This brings to the fore the important question of why certain types of technological innovations are adopted and others are not (e.g. fossil fuel energy versus solar energy) and more generally who controls the production of scientific knowledge and who benefits from it. To answer this question, we need to study power relations among individuals, social classes and among nations, for it is here that power is exercised, as Foucault (1980) has argued. Given that power and knowledge cannot be studied separately, the norms and directions for research and scientific knowledge as well as its technological applications are also set within these power relations.

McCormick (1998) gives a good summary of major historical events that led to important inventions during the first and the second industrial revolutions. The one event that truly revolutionized capitalist society was the introduction of *mass production* of commodities, which, as McCormick recounts, grew out of the idea of making interchangeable parts available for repairing guns – a project that was financed by the US government in 1798 under the Administration of President

Thomas Jefferson. From that time onward, and with the rise of industrial capital-ism, the norms and directions have clearly been set: technology would be designed primarily to perform specific tasks with the goal of reducing costs and increas-ing efficiency in order to make investment or the whole enterprise worthwhile. Technology of mass production is based on speed and efficiency, which have the obvious result of improving profitability – particularly by lowering costs in terms of human labour. In his book, *Fascism*, Mark Neocleous (1997) explains how the fascists and the Nazis were so fascinated and even obsessed by efficiency, speed and technological innovation under capitalism. They admired this triple combi-nation particularly because it permitted unprecedented increases in productivity under the 'scientific management' as applied by Taylorism and Fordism during the 1920s and 1930s. The development of capitalism and technological progress were, therefore, intertwined since the beginning of the industrial revolution, par-ticularly in Britain and in the United States.

The bourgeoisie in those countries, as opposed to the bourgeoisie of the "Eastern empires", had already developed a practical understanding of the empowering role of technology in the economy and in society – an understanding that is often attributed to the influence of the philosophical legacy of Francis Bacon who so much idealized the role of technology in enhancing the 'practical capabilities' of those who possess it; whence his emphasis on knowledge as power (see Leiss, 1994). This explains the rush by those who had "capital" to acquire the machines and set up the factory system.[3] In his meticulously detailed study of the industrial revolution in the eighteenth century, Mantoux (1928: 368) made the interesting observation that the inventors (or innovators) were not part of the rising class of manufacturers and, as he put it "One might expect to find, in this first generation of great manufacturers, the men who by their inventions had started the industrial revolution. But nothing of the sort happened". Mantoux did mention that there were perhaps two exceptions, which included the venture by James Watt, but he noted that the latter "certainly owed much to his partner Matthew Boulton [who was a businessman]".

The fact that the early inventors remained outside and did not become industri-alists was an indication of the culture that prevailed during this period. The new 'captains of industry' were eager to get any machine that would benefit them by improving their means of production, and in this haste, they could not care less for the inventor's patent rights. On the contrary, they behaved as if all inventions and any innovations thereupon were open and free for all to use. As Mantoux (1928: 373) writes:

> [f]ollowing the dictates of self-interest they worked untiringly to reduce the inventor's legitimate rights to nothing. This conduct, questionable though human enough, is abundantly illustrated by the behaviour of the spinners to Hargreaves and Crompton [who invented the spinning jenny and the "mule"], of the ironmasters to Henry Cort [who invented iron puddling], and by the innumerable lawsuits Boulton and Watt had to bring against those who used their engines.

This somewhat chaotic period, however, was a blessing; for the industrial revolution would not have developed at the pace it did had all the inventions been kept secret and protected by strict monopolistic patents.

As mentioned earlier, even though the major innovations were undertaken and financed by the state, with the rise of free-market capitalism, technological innovation itself had become an entrepreneurial activity that attracted the interest of wealthy businessmen and big corporations. Investors then sought not only to protect their products (through licensing for use) but especially to establish ownership over the idea itself that is behind the innovation – hence the establishment of intellectual property rights (IPRs). This has become particularly evident in late capitalism where property rights to every major 'innovation' are protected by universally recognized standard laws on intellectual property, with the exception of a few open source innovations that fall into the public domain. On this account, knowledge has clearly become a valuable asset that bestows power and economic advantage on its holder and can hardly be considered a public good.

In particular, access to scientific knowledge and to the technologies based on it is not free and this largely explains why those who cannot afford it remain at the bottom of the scale of progress. It also explains the retardation in progress, or at least the slow progress, towards higher processes and methods of securing our material commodities, such as through clean energy. The reason is in fact quite simple and was explained long ago by Michael Polanvyi[4] (1944: 62) who stated that:

> [t]he full benefit of knowledge is only reaped when its circulation is free. If it is necessary to provide a test for its economic value by charging a price for its use, and thereby to limit such use, society is made the poorer. The effect is the more severe, since limitations of this kind necessarily restrict the field in which a new industrial technique becomes known in practice and thus damps the stimulus which it may give to further technical development.

Michael Polanvyi (1944: 65) argued further that:

> It is in the nature of knowledge – in contrast to material resources – that the more people use it at the same time, the more it tends to grow and to benefit each of its users. The proper way to assure that an invention will be utilised best is to give it full publicity and allow its free application by everyone. Any proprietary management of useful knowledge is . . . both irrational and open to grave abuses.

In this excellent, but largely ignored, study of the patent system, Michael Polanvyi convincingly shows that the monopolistic rights conferred on the inventors and their backers through patents are against the best interest of society. While the harmful effects of such restrictive monopolies are, to some degree, obvious and have been studied by others, the *irrational* aspect of the patent law emphasized by Karl Polanvyi (1944: 70–1) is particularly insightful that it would be justified here to quote him *in extenso*

I believe the law is essentially deficient, because it aims at a purpose which cannot be rationally achieved. It tries to parcel up a stream of creative thought into a series of distinct claims, each of which is to constitute the basis of a separately owned monopoly. But the growth of human knowledge cannot be divided up into such sharply circumscribed phases. Ideas usually develop gradually by shades of emphasis, and even when, from time to time, sparks of discovery flare up and suddenly reveal a new understanding, it usually appears on closer scrutiny that the new idea had been at least partly foreshadowed in previous speculations. Moreover, discovery and invention do not progress only along one sequence of thought, which perhaps could somehow be divided up into consecutive segments. Mental progress interacts at every stage with the whole network of human knowledge and draws at every moment on the most varied and dispersed stimuli. Invention, and particularly modern invention which relies more and more on a systematic process of trial and error, is a drama enacted on a crowded stage. It may be possible to analyse its various scenes and acts, and to ascribe different degrees of merit to the participants; but it is not possible, in general, to attribute to any of them one decisive self-contained mental operation which can be formulated in a definite claim.

(Karl Polanvyi, 1944: 70–1)

This description elucidates one of the many contradictions upon which the capitalist society is built: if knowledge is necessarily a shared human activity that grows, expands and improves with the contribution of every member of society, then why should any one person or a group of persons claim its possession for themselves? Why should the rest of society forgo its share and contribution to what is a collective endeavour for the benefit of some individuals? This amounts to a *de facto* expropriation of a collectively produced resource, which is similar to the expropriation of land as a natural commons, which was achieved by the Enclosures Act (Karl Polanyi 1944). There is then an obvious tension between the reality of knowledge as a collective mental effort – an intellectual commons, and the need to transform that knowledge into a pure commodity that can be owned, bought and sold for personal gain (on this point, see also, Stiglitz, 2006: 108). This is not the first time in the history of the market economy that we witness an attempt to commodify something that is outside of the market, something that is not produced for sale. In his study, *The Great Transformation*, Karl Polanyi has shown that land, labour and money have also undergone such a process.

Karl Polanyi (1944: 72) has argued that land, labour and money are *not* commodities because, unlike capitalist commodities, they do not undergo a production process and, therefore, are not made in order to be sold:

Labor is only another name for a human activity which goes with life itself, which in its turn is not produced for sale but for entirely different reasons, nor can that activity be detached from the rest of life, be stored or mobilized; land is only another name for nature, which is not produced by man; actual money, finally, is merely a token of purchasing power which, as a rule, is not produced at all, but comes into being through the mechanism of banking or state finance.

Like land, labour and money, knowledge is also a fictitious commodity because it is a gift of nature that comes with life itself and is not produced for sale. In fact, knowledge is only another form of human labour – the intellectual as opposed to the manual labour, even though it is not possible to separate the physical and the cognitive abilities of the person.

Yet, there are now actual functioning markets for labour, land and money, all of which have been forcibly included in the market mechanism despite their being fictitious commodities. Knowledge also is now a commodity that has a great commercial value that is secured and sanctioned by law through the patent system and other IPRs.[5] Scholars like Dean Baker (2004, 2005) have strongly criticized the patent monopolies granted to pharmaceutical companies and the copyrights system as inefficient and argued that these are designed to serve the powerful interests in society. Furthermore, Katari and Baker (2015: 1) showed that pharmaceutical companies "had deliberately concealed or misrepresented evidence on the safety of the drug" they were selling. Baker (2005) and Stiglitz (2006), among others, proposed that IPR should be replaced by a system of compensation to the inventors that ranges from direct payments in the form of subsidies or salaries to the award of prizes, with the understanding that the results would become an open innovation available to anyone to use freely. Stiglitz (2006: 108, emphasis in original) emphasized the point by arguing that "Economic efficiency means that knowledge should be made freely available, but the intellectual property regime is *intended* to restrict usage".

The commodification of knowledge is particularly alarming for those who lose access to it because knowledge has the double characteristic of being both a product, an output whose consumption can enhance the human well-being and a means of production of other products, especially those that have come to be called knowledge-based products, which take the form of advances in technology that permit important discoveries and innovations in various fields from industrial-tech to bio-tech. It is here that one can see clearly the importance of not only acquiring knowledge but of owning knowledge and excluding others from sharing it – by making it scarce for them. It is thus that the power of knowledge is exercised. Those who are granted legal monopolies over 'detached pieces of knowledge' through patents and other IPRs accumulate power and secure domination by charging for licensing and earning super-profits on the sale of their products, such as in the case of pharmaceuticals and ICT (information and communication technology) sectors (see Baker, 2005). In this context, Leiss (1994: 121) rightly noted that:

> Advances in technology clearly enhance the power of ruling groups within societies and in the relations among nations; and as long as there are wide disparities in the distribution of power among individuals, social groups, and states, technology will function as an instrument of domination.[6]

This is another reason why the entrenched elite is actively establishing private research institutes and privatizing education and transforming universities and research centres into private corporations. The aim is to impose governance and management over the entire process from the initial research programmes to the final product – thus ensuring that the enclosure is complete. In this context, neoliberals argue that it is only natural that entrepreneurs earn rewards for their efforts and that such rewards serve as incentives to stimulate further research and innovation. But, as we discussed earlier, if monopolistic ownership of knowledge (inventions and innovations) is problematic and cannot be equated with ordinary capitalist commodities, its reward via patenting and other IPRs is even more problematic. It not only creates and perpetuates inequalities in the knowledge-based society by limiting access to inventions but it also stifles progress because of the restrictions on research programmes that are often geared to focus on what is already known and profitable. Baker (2005), for instance, has argued that "Drug patents also distort the direction of research by pushing it in the direction of patentable results". This is why Stiglitz (2006: 124) suggested that:

> A prize system, in which researchers are rewarded for the value of their innovations, would move incentives in the right direction. Those who make the really important discoveries – who, for example, tackle diseases with no known cure – would get big rewards.

Moreover, due to the nature of high risk and uncertainty inherent in the business of knowledge production, the logic of cost-benefit that is at the heart of capitalist entrepreneurship dictates the delay and even the scrapping of unprofitable projects; which could otherwise achieve breakthroughs (see Mazzucato, 2014). This is why Michael Polanvyi (1944: 65) suggested that we need state intervention to support and maintain the production of collective knowledge for the benefit of all members of society and all human societies. As he put it "In order that inventions may be used freely by all, we must relieve inventors of the necessity of earning their rewards commercially and must grant them instead the right to be rewarded from the public purse". This is what the Longitude Act sought to do and this is what current public policy on R&D should also do.

In a recent article in *Scientific American*, the co-founder of Microsoft Research, Nathan Myhrvold (2016) summed up the debate with such clarity and honesty. He wrote:

> Examine the detailed history of almost any iconic scientific discovery or technological invention – the lightbulb, the transistor, DNA, even the Internet – and you'll find that the famous names credited with the breakthrough were only a few steps ahead of a pack of competitors. Recently some writers and elected officials have used this phenomenon, called parallel innovation, to argue against the public financing of basic research . . . These arguments are dangerously wrong. Without government support, most basic scientific research will never happen . . . Even in applied fields, such as materials science and computer science, companies now understand that basic research is a form of charity – so they avoid it.

> When I created Microsoft Research, one of the largest industrial research labs founded in a generation, Bill Gates and I were very clear that basic research

was not our mission. We knew that unless our researchers focused narrowly on innovations we could turn into revenues quickly, we wouldn't be able to justify the R&D budget to our investors. The business logic at work here has not changed. Those who believe profit-driven companies will altruistically pay for basic science that has wide-ranging benefits – but mostly to others and not for a generation – are naïve.

If government were to leave it to the private sector to pay for basic research, most science would come to a screeching halt. What research survived would be done largely in secret, for fear of handing the next big thing to a rival. In that situation, Einstein might never have felt the need to finish his greatest work.

(Myhrvold, 2016)

Conclusion

Most scholars nowadays agree that innovation is key to progress, but if progress is to be pursued as a higher purpose of life and if it is to benefit all members of society, then innovation cannot be left to the whims of profit-seeking entrepreneurs. The benefits to society from scientific research and innovation are indeed the greatest when enclosure and appropriation are not permitted. For this reason, the production as well as the distribution or diffusion of knowledge must be a social responsibility – a collective task that, in modern society, should be carried out by the sovereign state. The chapter showed that historically the state has indeed played a central role not only by giving incentives to scientists and inventors but also by directly undertaking basic and fundamental research in public agencies and government departments. Several studies have documented the fact that the great discoveries of modern technology are the result of an active industrial policy designed and funded by the state. Such public and collective ownership of knowledge is consistent with the socialization project that seeks to put people before profits and workers in charge of their own enterprises where R&D would be carried out for the benefit of all humanity. Privatizing knowledge and innovation is a risky business that is doomed to stifle progress and lead to stagnation.

Notes

1 Wright (2008), for instance, noted that had the Europeans not occupied the Americas, used African slaves and adapted the highly productive crops of the New World for use in European farms, the industrial revolution would have been much slower. Wrigley (2010: 34) added that "Without the striking gains in manpower productivity in agriculture which took place in early modern England it is very doubtful whether the industrial revolution would have occurred". In his book, the *Great Divergence: China and Europe*, Pomeranz (2000: 264) argued that "western Europe, was able to escape the proto-industrial cul de sac and transfer handicraft workers into modern industries as the technology became available. It could do this, in large part, because the exploitation of the New World made it unnecessary to mobilize the huge numbers of additional workers who would have been needed to use Europe's own land in much more intensive and ecologically sustainable ways".

2 Noting that knowledge is the 'pursuit of truth', Foucault (1980: 131–2) wrote that "In societies like ours . . . [truth] is produced and transmitted under the control, dominant if not exclusive, of a few great political and economic apparatuses (university, army, writing, media); . . . it is the issue of a whole political debate and social confrontation ('ideological' struggles)".
3 Mantoux (1928: 365–6) noted that these were "Landowners, bankers, and merchants: apart from a few exceptions, every example of capitalism previous to the industrial revolution can be classified under one or other of these three heads".
4 Michael Polanvyi is the brother of Karl Polanyi, although the name is spelled differently in this particular publication.
5 This success, which coincides with the triumph of free-market ideology, required some profound transformations to society so as to make it become a market society and was not without challenges. As noted by Karl Polanyi (1944) and later emphasized by Jessop (2007), it has led to some social "protective counter-moves" seeking to preserve nature and to keep knowledge within the public realm. For instance, as a reaction against the proliferation of IPRs, there are now some strong movements advocating OA (open access) to science such as Sci-Hub, the Free and Open Source Software (FOSS), open development in Biotechnology (OpenBio) or the latest EU's Open Science initiative giving free access to scientific papers by 2020.
6 If progress means increased wealth that translates into increased consumption of new goods which are made possible through innovative techniques and processes, Perrotta (2003) has shown that, in fact, throughout the history of mankind since ancient times, consumption of new goods has always been the privilege of higher social classes and that only over time do these goods become available to middle and then to lower classes. This remained true in modern capitalist societies, where the use of new technologies is essentially concentrated in wealthy nations.

References

Asimakou, T. (2009) *Innovation, Knowledge and Power in Organizations* (New York: Routledge).
Baker, D. (2004) *Financing Drug Research: What Are the Issues?* (Washington, DC: Center for Economic and Policy Research).
Baker, D. (2005) "The Reform of Intellectual Property", *Post-Autistic Economics Review*, Vol. 32, No. 5, no page numbers given, online: www.paecon.net/PAEReview/issue32/Baker32.htm, accessed 20 March 2016
Breakthrough Institute (2010) *Where Good Technologies Come From: Case Studies in American Innovation* (Oakland, CA: Breakthrough Institute), available online: http://thebreakthrough.org/archive/american_innovation, accessed 20 March 2016.
Clowater, G. B. (2012) "Canadian Science Policy and the Retreat from Transformative Politics: The Final Years of the Science Council of Canada, 1985–1992", *Scientia Canadensis: Canadian Journal of the History of Science, Technology and Medicine*, Vol. 35, No. 1–2, pp. 107–34.
De Santillana, G. (1964) "The Role of Art in the Scientific Renaissance" in Marsak, L. M. (ed.), *The Rise of Science in Relation to Society* (New York: The Macmillan Company).
Foucault, M. (1980) *Power/Knowledge: Selected Interviews and Other Writings 1972–1977*, edited by Colin Gordon (New York: Pantheon Books).
Hall, R. (1964) "The Scholar and the Craftsman in the Scientific Revolution" in Marsak, L. M. (ed.), *The Rise of Science in Relation to Society* (New York: The Macmillan Company).

Jessop, B. (2007) "Knowledge as a Fictitious Commodity: Insights and Limits of a Polanyian Analysis" in Bugra, A. and K. Agartan, (eds), *Reading Karl Polanyi for the Twenty-First Century: Market Economy as a Political Project* (New York: Palgrave Macmillan, pp. 115–33).

Katari, R. and D. Baker (2015) *Patent Monopolies and the Costs of Mismarketing Drugs* (Washington, DC: Center for Economic and Policy Research).

Leiss, W. (1994) *The Domination of Nature* (Montreal: McGill-Queen's University Press).

Link, A. N. and J. R. Link (2009) *Government as Entrepreneur* (Oxford, UK: Oxford University Press).

Maddison, A. (2006) *The World Economy: Vol. 1 A Millennial Perspective, Vol. 2 Historical Statistics* (Paris: OECD).

Madrick, J. (2014) "Innovation: The Government was Crucial After All", *The New York Review of Books*, 24 April 2014, online: www.nybooks.com/articles/2014/04/24/innovation-government-was-crucial-after-all/, accessed 20 March 2016.

Mantoux, P. (1961 [1928]) *The Industrial Revolution in the Eighteenth Century* (London: University Paperbacks).

Marsak, L. M. (ed.) (1964) *The Rise of Science in Relation to Society* (New York: The Macmillan Company).

Mazzucato, M. (2014) *The Entrepreneurial State: Debunking Public vs. Private Sector Myths* (New York: Anthem Press).

McCloskey, D. N. (2010) *Bourgeois Dignity: Why Economics Can't Explain the Modern World* (Chicago, IL: The University of Chicago Press).

McCormick, A. L. (2014 [1998]) *The Industrial Revolution in the United States History* (Berkeley Heights, NJ: Enslow Publishers).

Myhrvold, N. (2016) "Basic Science Can't Survive without Government Funding: Without Government Resources, Basic Science Will Grind to a Halt" in *Scientific American* (1 February), online: www.scientificamerican.com/article/basic-science-can-t-survive-without-government-funding/, accessed 20 March 2006.

Neocleous, M. (1997) *Fascism* (Minneapolis, MN: University of Minnesota Press).

Nicholas, T. (2011) "What Drives Innovation?" *Antitrust Law Journal*, Vol. 77, No. 3, pp. 787–809.

Perrotta, C. (2003) "The Legacy of the Past: Ancient Economic Thought on Wealth and Development", *European Journal of History of Economic Thought*, Vol. 10, No. 2, pp. 177–229

Polanyi, K. (1944) *The Great Transformation: The Political and Economic Origins of Our Time* (Boston, MA: Beacon Press).

Polanvyi, M. (1944) "Patent Reform", *The Review of Economic Studies*, Vol. 11, No. 2, pp. 61–76.

Pollard, S. (1968) *The Idea of Progress: History and Society* (Harmondsworth, UK: Penguin Books).

Pomeranz, K. (2000) *The Great Divergence: China, Europe, and the Making of the Modern World Economy* (Princeton, NJ: Princeton University Press).

Potter, V. R. (1962) "Bridge to the Future: The Concept of Human Progress", *Land Economics*, Vol. 38, No. 1, pp. 1–8.

Schumpeter, J. (2003 [1943]) *Capitalism, Socialism and Democracy* (New York: Routledge).

Sobel, D. (1995) *Longitude: The True Story of a Lone Genius Who Solved the Greatest Scientific Problem of His Time* (New York: Penguin Books).

Spencer, R. W. (2012) "Open Innovation in the Eighteenth Century: The Longitude Problem" in *Research-Technology Management*, pp. 39–43 (July–August).

Spier, F. (2010) *Big History and the Future of Humanity* (Chichester, UK: John Wiley & Sons, Ltd).

Stiglitz, J. E. (2006) *Making Globalization Work* (New York: W. W. Norton & Co.).

Vries, P. (2015) *State, Economy and the Great Divergence: Great Britain and China, 1680s–1850s* (New York: Bloomsbury Academic).

Wright, R. (2008) *What is America?: A Short History of the New World Order* (Toronto: Random House of Canada).

Wright, R. (2011 [2004]) *A Short History of Progress* (Toronto: House of Anansi Press, Inc.).

Wrigley, E. A (2010) *Energy and the English Industrial Revolution* (Cambridge, UK: Cambridge University Press).

6 Industrial backwardness, international trade and finance

> Mohamed Ali [of Egypt] began a state-led modernization of the Egyptian economy and society that can be compared only to those of Peter the Great in Russia and the Meiji Emperor in Japan . . . *By the 1830s Egypt was second only to England in its modern industrial capacity.*
>
> Mohamed Ali's state-centred autarky had been weakened by European commercial penetration; . . . Nevertheless, Mohamed Ali's descendants retained considerable wealth and power until their political and military defeat by the British. *Indeed, a further and much more severe collapse of the modern economy came only after the British takeover in 1880.*
>
> (Martin Bernal, 1991, *Black Athena*, pp. 246, 249)

Introduction

The industrial revolution was a defining moment in the history of Europe not only because of the internal social and economic transformations to which it had contributed. Technological development had also empowered European countries militarily and redefined their relations with the rest of the world since the nineteenth century. While technology in itself cannot be regarded as a cause of imperial expansion, historians have documented the fact that the discovery of firearms and other killing machines played a key role in the conquest of Africa, Asia and the Americas (see Headrick, 1981). In other words, technology was not necessarily a motive that fomented the desire to acquire colonies, but it certainly was an effective means that asserted domination and permitted the exploitation of plantations, farms, mines and forests. Since colonial times, techno-industrial development appeared as a distinctive characteristic of the superiority of the 'West' over much of the 'rest' – which immediately came into being in a state of backwardness.

It is not the aim of this chapter to give a historical account of technological backwardness in Africa and other parts of the world, but rather to emphasize that it has historical reasons – an issue which has been studied in depth and documented at length by economic historians (see Rodney, 1972; Maddison, 2006; Studer, 2015; Vries, 2015). The conclusion of these studies is that colonial hegemony determined the pattern of trade and development – that is, who gets to import and export what – and, therefore, the type of 'industrial' activity in which the colonies had to specialize (Amin, 1974).

While David Ricardo and his colleagues were busy formulating the theory of comparative advantage according to which specialization should be based on considerations of pure economic efficiency, colonial powers designed, according to their business and political interests, what would become the *de facto* 'international economic order'– by assigning to colonies the role of producing primary commodities and preserving manufacturing in the old industrial centres (see Nurkse, 1954).[1] Svedberg (1981) has shown that the patterns of both trade and investment were actually dictated and "enforced" by colonial powers and have, therefore, roughly revolved around this division of labour, which has been only slightly altered today. Recently, the US President Obama (2016) put it blatantly when he emphasized this point by stating unambiguously that "America should write the rules. America should call the shots. Other countries should play by the rules that America and our partners set, and not the other way around".

It would, obviously, be more informative and more accurate to study trade and foreign investment by country of origin, but the intent here is not to reveal the idiosyncrasies in the behaviour of a particular colonial power. Rather, our aim is to discern the general pattern of trade and investment during the colonial era and examine the role it played in the divergence between Western Europe and its colonies. A popular explanation in development economics for the divergence between industrialized and underdeveloped countries is the role played by institutions.

Other studies emphasize the importance of the democratic rule in the political process and the prevalence of property rights as key factors that promote private entrepreneurship – seen as the engine of industrialization and growth (see McCloskey, 2010). Many of these studies claim that Africa, for instance, is underdeveloped because it lacks these institutions: for instance, Acemoglu and Robinson (2012) have pointed to the totalitarian nature of political regimes in Africa and in most of the underdeveloped countries where there is little or no respect for the due process and rule of law, while Radelet (2010) has argued that success in Africa requires more democracy and an accountable governance.

However, the current regimes did not just emerge from a vacuum and certainly did not develop independently of outside influence. The pioneers in the study of underdevelopment have emphasized the importance of colonial exploitation through slavery and Atlantic Trade (Gunder Frank, 1998, 1978; Wallerstein, 1974; Amin, 1974). Taking this argument further, Vries (2015) and Fields and Vernengo (2016), among others, have argued that the military and fiscal powers of the state may have played a central role in the rise of Western Europe's hegemony. The current regimes prevailing in the underdeveloped world are the legacy of a long process of colonialization during which Europeans took care to set up the legal, economic and political institutions that helped secure domination and make the "colonies politically submissive and economically profitable to their European metropoles" (Headrick, 1981: 11). With the notable exception of the 'new' countries, which were settled by Europeans (Canada, Australia, New Zealand and the United States), all the 'old' colonies were subjected to the colonial pattern of trade and investment through what Acemoglu *et al.* (2001) and Acemoglu and Johnson (2005) called "extractive" institutions, which were designed and used as tools to exploit native populations and their resources.[2] It is not a surprise that the least developed and non-industrial countries today are those which are extremely rich in all sorts of natural resources. Canada, the United States and the other 'new' countries also relied on export of natural resources, but the difference is that these countries benefited immediately, even during the process of their creation, from European support to finance and develop their industrial base and the needed public infrastructure.

The idea that countries outside of Western Europe simply failed to have an industrial revolution at the same time and did not develop at the same pace as Britain is not true. Let us not forget, for instance, that until recently, many European historians had been considering China a backward and underdeveloped country but that has turned out to be a figment of their Eurocentric imagination and a prejudiced cliché (see Vries, 2015: 1–2; see also Mokyr, 1990: chapter 9; Maddison, 2006: 119; Amin, 2009). This chapter argues that regardless of the level of industrial development prior to colonization, the *persistence* of industrial backwardness into the twenty-first century has a lot do with how these colonial extractive institutions have evolved.

In any case, the problem today, which has preoccupied intellectuals and policymakers for a long time, is how to break away from this vicious circle of extraction and transfer of value whose goal and outcome have been – and still are – the creation of wealth for an entrenched elite and poverty for the rest of the population.[3] The chapter proposes a solution which may be useful for addressing what are considered to be the two key aspects of this question: industrialization and international financing. The first aspect, covered in the following section, deals with ways to overcome the technological constraint by building a productive economy that is capable of inducing development and closing the divergence between the industrial and non-industrial economies. In the third section, recognizing that the latter countries also face an external financing constraint, we look at alternative methods of securing financing for industrialization through a radical reform of the international monetary system. Concluding remarks are found in the last section.

The weight of history, the great divergence and industrial policy

Since the Stone Age, humans have been making tools and using them to increase their capacity to accomplish certain tasks (for survival or for amusement). The nature of tools, techniques and procedures has evolved to reflect the improvement in skills and knowledge accumulated over time (see Maynard *et al.*, 2005). Technology, primitive as it was, travelled freely as tribes, wandering around, could easily lend and borrow tools, copy them from each other and adapt them to their own needs – often resulting in an improvement, thus making technological progress cumulative. There were no barriers to technological diffusion and often, there was no need to re-invent the wheel since as Morgan (1877: 540) noted:

Some of these inventions were borrowed, not unlikely, from tribes in the Middle Status; for it was by this process constantly repeated that the more advanced tribes lifted up those below them, as fast as the latter were able to appreciate and to appropriate the means of progress (see also De Gregori, 1968).

With the advent of the industrial revolution and the rise of the European tribe, the diffusion of technology took on a different twist. The social institutions that developed with the triumphal arrival of capitalism put heavy emphasis on private property rights, which included patents to protect technological "inventions". Even though James Watt had only improved on a previously existing steam engine, he and his business partner Matthew Boulton became involved in numerous lawsuits over patents – claiming originality and, therefore, intellectual property of the engine (see Mantoux, 1928).

What about technological diffusion to the rest of the world? Economists of all persuasions agree that the logic of capital, understood as money-cum-technology, is that it goes where profits can be made. Foreign investment, then, would flow to areas and countries where such opportunities exist. However, as we shall see below, there are other important considerations, particularly when we include public and state-sponsored foreign investment. A mapping of European foreign investment during the last part of the nineteenth century reveals that investment by colonial powers during that period was particularly biased as, for instance, most of Britain's foreign investment went to the so-called 'new' countries, which were sparsely populated and to which European entrepreneurs and skilled workers had migrated (Canada, the US, New Zealand, Australia). As noted by Nurkse (1954: 250, emphasis added):

> The capital that came into these regions . . . was employed above all in *building up the costly framework of public services*, including especially transport, which laid the *basis for domestic industrial development*, as well as for the production of raw commodities for export. These areas are now, and have been for some time, predominantly industrial.

By contrast, in the 'old' colonies which had "ancient civilizations of their own", investment was essentially restricted to extractive industries producing raw materials and foodstuffs for the industrial centres and no such "building up of the costly framework of public services" ever took place. Hirschman (1958) added that when these investments occurred, they often lacked any backward and forward linkages with the rest of the economy and so did not contribute much to the industrial development of the 'old' colonies. The 'colonial' pattern of investment begs explanations outside of the box of mainstream economic principles. Perhaps we need to study, among other aspects, the psychology of colonialism to understand the motivations and the aspirations of the colonizers – then and now.

The institutional approach to economic development – and lack of it – provides an interesting framework for studying the colonization strategy and the consequences of what European colonizers did to the indigenous populations, during what McCloskey (2010: 105) called "their fanatical and profitable peregrinations". European expeditions may have looked fortuitous in their beginnings when sailors were riding high seas not knowing exactly where they may end up, but those behind the expeditions knew what they were after: land and its riches. Access to land was a priority in the colonization strategy because it permitted immediate settlement – and therefore, expansion.

Territories that were sparsely populated were easy to conquer and more favourable for setting up 'new' countries, which were direct offshoots of European civilization and regarded as mere extensions of colonial powers' territories: New France, New England, New Holland and so on (which later became Canada, the US, Australia, New Zealand). Countries with "ancient civilizations of their own" obviously presented risks: the project of setting up a 'new' European country in an 'old' colony with its "teeming millions" is problematic and may have little chance of success as the experiences of Rhodesia, South Africa and Israel have shown. Acemoglu *et al.* (2001) and Acemoglu and Johnson (2005) refer to this as the "feasibility of settlements" which, in the case of Africa, was limited by factors such as the high risks of mortality for Europeans due to "the tropical diseases such as malaria and yellow fever that had turned much of Africa into the 'white man's graveyard' and prevented Europeans from settling or even setting up permanent outposts" (Acemoglu and Robinson, 2012: 260).

Now the picture is clearer: wherever colonizers were able to set up a new country with a homogenous European population, foreign investment 'followed the flag' and money and technology poured in. Nurkse (1954: 253) has noted that public infrastructure investments – financed by colonial governments – in railways, roads, bridges, hospitals and schools were actually "deliberately planned and built in *advance*" so as to attract European migrants and facilitate settlement. Thereafter, inclusive political and economic institutions that are conducive to progress and development were readily put in place. By contrast, Indian railways, as late as 1914, "accounted for less than one-tenth of the total of overseas railway securities held by British investors" Nurkse (1954: 253). For the same reasons, France never built that "costly framework of public services", the basis for industrial development, in any of its African colonies even though Algeria, for instance, was under French rule for more than 130 years and was officially considered a French department for much of that period. In African colonies, railways and road networks were strictly limited to areas declared '*zones utiles*' to transport primary commodities, mainly destined for export: they are direct links between the mines/ plantations and seaports. In other instances, railroads were dictated by geostrategic calculations during the colonial rivalry and the 'Scramble for Africa'.[4]

It is important to emphasize here that these state-sponsored advantages accorded to the settlers (and not to the 'old' colonies) exerted a strong impact on subsequent investments via the well-known agglomeration effect and, therefore, created a path dependence in the future development of colonies.[5] This explains why the 'new' countries like Canada and the United States, even though also they relied on export of primary commodities in their early stages of development, have nonetheless emerged as industrial countries in a very short period of time;

whereas the 'old' colonies in Africa, for instance, remained essentially "hewers of wood and drawers of water". In fact, just as Cecil Rhodes had envisioned (see footnote 2 above), they became suppliers of cheaply-priced primary commodities and consumers of manufactured products imported from Europe – interacting in a regime that Maddison (2006: 27, 100) called "free trade imperialism" and which has played an important role in the industrial development of Western Europe.

Free trade imperialism actually represented an important component of industrial policy in Western Europe and, up until recently, was defended even by some fair-minded economists. Keynes (1941: 25–6), for instance, wrote that:

> Of the special measures which it is open to us to employ by far the most potent is to use the importance of the British market to producers of food and raw materials overseas as an inducement to them to make equivalent purchases of manufactured articles from us. The Argentine, for example, cannot hope to market her wheat and maize and meat . . . unless she can sell substantial quantities in Britain. We may have to tell her that we are not in a financial position to purchase these substantial quantities unless she is prepared to expend the proceeds on taking textiles and engineering products from us.

To secure a continuous flow of these supplies, colonial powers did not rely only on political bargaining and persuasion. They also resorted to the use of force and violence – and for that they needed to put in place extractive institutions, which took the form of repressive political regimes whose mission was, and still is, to maintain an economic structure designed to serve the interests of the elite. Violence and repression against indigenous populations of Africa, Asia and the Americas were so flagrant and repulsive that any sane person would refuse to believe that European colonizers did actually commit such crimes. In the words of Shakespeare, their "cannons were bent against the brows of any resisting town", because in their view they were fighting "just and charitable wars" (Shakespeare's *King John*, Act 2, scene 1). As far as the populations of the 'old' colonies are concerned, these institutions are modern replicas of Roman imperialism, which "was based on plunder, enslavement and ability to exercise control through military force" (Maddison, 2006: 52).[6] In his analysis of the present situation, Amin (2004: 24) concluded that "The globalized 'liberal' economic order requires permanent war – military interventions endlessly succeeding one another – as the only means to submit the peoples of the periphery to its demands". Polanyi-Levitt (2016) described this recurring practice since early colonial times as "commerce and conquest, trade and war, finance and warfare" – all of which are analysed in great detail by Amin (1974) in his book *Accumulation on a World Scale*.

Repressive, extractive institutions may succeed in subjugating and exploiting people for quite some time, but they can never create an atmosphere that is conducive to progress, social stability and long-term growth – because people revolt. As history shows, the Roman Empire collapsed and disintegrated and the 'old' colonies are now left in a state of economic sclerosis. Among these, the countries that did well on the scale of industrial development are those that were able to break away from the colonial trap and build their own institutions with a clear development strategy. And that they could do only through a strong national state motivated by what we can call the population's 'democratic aspirations' for prosperity. Can African countries then have a successful industrial policy?

Interest in industrial or technological development is justified on the grounds that it allows the diffusion of technology to underdeveloped areas so as to defeat technological backwardness through the absorption of the most up-to-date knowledge. Industrial development is also desirable because it has the potential of creating growth opportunities in agriculture and other sectors of the economy – as historically proven – and, therefore, of generating good-paying jobs that are essential in the fight against unemployment and poverty. Industrialization, however, should not be idealized, neither should it be regarded as a difficult or impossible task. There are now examples of several countries that have achieved high levels of technological development in less than one generation. The one essential ingredient in this process is the acquisition of scientific knowledge, which can be obtained through the provision of a good education and the generalization of the teaching of *science* to broaden the knowledge base of the economy – thus improving skills and learning within the production units (see Greenwald and Stiglitz, 2013a). Much of all this can be achieved using domestic resources and, therefore, the national currency. However, there is often the need for foreign technology whose import requires international currencies – mainly the US dollar. The traditional methods used up until now have been to earn these reserves through exports or to borrow them on international markets. The limits to both of these methods are well known by now. The international financing constraint is the subject of the next section, but let us first deal with industrial policy and examine ways to overcome the technological constraint.

Policymakers who are concerned about the state of underdevelopment and industrial backwardness in their countries should learn the crucial lesson that there is no economy on this planet that functions – or has ever functioned – according to 'pure' market forces. They should not be duped into thinking that industrialization and development will occur if only they improved institutions and allowed markets to work efficiently (Storm, 2015). Historically, industrialization and successful development occurred in countries where the state actively intervened to create and shape markets by providing the legal framework, public infrastructure and social services, by setting standards and regulating industrial relations and above all by acting as entrepreneur, particularly in high-risk activities.

Indeed, every developed country has relied on industrial policy: as noted earlier, advanced industrialized countries of Western Europe and North America have systematically relied on heavy state intervention for their development throughout their history and continue to do so. The recent success stories of the East Asian "miracle" economies have been based on the implementation of carefully designed trade and investment policies (Amsden, 1996, 1997; Amsden and Chu, 2003; Wade, 2004). The same is also true of Japan and to some extent other newly industrialized countries (NICs). In all these cases, contrary to the much-celebrated *laissez-faire* principles, the state planned, subsidized and protected by tariffs or quotas what it considered vital sectors of the economy. Only the naïve believe in the virtues and powers of free markets. So the first requirement for designing a successful industrial policy is making sure that the state is not captured by the interests of those who stand behind the free-market ideology.

Stiglitz (2015: 10) has recently made the astute observation that "all governments, whether they know it or not, are engaged in industrial policy" – the point being that whatever a government does or does not do, that is, all government's (in)actions necessarily reflect the policymakers' view of how the economy should function and how society should develop. For example, when a government chooses to privatize education and health care, to encourage the creation of monopolies in trade, finance, insurance and real estate (T-FIRE) and not to invest in physical public infrastructure, it is opting for a particular industrial policy that seeks to maintain in place a regime based on extraction of rents and whose goal is to further the interests of a particular class at the expense of the wider population (for a typical example, see *Saudi Gazette*, 2016). By contrast, a government that sets as its objective the elimination of social and economic inequalities through income and wealth redistribution schemes, putting emphasis on science and technology by subsidizing and investing directly in these areas would be opting instead for an inclusive industrial policy that has the potential of generating long-term growth and creating wealth for the masses. The choice of policy is never neutral. Economic and social policies, of which industrial policy is only one component, always have concrete effects on our lives.

While there is no blueprint for a successful industrial policy, there are recognizable traits and features of past and existing successful experiences that can inspire African and other policymakers wishing to embark on the road of industrialization. Consider for instance the well-known case of South Korea. In the early 1960s, Korea was one of the poorest countries in the world and its level of industrial development was comparable to that of Egypt or Argentina – to give but those two examples. Today, it stands out as a highly industrialized country, capable of manufacturing the most sophisticated technological products. What makes the Korean model of industrialization so noticeable and perhaps worthy of emulation is that it was able to shatter three related myths that had long dominated policymaking and the literature on development economics: (a) the supremacy of free, unfettered markets in the process of growth and development, (b) only a liberal democracy of the Western type is compatible with growth and development and (c) the road to development is long and winding and the learning process slow and complex.

Indeed, right from the beginning in the 1960s, the state – which took charge of disciplining the market by subjecting private firms to performance standards – was not exactly a liberal democracy, but rather a 'political dictatorship' that lasted until 1987 (see Cheon *et al.*, 2014). The state started by outlining the objectives of industrialization, listing the instruments to be used and determining the time span to achieve those objectives – actions which were formulated in consistent short and long-term plans and which earned the state the adjective 'developmental'. Aware of the central role of finance in the process of development, the state immediately took control of the banking system (see Lim, 2013). It then resorted to the policy of sticks and carrots, rewarding performance of those firms that meet the set standards and promoting new industries. The vision was clear: make Korea an industrialized country in a short period of time. One of the insights of the Korean success story is that policymakers did not neglect the crucial role of agriculture in development. In the 1970s, Korea pursued a strategy that aimed to increase agricultural production and incomes of rural communities (the *Saemaul Undong* or New community movement), which contributed to the increase in domestic demand and further promoted innovations in agricultural industries. Consequently, the instruments – or the means towards the structural transformation – were chosen carefully. The following examples, not an exhaustive list, indicate the coherence of the strategy:

(a) Primary and secondary education received a high priority in the early planning process, with an emphasis on the technical content in an effort to increase the number of scientists and engineers,
(b) Since the goal was to develop a home-grown industrialization, Korean policymakers did not encourage foreign direct investment. Instead, they focused on increasing the local technological base through the transfer of foreign technology via licensing and reverse engineering and in a later stage by encouraging research and development (R&D),
(c) Given the small size of the Korean market, external demand was identified as a solution and so the industrialization programme had to be based on an export-led growth strategy. To ensure that it did not remain at the bottom of the value chain as a supplier of cheap manufacturing exports, Korea sought to increase the value-added content of its exports and encouraged the move into more sophisticated industries. Such a move requires a highly educated and skilled labour force, which is met by instrument (a) above.

Although Korea evolved within a globalized world economy in which access to trade and capital markets were essential for its development, policymakers did not shy away from using tariffs and subsidies to protect sectors and industries, either because they were strategic or in their 'infant' stage (Stiglitz *et al.*, 2013). Moreover, imports were linked to exports in such a way that permits to import or tariff exemptions were used in a discriminatory way and given to firms that reached export targets. The ubiquitous involvement of the government in the economy made it possible to forge strategic alliances between state-owned enterprises and industry conglomerates, known as *chaebol* and which occupied oligopolistic positions in the economy – not exactly the image of the competitive market idealized in textbooks. This corporatism allowed strategic companies, though under monitoring and performance requirements, to benefit from state guarantees of foreign loans which gave them easier access to international financial markets.

The shortcomings of the Korean model are typical of any capitalist economy. The objectives of industrial policy were mainly focused on promoting growth and not so much on redistribution and elimination of inequality and had even less concern for the environment. Data from the OECD indicate that inequality in Korea has increased and that the size of the middle-income class as a proportion of the total population declined substantially from 75.4 per cent in 1990 to 67.5 per cent in 2010, while the size of the low-income class has increased (see OECD, 2014: 31, figure 15). This change in income distribution had a direct impact on poverty in the country and, as a result, relative poverty increased from about 8 per cent in the early 1990s to 15 per cent in 2010 (OECD, 2014: 7, 31). It is interesting to note that the Gini coefficient followed a U-shaped curve as inequality decreased in the early phase of the industrialization programme due to an improvement in wages and job creation, but started to rise in the early 1990s when Korea adopted neoliberal policies – a trajectory referred to as the Great U-turn by Cheon *et al.* (2014: 421).

Neoliberal policies have quite a long history in Africa where they have been popularized under the misleading name of 'Structural Adjustment Programmes' (SAPs) and where they forced a much worse turn of events. The available data show that the process of industrialization, growth and development in most of Africa, and particularly in the sub-Saharan region, has actually followed an inverted V-shaped path. Inspired by the principles of the Bandung Conference[7] (1955), leaders of the liberation movements in Africa strongly advocated and pursued a state-led development strategy in the era immediately following independence. Throughout the 1960s and 1970s, most governments in Africa implemented five-year plans and there was a surge in economic growth and industrialization (see Heidhues and Obare, 2011; Storm, 2015). The turning point occurred in 1980, when international institutions, led by the World Bank and the IMF, in the context of high interest rates and a strong US dollar, imposed *contractionary* SAPs, which practically aborted any serious development project. For Amin (1997: 148), however, the "Bandung project" was doomed to fail because it never sought to break away from that "gigantic sub-contracting enterprise" which is global capitalism.

The new approach to development was enunciated in a 'white paper' by the World Bank (1981) entitled *Towards Accelerated Development in Sub-Saharan Africa*. The basic recommendations, which became instructions, specifically required a return to specialization in the export of agricultural and primary commodities, i.e. a return to the 'colonial pattern of trade' and the *withdrawal* of the state from all vital sectors of the economy (liberalization, deregulation and privatization). Loans and financial assistance were made conditional on such withdrawal (Loxley, 1983), specifically targeting the support of primary exports (mining and agriculture) and showing a clear prejudice against industrialization (Amin, 1997). In addition, as argued by Chang (2015), the industrial policy space was also, later on, severely constrained by the World Trade Organization and other free trade agreements. The net result of these policies is that development in Africa was not 'accelerated' but instead *'arrested'* (Fieldhouse, 1986), which led to a process of deindustrialization (as documented by United Nations, 1998; Greenwald and Stiglitz, 2013b; Stiglitz and Greenwald, 2014), slow or negative growth and intolerable poverty in most African countries (Artadi and Sala-i-Martin, 2004). If in 1970, one in ten poor people in the world lived in Africa, by 2012 the number was closer to one in two (see World Bank, 2016a). The World Bank (2016b) also tells us that since 1990, the number of the poor in Africa has increased by at least 100 million.

The power of finance: removing the external constraint

If you think that the international trade system has been rigged and made to work for the interest of the powerful nations and their allies, then welcome to the world of finance. Let us not forget that trade and finance are intimately tied to each other as every export/import requires a payment – a flow of funds. The links between transactions in international trade and finance are often summarized in an accounting statement known as the balance of payments, which captures commercial and financial transactions of a given country with the rest of the world, as shown in Table 6.1.

The difference between credits and debits of lines 1, 2 and 3 gives the balance of the current account whereas that of lines 4, 5 and 6 gives the balance of the capital account. If the current account is in deficit, then the capital account must be in surplus – therefore reflecting the inflows or sources of financing. When the terms of trade deteriorated so much for developing countries that they were increasingly unable to buy the same quantity of manufactured products with the same earnings from their exports (higher value of line 1 on the debits side), such as occurred during the 1960s and 1970s, they received loans denominated in US dollars (line 4 on the credits side) on which they paid hefty interests (line 2 on the debits side) – thus adding to their current account deficit. As export proceeds dwindled, more loans were needed to service the initial loans and to finance imports but interestingly enough not much inflows in terms of long-term investments (line 5 on the credits side) that could finance the capital development and serve as a basis for industrialization.

The deteriorating terms of trade have been a central argument by the dependency school since the 1950s and was recently re-confirmed for the whole twentieth century in an updated study by a group of economists from the United Nations (see Ocampo and Parra, 2003; UNCTAD, 2005). In this way, most developing countries were caught in a spiral of loans-imports-loans that partially broke but did not end with the infamous debt crisis of the 1980s. Although the context is different, a somewhat similar and perhaps more tragic scenario was re-enacted more recently with Greece (see Galbraith, 2016).

The same ideology behind 'SAPs' continued after the 1980s, with the IMF and the World Bank advising policymakers in developing countries to balance their public budgets by cutting spending on such things as public infrastructure and social services (austerity), by selling public corporations (privatization) and by

Table 6.1 Balance of payments accounting statement

Credits (claims on foreigners)	Debits (debts due to foreigners)
1 Exports of goods and services	1 Imports of goods and services
2 Investment income received from abroad	2 Investment income paid to foreigners
3 Unilateral transfers received from abroad	3 Unilateral transfer to foreigners
4 Short-term credit from foreigners	4 Short-term credit to foreigners
5 Long-term investment coming in	5 Long-term investment going abroad
6 Change in foreign reserve holdings	

dismantling all government's involvement in economic affairs (deregulation); in short, they were advised to implement the neoliberal model of economic management. It is now widely recognized that such policies resulted in a deindustrialization of certain countries (Noman and Stiglitz, 2012) and a worsening of the finances of many more, which contributed to a series of banking and financial crises such as the Asian crisis (1997–8) and the Argentinian crisis (2001–2), among others.

When certain countries were unable to meet their excessive interest payments and tried to link these to the proceeds from their exports, as Mexico did in the 1980s, international credit rating agencies downgraded these countries' standing to 'C' – therefore severing their access to international financial markets by signalling to international lenders that these are high-risk, and perhaps bankrupt, countries. This brings us to the heart of the problem. Why does a poor, developing country have to rely on borrowing the currency of a developed country to finance the importation of goods and services that are essential for its industrialization and development?

Under the current system, a small start-up firm in a remote area in any industrial country, say the United States, can apply for a loan and get the needed funds to finance the acquisition of the most sophisticated machinery and equipment. By comparison, even the largest corporation in a developing country faces a binding constraint because only some major reserve currencies are accepted for payment in international transactions – a fact referred to as the 'Original Sin' (see Eichengreen and Hausmann 1999; Hausmann and Panizza, 2003). Since foreign lenders often impose strict credit standards on borrowers from developing countries, industrialization and development projects in general are frustrated, delayed or abandoned – a state of affairs that goes a long way in explaining retardation and backwardness (see Bougrine and Seccareccia, 2009–10). If the answer to the above question is 'well, that is the system!', then the system is flawed and needs to be reformed. A radical reform of the international monetary system is necessary for a successful industrialization of poor countries.

In an interview at the Wharton School at the University of Pennsylvania on 3 April 2012, the managing director of the IMF, Christine Lagarde, was asked what she was most passionate about and what she would like to see happen at the IMF. She replied:

> That's complicated . . . You see, this is a very fascinating institution because it's completely counter-cyclical. When the world around the IMF goes downhill, we thrive. We become extremely active because we lend money, we earn interest and charges and all the rest of it, and the institution does well. When the world goes well and we've had years of growth, as was the case back in 2006 and 2007, the IMF doesn't do so well both financially and otherwise.
>
> (see Lagarde, 2012).

Now, an institution that is *designed* to thrive on poor countries' misery isn't exactly what a civilized world needs. On this account, the IMF is another extractive institution in international finance. And that is why a reform of the system is an urgent matter, as many have insisted (see, among others, Smithin, 2001; UN Commission of Experts, 2009; UNCTAD, 2009; Stiglitz and Greenwald, 2010; Hudson, 2010; Rossi, 2015). While most of these scholars advocated a return to Keynes' original plan and the adoption of an international currency unit as the means of payments in order to give poor countries direct access to international financing, others like Mehrling (2016) considered the plan to be outdated and proposed instead the continued reliance on existing major national currencies, with the US dollar at the top of the pyramid and the IMF playing the role of a walking cane.

The story behind the creation of the IMF is indeed a 'fascinating' one but not for the reasons mentioned by Lagarde (2012). In 1942–3, just before the end of the Second World War, the Allies – led by Britain and the United States – began preparing for a new post-war economic order. The aim was to develop a payments system that would ensure stability and growth throughout the world; and so the discussions centred on the creation of an international currency, universally accepted as a means of payment, for the purpose of properly managing the problems arising from imbalances in international transactions of trade and finance. The system that had prevailed until then was fundamentally mercantilist in that international payments for settlement of debts were still based on the transfer of some *reserve* currency that was supposed to be a store of value ultimately represented by gold (see De Cecco, 1979). On that account, imports were immiserating whereas exports increased wealth as they led to the accumulation of reserves and more gold. The hoarding of such assets for long periods of time had the obvious consequence of maintaining global imbalances in trade and finance and of stifling economic expansion and growth worldwide but particularly in the deficit countries (see Keynes, 1942; Hudson, 2010).

Even though the Bretton Woods system had departed markedly from Keynes' original plan, the period from 1945 to 1971, known as the 'golden age' of capitalism, was still characterized by (a) fairly stable exchange rates, which were fixed but adjustable, (b) extensive regulation and capital controls, with most national governments pursuing (c) domestic expansionary fiscal and monetary policies. Soon after the Bretton Woods system collapsed in 1971, however, exchange rates started floating again and free capital mobility returned with full force as free-market advocates called for the removal of all barriers to capital flows. The next two decades of the 1980s and 1990s were marked by a general shift towards free markets and coincided with the rise of neoliberal policies which put strong emphasis on financial deregulation and liberalization.

The new wisdom for policymaking now came in the form of a *trilemma*: a country cannot have at the same time an independent monetary policy to deal with domestic issues, fixed exchange rates and free capital mobility – implying that it must choose at most two of these options. But the debate that surrounded the trilemma issue has been highly misleading, because if a country establishes its monetary sovereignty and sets out to implement expansionary fiscal and monetary policies while managing the value of its currency, then it must enforce capital controls (see Epstein, 2010). An empirical assessment of the two episodes following the Second World War is given by Reinhart and Rogoff (2008: 23) who find that the first episode (1945–71) of regulation and capital controls was characterized by calm and stability, whereas after 1971 higher capital mobility was associated with more banking crises. In their updated study, Reinhart and Rogoff (2013: 4558, emphasis in original) noted that "*Since the early 1970s, financial and international capital account liberalization took root worldwide. So, too, have banking crises*".

The theoretical discussions prior to the Bretton Woods conference in 1944 – which led to the creation of the IMF – were mainly between Harry Dexter White representing the United States and John Maynard Keynes representing Britain and other delegations.[8] The proposals for reforming the international monetary system initially suggested by White and Keynes were somewhat similar, but as negotiations proceeded, the differences became sharper: Keynes was arguing for an international *currency unit* to be used principally as a means of payments whereas White pushed for the adoption of a national *reserve currency* – namely the US dollar – that can also be a store of value (Amato and Fantacci, 2014). As we shall see below, the difference between the two proposals is enormous in terms of the type of international monetary system it entails and of its consequences for the world economy.

The historical details surrounding the rejection of Keynes' plan and the adoption of the US dollar as the international currency are indeed intriguing and fascinating but too lengthy to relate here and have been discussed by others, including Moggridge (1980), Rosenberg and Schuler (2012) and Steil (2013). It is important to recall that Keynes was not present at the discussions when the decision was made to adopt the US dollar as the international currency. Keynes was preoccupied managing the World Bank proceedings when White, in Keynes' absence, abruptly ended the discussion on the issue of replacing gold with the US dollar and declared "Unless there are any objections, this question will be referred to the special committee. Any objection? Then we pass to the next problem", quoted in Steil (2013: 216). Commenting on this incident, Amato and Fantacci (2014: 1435) wrote that:

> In this sense, the story of Bretton Woods, with respect to the goals that it was supposed to achieve, is the story of a failure: it is the story of how, instead of an international currency unit, a national reserve currency was eventually established as international money.

Still, a brief summary is needed in order to appreciate the difference Keynes' proposal would have made for the history of the world economy had the plan been adopted. By the 1930s Keynes had already become a fierce opponent of the Gold Standard, and the Bretton Woods conference was an opportunity for him to put forth his alternative theory of money and to propose a solution to what he called the *secular* international problem, which has plagued the balance of payments between countries ever since the introduction of 'money and bills of exchange' as means of settlement (Keynes, 1941: 21). Keynes noted that the world economy had been in "a state of extreme disequilibrium" even prior to the war and attributed that to a single reason: transfer of value from the debtor country to the creditor countries in a system that "throws the main burden of adjustment on the country which is in the *debtor* position on the international balance of payments" and which therefore sought "to force adjustments in the direction most disruptive of social order, and to throw the burden on the countries least able to support it, making the poor poorer" (Keynes, 1941: 29). Having identified this compulsory flow of capital funds out of the debtor countries as the major source of instability, his solution was then to come up with a system that would force both debtor and creditor countries to share the burden of adjustment. That system was what Keynes called the *International Clearing Union*.

The idea of an International Clearing Union is quite simple, but has far-reaching consequences. It is based on the idea of the role of a commercial bank in a closed system. As we have seen in Chapters 3 and 4, commercial banks today create money out of thin air simply by accepting to extend credit to creditworthy borrowers who then use these credits to pay for goods and services and to extinguish their debts. If both the payers and the payees are clients of the same bank, then the settlement of debts consists of simply moving credits from one account to the other and the bank would never face any difficulty honouring cheques drawn upon it. The International Clearing Union would function in essentially the same way and "international money" would be moved from the account of the importing country to the account of the exporting country. There are, however, some crucial differences and these are perhaps what made Keynes' brilliant plan so unconventional that it was not adopted – although we know now that the plan was sidelined by dodgery and trickery rather than by honest intellectual argumentation (see Steil, 2013: chapter 8).

The "international money", which Keynes called *bancor*, resembles commercial bank money in that it can be created to accommodate the needs of commerce. For this purpose, every member country would have an account with the Clearing Union, with all accounts initially set to zero bancor. Countries will agree among themselves on "the initial values of their own currencies in terms of bancor and also the value of bancor in terms of gold" and these values, that is, exchange rates, will remain fixed and cannot be altered without the permission of the Governing Board of the Clearing Union (Keynes, 1942: 172). Just like private citizens have access to a line of credit and can borrow funds in their national money from a local bank, all member countries have access to an overdraft with the Clearing Union, with a maximum amount designated as their *quotas* – the quota of each country being relative to its weight in international trade.

Unlike the current system which requires importing countries to have a prior deposit of reserves, the Clearing Union allows the importing country to use its overdraft facility and the payment is made simply by recording a 'minus' in the account of the importer and a 'plus' in the account of the exporter – thus making bancor a purely scriptural money, which is created each time an importing country uses its overdraft facility to pay for its imports. This is of paramount importance for poor and developing countries because it effectively removes their external constraint by allowing them direct access to financing imports of foreign technology. Countries with a negative (positive) balance would be in a deficit (surplus) position vis-à-vis the Clearing Union as a whole and *not* vis-à-vis other countries, which "means that overdraft facilities, whilst a relief to some, are not a real burden to others". However, the use of overdraft facilities is not unlimited, neither is it free. A deficit country is allowed a 'defined amount' and an "interval of time within which to effect a balance in its economic relations with the rest of the world" (Keynes, 1942: 176).

Since the main purpose of the International Clearing Union is to avoid the systematic build-up of long-lasting imbalances, both deficit and surplus countries are subject to certain conditions by which they are required to take appropriate measures to restore equilibrium of their international balances.[9] For this purpose, the Clearing Union would charge interest on both negative and positive balances when these reach a certain percentage of the country's quota. The idea of charging surplus countries a negative interest or a 'carrying cost' on their accumulated credit balances did not sit well with the orthodoxy since these balances would be gradually depleted over time. But from the Keynesian perspective, the point is not to penalize surplus countries for having conducted successful transactions in international trade. Rather, the point is to induce them to spend these credits instead of withholding them from circulation and thus forcing a "deflationary and contractionist pressure on the whole world, including in the end the creditor country itself" (Keynes, 1942: 177). This measure is consistent with the general Keynesian paradigm of putting demand at the centre of economic expansion. That is why creditor countries cannot be permitted to hoard their surpluses indefinitely. Therefore, surplus countries will have three options:

1   Spend their credit balances on buying goods and services, including from deficit countries, thereby contributing to the expansion of world trade and to a return towards equilibrium.
2   Invest these balances on a long-term basis in the form of direct investments as per line 5 of the balance of payments in Table 6.1 and, therefore, contribute to the capital development of other, particularly the poor and developing, countries.
3   Continue to hold their balances at the Clearing Union but pay the carrying costs, which, as noted earlier, act as a tax that gradually reduces the outstanding amount of credit balances. This last option should be the least favoured, which means that the creditor country will not remain passive and that is the idea behind the plan.

Amato and Fantacci (2014: 1445) noted that the provisions outlined above have the advantage of encouraging the "continuous circulation of international money" and avoiding the "accumulation of idle balances and the generation of rents" in order to "ensure an adequate funding for international trade and investment". But it is interesting to note that the plan puts a particular emphasis on long-term capital movements, because these are considered the "genuine new investment for developing the world's resources", which will help prevent world trade imbalances (Keynes, 1942: 186–7). In this context, short-term capital movements are obviously considered a source of disturbance and, therefore, surplus countries are not permitted to engage in speculative transactions such as using their bancor balances to purchase financial securities (see De Cecco, 1979; Amato and Fantacci, 2014;).

There are many other interesting features of the plan but the most relevant to us here are those dealing specifically with access to international financing and the role of the latter in the capital development of poor countries. It can be said here that the overriding goal was to create favourable conditions for states to curtail the harmful effects of speculative capital and to channel finance towards a structural transformation of their economies, while pursuing full-employment policies – a task that was crucial to industrialization strategies, as later argued by the pioneers of development economics such as Raul Prebisch, Albert Hirschamn and Ragnar Nurkse, among others (see Gallagher, 2014). John Maynard Keynes should be credited for having had the foresight that the accumulation of idle resources and the generation of rents through interest and speculation would lead to a disproportionate growth of finance and the divorce between the latter and the real economy – which is a major feature of capitalism today and a source of its ailments.

Conclusion

The colonial pattern of trade and investment that required the 'old' colonies to specialize in the production and export of primary commodities and to import manufactured products from the metropoles has recently received new backing from the proponents of the so-called post-industrial economy. This argument plainly suggests that, since we now live in a knowledge economy, it is pointless for the old colonies to seek industrialization. After centuries of colonial exploitation, the message today seems to be that it is too late to build the costly infrastructure for manufacturing industries and pursue development strategies based on industrialization. Active industrial policy is then rejected out of hand because of what is called state capacity – a convenient term for discounting the fiscal and administrative powers of the state to manage the economy. The underlying argument is that the market, not the government, is the driving force of the economy and consequently there is no need for government intervention, particularly when we know that such intervention requires the use of 'public funds', which are supposed to be scarce.

While it is true that the share of manufacturing in gross domestic product has declined in most industrialized countries, it does not mean that we are about to give up the material production of technology, just as we can never stop the production of food because of the decline of agriculture. In fact, the decline of these sectors and the rise of the service sector are mainly due to technological advances which have increased productivity and liberated labour from these primary and secondary activities. Industrialization remains – and shall continue to be – the main driver of progress and the march towards a higher level of human development. Poor countries, however, continue to face two major constraints: access to technological knowledge and international finance. The chapter offered ideas on how to overcome these constraints by pursuing well-designed development strategies that include the struggle for revamping the current international monetary system.

Notes

1 In the case of India, Dutt (1992: 147) noted that "When the British began their colonization, India was an exporter of industrial goods and an importer of primary and intermediate goods. Before 1800, India was the major supplier of cotton and silk textiles (fine clothes as well as everyday wear for the masses) in international markets, including Europe; Indian textiles were considerably cheaper than British woollens because of India's lower wages and technical advantages". But "India's pattern of trade changed drastically after a few decades of colonial rule . . ." as "Indian handicraft industries were adversely affected . . ." and artisans were subjected to "flogging, imprisonment, and worse (cutting off the thumbs of winders of raw silk has been documented)".

2 For those who have any doubts about the goals and intentions of colonialism, Cecil Rhodes, the "founder" of ex-Rhodesia, present-day Zimbabwe, has blatantly summarized these as follows: "We must find new lands from which we can easily obtain raw materials and at the same time exploit the cheap slave labour that is available from the natives of the colonies. The colonies would also provide a dumping ground for the surplus goods produced in our factories". Quoted in Roberts, P. (1981) "Rural Development and the Rural Economy in Niger, 1900–75" in Heyer, J., P. Roberts and G. Williams (eds), *Rural Development in Tropical Africa*, New York: St Martin's Press, p. 195.

3 For instance, according to the World Bank in 2009, more than 76 per cent of the population in Nigeria live on less than \$3.10 a day. Nigeria is one of the top producers of oil in the world, with an average of 2.5 million barrels a day.

4 For instance, to secure its control over the source of the Nile river, Britain built a railroad line running from the coast through Kenya to the Great Lakes region of central Africa. Jedwab *et al.* (2015: 3) show that this railroad in Kenya "had a strong impact on European settlement, establishing cities from where the *European settlers* managed their commercial farms and specialised in urban activities".

5 Donaldson and Hornbeck (2016), among others, have documented the important impact of nineteenth-century railroads on economic growth in the United States.

6 Plunder and violence are not tales of times past. During the first 15 years of the twenty-first century, we have witnessed military invasions and barbaric destruction of a number of countries and their ancient civilizations (Iraq, Libya, Syria, etc.) by the United States and its allies for the purpose of securing access to vital resources such as oil and gas. In a clear reference to the conquest by Julius Caesar who declared "veni, vidi, vici: we came, we saw, we conquered", the US Secretary of State Hillary Clinton, who was in Libya to oversee the overthrow of Muammar Gaddafi in 2011, mimicked the Roman emperor and announced viciously on TV: "We came, we saw, he died": www.cbsnews.com/news/clinton-on-qaddafi-we-came-we-saw-he-died/, accessed 20 March 2016. It is ironic that in the midst of a permanent, savage war that has been ongoing since the turn of this century and in spite of all the destruction and loss of life that ensued, Barack Obama declared recently that we are "living in *the* most peaceful, most prosperous and most progressive era in human history": www.dw.com/en/obama-stresses-importance-of-eu-us-partnership-in-landmark-speech/a-19212444, accessed 25 April 2016.

7 The Bandung Conference (1955) called for an end to colonialism and encouraged newly independent countries in Africa and Asia to embark on industrialization and development through state intervention, negotiation of fairer trade arrangements and a

favourable international financial system through, among other things, the establishment of a special United Nations fund for development. See the full communiqué here: www. ena.lu/final_communique_asian_african_conference_bandung_24_april_1955-2-1192, accessed 5 May 2016.

8 In the early days of the preparations for negotiating a new international monetary system, Keynes (1942: 152) was reluctant to engage in an 'Anglo-American bloc' and wanted to include as many delegations as possible (e.g. Russia, the Dominions, the rest of Europe) in the formulation of the plan so that it would have an 'international character' but for practical reasons, he agreed that "the actual constitution of particular plans must be agreed and established by as few cooks as possible, with the others invited to the dinner table after they have smelt the broth". Ironically, even the British position as represented by J. M. Keynes was sidelined by the United States delegation (see Rosenberg and Schuler, 2012).

9 Keynes (1942: 169) has stated very clearly that "We need a system possessed of internal stabilizing mechanism, by which pressure is exercised on any country whose balance of payments with the rest of the world is departing from equilibrium in either direction, so as to prevent movements which must create for its neighbours an equal but opposite want of balance".

References

Acemoglu, D. and S. Johnson (2005) "Unbundling Institutions", *Journal of Political Economy*, Vol. 113, No. 5, pp. 949–95.

Acemoglu, D. and J. A. Robinson (2012) *Why Nations Fail: The Origins of Power, Prosperity, and Poverty* (London: Profile Books Ltd).

Acemoglu, D., S. Johnson and J. A. Robinson (2001) "The Colonial Origins of Comparative Development: An Empirical Investigation", *American Economic review*, Vol. 91, No. 5, pp. 1369–401.

Amato, M. and L. Fantacci (2014) "Back to Which Bretton Woods? Liquidity and Clearing as Alternative Principles for Reforming International Money", *Cambridge Journal of Economics*, Vol. 38, pp. 1431–52.

Amin, S. (1974) *Accumulation on a World Scale*, 2 volumes, (New York: Monthly Review Press).

Amin, S. (2004) *The Liberal Virus: Permanent War and the Americanization of the World* (New York: Monthly Review Press).

Amin, S. (2009) *Eurocentrism: Modernity, Religion, and Democracy: A Critique of Eurocentrism and Culturalism* (New York: Monthly Review Press).

Amin, S. (2014 [1997]) *Capitalism in the Age of Globalization: The Management of Contemporary Society* (New York: Zed Books).

Amsden, A. (1996) "A Strategic Policy Approach to Government Intervention in Late Industrialization" in Solimano, A. (ed.), *Road Maps to Prosperity: Essays on Growth and Development* pp. 119–41 (Ann Arbor, MI: University of Michigan Press).

Amsden, A. (1997) "South Korea: Enterprising Groups and Entrepreneurial Government" in Chandler, A., F. Amatori and T. Hikino (eds), *Big Business and the Wealth of Nations,* pp. 336–67 (Cambridge, UK: Cambridge University Press).

Amsden, A. and W. Chu (2003) *Beyond Late Development: Taiwan's Upgrading Policies* (Cambridge, MA: MIT Press).

Artadi, E. V. and X. Sala-i-Martin (2004) "The Economic Tragedy of the Twentieth Century: Growth in Africa" in Hernández-Catá, E., K. Schwab and A. Lopez-Claros (eds), *The Africa Competitiveness Report 2004* (Geneva: World Economic Forum, pp. 1–18).

Bernal, M. (1991) *Black Athena: The Afroasiatic Roots of Classical Civilization* (London: Vintage).

Bougrine, H. and M. Seccareccia (2009–10) "Financing Development: Removing the External Constraint", *International Journal of Political Economy*, Vol. 38, No. 4, pp. 44–65.

Chang, H. J. (2015) "Is Industrial Policy Necessary and Feasible in Africa?: Theoretical Considerations and Historical Lessons" in Noman, A. and J. E. Stiglitz (eds), *Industrial Policy and Economic Transformation in Africa* (New York: Columbia University Press).

Cheon, B. Y., J. Chang, G. S. Hwang, J. W. Shin, S. W. Kang, B. H. Lee and H. J. Kim (2014) "Korea: The Great U-Turn in Inequality and the Need for Social Security Provisions" in *Changing Inequalities and Societal Impacts in Rich Countries: Thirty Countries' Experiences* (Oxford, UK: Oxford University Press).

De Cecco, M. (1979) "Origins of the Post-War Payments System", *Cambridge Journal of Economics*, Vol. 3, pp. 49–61.

De Gregori, R. T. (1968) "Foreign Investment and Technological Diffusion: The Case of British Colonial Africa", *Journal of Economic Issues*, Vol 2, No. 4, pp. 403–15.

Donaldson, D. and R. Hornbeck (2016) "Railroads and American Economic Growth: A 'Market Access' Approach", forthcoming in *The Quarterly Journal of Economics*, doi: 0.1093/qje/qjw002.

Dutt, A. K. (1992) "The Origins of Uneven Development: The Indian Subcontinent", *American Economic Review*, Vol. 82, No. 2, pp. 146–50.

Eichengreen, B. and R. Hausmann (1999) *Exchange Rates and Financial Fragility*, NBER Working Paper, no. 7418.

Epstein, G. (2010) "Financial Flows Must be Regulated" in Bougrine, H. and M. Seccareccia (eds), *Macroeconomic Analysis: Issues, Questions, and Competing Views* (Toronto: Emond Montgomery Publications).

Fieldhouse, D. K. (1986) *Black Africa 1945–1980: Economic Decolonisation and Arrested Development* (London: Allen and Unwin).

Fields, D. and M. Vernengo (2016) "DisORIENT: Money, Technological Development and the Rise of the West", Working paper presented at the ASSA Meetings in San Francisco, (January 4) (Department of Economics, Bucknell University).

Galbraith, J. K. (2016) *Welcome to the Poisoned Chalice: The Destruction of Greece and the Future of Europe* (New Haven, CT: Yale University Press).

Gallagher, K. (2014) "The Economics of Regulating Cross-border Finance: Two New Views", *Review of Political Economy*, Vol. 26, No. 4, pp. 594–617.

Greenwald, B. C. and J. E. Stiglitz (2013a) "Industrial Policies, The Creation of a Learning Society, and Economic Development" in Stiglitz, J. E. and J. Y. Lin (eds), *The Industrial Policy Revolution I: The Role of Government Beyond Ideology* (New York: Palgrave Macmillan).

Greenwald, B. C. and J. E. Stiglitz (2013b) "Learning and Industrial Policy: Implications for Africa" in Stiglitz, J. E., J. L. Yifu and E. Patel (eds), *The Industrial Policy Revolution II: Africa in the 21st Century* (Basingstoke, UK: Palgrave Macmillan).

Gunder Frank, A. (1978) *World Accumulation 1492–1789* (New York: Monthly Review Press).

Gunder Frank, A. (1998) *ReOrient: Global Economy in the Asian Age* (Berkeley, CA: University of California Press).

Hausmann, R. and Panizza (2003) "On the Determinants of Original Sin: An Empirical Investigation", *Journal of International Money and Finance*, Vol. 22, pp. 957–90.

Headrick, D. R. (1981) *The Tools of Empire: Technology and European Imperialism in the Nineteenth Century* (Oxford, UK: Oxford University Press).

Heidhues, F. and G. Obare (2011) "Lessons from Structural Adjustment Programmes and Their Effects in Africa", *Quarterly Journal of International Agriculture*, Vol. 50, No. 1, pp. 55–64.

Hirschman, A. O. (1958) *The Strategy of Economic Development* (New Haven, CT: Yale University Press).

Hudson, D. (2010) "Financing for Development and the Post Keynesian Case for a New Global Reserve Currency", *Journal of International Development*, Vol. 22, pp. 772–87.

Jedwab, R., E. Kerby and A. Moradi (2015) "History, Path Dependence and Development: Evidence from Colonial Railroads, Settlers and Cities in Kenya", forthcoming in *The Economic Journal*, doi: 10.1111/ecoj.12347.

Keynes, J. M. ([1941] ([1942], in Moggridge, D. (ed.), 1980, *The Collected Writings of John Maynard Keynes*, Volume XXV (New York: Macmillan).

Lagarde, C. (2012) *Emerging Market Nations Will Get More Power in the IMF*, online interview available at: http://knowledge.wharton.upenn.edu/article/christine-lagarde-emerging-market-nations-will-get-more-power-in-the-imf/, accessed 5 May 2016.

Lim, W. (2013) "The *Chaebol* and Industrial Policy in Korea" in Stiglitz, J. E. and J. Y. Lin (eds), *The Industrial Policy Revolution I: The Role of Government Beyond Ideology* (New York: Palgrave Macmillan).

Loxley, J. (1983) "The Berg Report and the Model of Accumulation in Sub-Saharan Africa", *Review of African Political Economy*, No. 27/28, pp. 197–204.

Maddison, A. (2006) The World Economy: A Millennial Perspective (Paris: OECD Development Center Studies).

Mantoux, P. (1961 [1928]) *The Industrial Revolution in the Eighteenth Century* (London: University Paperbacks).

Maynard, A. E., K. Subrahmanyam and P. M. Greenfield (2005) "Technology and the Development of Intelligence: From the Loom to the Computer" in Sternberg, R. J. and D. D. Preiss (eds), *Intelligence and Technology: The Impact of Tools on the Nature and Development of Human Abilities* (Mahwah, NJ: Lawrence Erlbaum Associates, Inc., Publishers).

McCloskey, D. N. (2010) *Bourgeois Dignity: Why Economics Can't Explain the Modern World* (Chicago, IL: The University of Chicago Press).

Mehrling, P. (2016) "Beyond Bancor", *Challenge*, Vol. 59, No. 1, pp. 22–34.

Moggridge, D. (ed.) (1980) *The Collected Writings of John Maynard Keynes*, Volume XXV (New York: Macmillan).

Mokyr, J. (1990) *The Lever of Riches: Technological Creativity and Economic Progress* (Oxford, UK: Oxford University Press).

Morgan, L. H. (1877) *Ancient Society: Or Researches in the Lines of Human Progress from Savagery through Barbarism to Civilization* (New York: Holt & Co.), available online from the *Internet Archive*: https://archive.org/details/ancientsociety00morg, accessed 20 March 2016.

Noman, A. and J. E. Stiglitz (2012) "Strategies for African Development" in Noman A., K. Botchwey, H. Stein, and J. E. Stiglitz (eds), *Good Growth and Governance for Africa: Rethinking Development Strategies* (New York: Oxford University Press, pp. 3–47).

Nurkse, R. ([1954]), in Kattel, R., J. A. Kregel and E. S. Reinert, (eds) (2009, *Ragnar Nurkse: Trade and Development* (New York: Anthem Press).

Obama, B. (2016) "The TPP Would Let America, Not China, Lead the Way on Global Trade", online: www.washingtonpost.com/opinions/president-obama-the-tpp-would-let-america-not-china-lead-the-way-on-global-trade/2016/05/02/680540e4–0fd0–11e6–93ae-50921721165d_story.html, accessed 3 May 2016.

Ocampo, J. A. and M. A. Parra (2003) "The Terms of Trade for Commodities in the Twentieth Century", *CEPAL Review* 79, pp. 7–35.

OECD (2014) *OECD Economic Surveys: Korea*, (June) (Paris: OECD).

Polanyi-Levitt, K. (2016) "Economics, Development and Ideology in Historical Perspective", paper presented at the Canadian Economics Association meeting, Ottawa, 2–5 June 2016.

Radelet, S. (2010) *Emerging Africa: How 17 Countries Are Leading the Way* (Washington, DC: Centre for Global Development).

Reinhart, C. M. and K. S. Rogoff (2008) *Banking Crises: An Equal Opportunity Menace*, National Bureau of Economic Research, Working Paper 14587, online: www.nber.org/papers/w14587, accessed 20 May 2016.

Reinhart, C. M. and K. S. Rogoff (2013) "Banking Crises: An Equal Opportunity Menace", *Journal of Banking & Finance*, Vol. 37, No. 11, pp. 4557–73.

Rodney, W. (1972) *How Europe Underdeveloped Africa* (London: Bogle-L'Ouverture).

Rosenberg, A. and K. Schuler (eds) (2012) *The Bretton Woods Transcripts* (New York: Center for Financial Stability).

Rossi, S. (2015) "Structural Reforms in Payment Systems to Avoid Another Systemic Crisis", *Review of Keynesian Economics*, Vol. 3, No. 2, pp. 213–25.

Saudi Gazette (2016) *Saudi Arabia's Vision 2030*, online: http://saudigazette.com.sa/saudi-arabia/full-text-saudi-arabias-vision-2030/, accessed 5 May 2016.

Smithin, J. (2001) "International Monetary Arrangements" in Holt, R. P. F. and S. Pressman (eds), *A New Guide to Post Keynesian Economics* (New York: Routledge).

Steil, B. (2013) *The Battle of Bretton Woods: John Maynard Keynes, Harry Dexter White, and the Making of a New World Order* (Princeton, NJ: Princeton University Press).

Stiglitz, J. E. (2015) *Industrial Policy, Learning, and Development*, WIDER Working Paper 2015/149, World Institute for Development Economics Research, online: www.wider.unu.edu/publication/industrial-policy-learning-and-development, accessed 8 May 2016.

Stiglitz, J. E. and B. C. Greenwald (2010) "Towards A New Global Reserve System", *Journal of Globalization and Development*, Vol. 1, No. 10, pp. 1–24.

Stiglitz, J. E. and B. C. Greenwald (2014) *Creating a Learning Society: A New Approach to Growth, Development, and Social Progress* (New York: Columbia University Press).

Stiglitz, J. E., J. Y. Lin and C. Monga (2013) "Introduction: The Rejuvenation of Industrial Policy" in Stiglitz, J. E. and J. Y. Lin (eds), *The Industrial Policy Revolution I: The Role of Government Beyond Ideology* (New York: Palgrave Macmillan).

Storm, S. (2015) "Structural Change", *Development and Change*, Vol. 46, No. 4, pp. 666–99.

Studer, R. (2015) *The Great Divergence Reconsidered: Europe, India, and the Rise to Global Economic Power* (Cambridge, UK: Cambridge University Press).

Svedberg, P. (1981) "Colonial Enforcement of Foreign Direct Investment", *The Manchester School*, Vol. 49, No. 1, pp. 21–38.

UN Commission of Experts (2009) *The Commission of Experts on Reforms of the International Monetary and Financial System*, available online: www.un.org/ga/president/63/commission/meetings.shtml, accessed 5 May 2016.

UNCTAD (2005) "Evolution in the Terms of Trade and Its Impact on Developing Countries", *Trade and Development Report, 2005* (New York: United Nations), online: www.unctad.org/en/docs/tdr2005ch3_en.pdf, accessed 5 May 2016.

UNCTAD (2009) *Trade and Development Report 2009* (New York: United Nations).

United Nations (1998) *African Industrialization Tops UNIDO's Agenda*, online: www.un.org/en/africarenewal/subjindx/113indus.htm, accessed 5 May 2016.

Vries, P. (2015) *State, Economy and the Great Divergence: Great Britain and China, 1680s–1850s* (New York: Bloomsbury Academic).

Wade, R. (2004) *Governing the Market: Economic Theory and the Role of Government in East Asian Industrialization* (Princeton, NJ: Princeton University Press).

Wallerstein, I. (1974) *The Modern World-System I: Capitalist Agriculture and the Origins of the European World-Economy in the Sixteenth Century* (New York and London: Academic Press).

World Bank (1981) *Accelerated Development in Sub-Saharan Africa: an Agenda for Action* (Washington, DC: The World Bank), online: http://documents.worldbank.org/curated/en/1981/01/438047/accelerated-development-sub-saharan-africa-agenda-action, accessed 5 May 2016.

World Bank (2016a) *Poverty: Overview*, online: www.worldbank.org/en/topic/poverty/overview, accessed 5 May 2016.

World Bank (2016b) *Poverty in a Rising Africa: Africa Poverty Report*, authored by Beegle, K., L. Christiaensen, A. Dabalen and I. Gaddis (Washington, DC: The World Bank).

7 Industrialization and the environmental crisis

Surely, We have made all that is on the earth an embellishment for it in order to test people as to who of them is better in conduct.

(Quran (18:7))

Introduction

Concern with the environment is a personal issue – for everyone that is. It starts with the quality of the air we breathe every day, the contaminated water in the lakes and in the seas, and with the chemicals found in our food. The toxic contaminants are often 'unintended' by-products of industrial activity when making goods and services or extracting resources from underground by methods such as fracking. These contaminants are called 'externalities' and those who produce them often do not want to be held accountable: they reject any responsibility, arguing that externalities should be seen as part of life and be either ignored or accepted as such – which makes them a cost to society while the profits made during the process that generates them remain private. This contradiction alone should arouse interest in environmental issues even among climate change skeptics.

Some economists argue that such externalities are a market failure which remains unresolved because of the absence of property rights to air, space, water and other spheres of nature (see Bator, 1958; Coase, 1960) and suggest that environmental problems result from the failure to implement capitalism fully[1] (see Kula, 1998). But toxic chemicals are also often intentionally used to enhance productivity and profitability when seeking, for instance, to increase the yield of agricultural crops. In this instance, such chemicals are direct inputs and become part of the production process and, therefore, cannot be regarded as 'externalities'. Yet, the producers want them accepted and are often ready to provide the 'scientific' data to prove that they are safe.[2]

In Chapter 5, we showed that the industrial revolution played a crucial role in the rapid economic progress of the West. Here, we argue that the industrial revolution itself would not have happened at the pace it did, without an energy revolution, which marked the shift from an economy that was largely based on human and animal power to one based on steam power. This was the transition from a pre-industrial *organic* economy to a *fossil* economy.[3] Wrigley (2010) has noted that mechanical energy was in a later stage of the organic pre-industrial economies supplemented by wind and water, but the burning of wood and charcoal remained the main source of energy. Mantoux (1928: 280–1) reported that the development of manufacturing in Britain towards the middle of the eighteenth century relied so heavily on the use of wood that entire forests had disappeared and wood became scarce even for household use, which prompted the promulgation by the government of several Acts seeking to limit "the number of ironworks allowed to be set up in certain counties".

This lack of fuel hastened the turning point in the history of Britain, and in the history of humanity, which occurred when burning coal became the alternative and primary source of thermal and mechanical energy (heat and motion). In the early nineteenth century, steam engines became widely used in industry and transportation in Britain and quickly spread to the rest of Western Europe. Powered by coal, these 'fascinating' machines performed well and accomplished wonders. Wrigley (2010: 28) quoted the French historian Levasseur (1889) as having estimated that "one steam horsepower performed work equivalent to twenty-one labourers". But what was really important is that these machines, unlike human labourers, could work continuously and not complain (unless they broke down) as long as you kept feeding them coal.[4] Coal was dirty, but it was effective: it served the purpose of increasing the power and the capacity to produce things and to move them around. Even space seemed to shrink as the time to travel and ship commodities was shortened by moving trains powered by coal. This was the industrial revolution and the steam engine changed everything.[5]

The new economy was hungry for energy and its factories gobbled a lot of coal. Smokestacks started sprouting at a fast pace and the landscape changed quickly. Thick smoke literally 'poisoned the atmosphere' and polluted the rivers, nearby and far afield. The immediate fatalities showed as increases in the number of deaths and diseases suffered by the workers, but a far greater danger was looming ahead: an environmental crisis affecting the future of humanity and the biological evolution as we fast-forward into the twenty-first century and beyond. The science of climate change, though still contested by some, has documented the extinction of several animal species and projects that global warming, the result of cumulative emissions of greenhouse gases, particularly carbon dioxide (CO_2), will continue to cause more droughts, famines, floods and wars. The death toll from these calamities, singularly or combined, is often in the millions and impacts not only humans but also other species of the earth's ecosystems (United Nations, 2014; World Health Organization, 2015) – which leads us to question the nature and the merits of the progress we have accomplished thus far.

There is now a general agreement among climate scientists that the conventional industrialization based on fossil fuels, namely coal, oil and gas, has done great damage to the environment and that it is constantly lowering the quality of life because of the costs it imposes in terms of pollution, congestion, stress and the destruction of the "natural capital". Some crude estimates suggest that if such costs were taken into account, even the top performing industries would not be profitable – thus framing the whole issue of environmental degradation and climate change in purely economic terms. But this narrow focus on costs and benefits is misleading because, for all we know, there can be no meaningful prices for the benefits of a healthy environment or for the costs of damages to it (see Ackerman, 2008). In this analysis, we also detect the implicit assumption, still popular in the economics of climate change, that should these industries become profitable then concern with the environment should disappear and no action need be taken to protect the environment – except perhaps for a small carbon tax that could discourage the emissions of greenhouse gases. Acemoglu *et al.* (2016) find that relying on carbon taxes only will result in welfare costs and thus they advocate the additional use of subsidies to encourage R&D and speed up the transition to a clean technology. However, we argue here that concern with the environment goes beyond questions of profitability and pecuniary gains or losses and can be considered as a moral issue since it seeks to preserve biodiversity by protecting (human and animal) life in its natural habitat.

Since these gases are responsible for global warming, as science has proven, then the scale of the threat to biodiversity requires immediate policy responses. It is argued here that, given the progress and knowledge accumulated since the industrial revolution, modern societies have reached a degree of maturity that makes it not only desirable but also necessary to finally make the switch from the fossil economy to the *green* economy and to start building the needed infrastructure to facilitate the transition by investing increasingly in technologies that do not damage the ecological system. Furthermore, the chapter demonstrates that the alternative of a green economy is feasible, viable and economically more efficient than the current system based on fossil fuels. It also shows that green industrialization is good for jobs and for a socially sustainable development. Obviously, the democratic state is expected to play a crucial role in making it all happen by supporting the green economy through public policy initiatives that are integrated within the overall development strategy.

The fossil economy and the rise of capitalist industrialization

For obvious reasons, the long history of humanity is often shortened to the last 10,000 years or so, which marks the beginning of our civilization – a period which scientists call the *Holocene* era[6] and which the physicist and Nobel prize laureate Burton Richter (2014: 46) described as "a time period so short as to be only the blink of a geological eye". The geological perspective is useful because it informs us that other climate changes have occurred in the past and have drastically transformed life on earth: ice ages, global warming and mass extinctions. As Richter (2014: 45) put it "Our planet Earth is 4.5 billion years old, and over the planet's lifetime changes in temperature, greenhouse gas concentration, and sea level have occurred that dwarf any of the changes being discussed now". Still, the rapid and unprecedented increase in human population and in the size of its economic activity since the beginning of the industrial era has made history even shorter and the focus now is mainly on the last 300 years. As mentioned earlier, different accounts have been given of the industrial revolution, but everyone seems to agree that it was, as Wrigley (2010: 2) put it, "one of the two greatest transformations of human society since hunter-gatherer days" – the first one having been the Neolithic agricultural revolution.

The industrial revolution has indeed greatly transformed human society in many ways and succeeded in building an entirely new civilization; one that is based on hard science and technological progress and which has pushed aside spiritual explanations of the universe and of how humans should relate to each other and to their environment. It is not an exaggeration to say that the first monuments of this new civilization were the chimney stacks and factories that changed the landscape of Britain and later of Western Europe and the rest of the world. Prior to the factory system, the capitalist-entrepreneur assigned *tasks* to workers who performed these in their own homes and did so at their own pace, which allowed them also to care for their children and other family members.

Under the new production system in the factory, the capitalist assigned *workers* to tasks, which needed to be completed within a set timeframe. Forced to compete against the running machines and with their peers, the worker now must show diligence and obedience to keep the job and receive the wage. It was the beginning of mechanization and rationalization of work – the prelude to Fordism and Taylorism, whose effects we discussed in Chapter 5. Self-employed workers and artisans who were once independent workers became salaried and needed to spend long hours at the factory – a new routine that had important implications for the structure of the economy, the family, the system of education and many other new institutions that became necessary for building the new civilization.

Nell (1998) has characterized this phase in the development of capitalism as the shift from a 'craft-based economy' to 'mass production' – a system that requires large pools of labour and the concentration of people in towns and cities. In turn, the rapid growth of such agglomerations meant the need for – and the development of – new services from child care to schooling, transportation, housing, public utilities and a host of other urban services. Writing in the midst of these changes, Barnett and Barnett (1895: 138) observed that:

> Sometimes the unwedded mother . . . honestly tries to get work at sack-making, factory-work, anything which will enable her to keep her little one near her; but it is a hard, and an almost impossible, task. The care of the child impedes the work, and thus it has to be put out to daily nurse.

By this time, however, new divisions of labour had appeared and most of the economic functions of the family were rapidly lost. In parallel, as noted by Nell (1998), there was a dramatic increase in the role of the state, which expanded by developing the necessary infrastructure and the appropriate institutions required for managing the new economy and the social changes brought with it.

One of the best characterizations of the industrial revolution, however, is that given by Wrigley (2010) who considered it to be primarily an *energy revolution*. He concurs with other studies that social, political, cultural and institutional factors did play an important role in the industrial revolution, but argues that it is important to consider also physical and biological factors. Wrigley (2010: 9, 14) maintains that the productive capacity of an economy and its growth potential depend in a crucial way on the amount and type of energy available for use. Organic economies, he argues, depended on energy which was essentially derived from human and animal power, waterwheels and plant photosynthesis, namely the burning of wood and charcoal whose limited scope is easily recognized and well known by now.[7] Such physical and biological constraints impeded growth and condemned these economies in the long run to perpetual simple reproduction, if not decline. To put things in perspective, Wrigley (2010: 249) makes the following comparison:

> The type of infrastructural investment which underwrites a wide range of the activities taking place in modern societies could not have been provided in the organic era. This is readily demonstrable in some contexts. The quantity of iron and steel needed to build a railway network or to construct bulk carrier ships, for example, could not have been produced even if all the forested land had been denuded of timber.

By contrast, the use of coal as an alternative source of energy expanded the powers of industry to produce things by supplying the new economy with abundant energy – and that provided an escape from the constraints of the organic economy. This may not have been a sufficient reason, but it was necessary for the industrial revolution to take off. Once the benefits of coal were discovered, its use in Britain grew so rapidly that it more than quadrupled between 1800 and 1859, representing more than nine-tenths of total consumption, whereas the use of other sources (wind, water, human) only marginally increased or declined sharply such as in the case of firewood (see Wrigley, 2010: table 4.2). The quantity of energy needed to sustain all the activities of the new economy (industries and home consumption) was a great deal more than what the organic economy could ever supply. Coal energy effectively liberated industry from the constraints and limitations imposed by traditional sources and *that* opened new horizons for unparalleled growth and expansion. It is in this sense that the industrial revolution was really a revolution in energy use.

The search for new sources of energy continued unabated, and towards the end of the nineteenth century coal, was already supplemented with oil and in the beginning of the twentieth century with gas. Today, the world economy literally runs on this trio – roughly, coal for electricity generation, oil for transportation and gas for heating. Indeed, life in modern society depends in a crucial way on the use of energy since we need it in every activity of our daily life: heating, cooking, lighting, transportation, communication and producing the goods and the bads. In this regard, Richter (2014: 11) rightly commented that "While poets and song writers say it is love that makes the world go round, and bankers say it is money, it is really energy that makes the world go round". The heavy reliance on these fossil fuels as sources of energy has certainly served humanity well in the sense that it sustained growth and expansion for several generations, but it has also brought with it serious environmental dangers – of which the most talked about is global warming.

What is climate change and why should we be concerned about it? The basic scientific explanation for climate change – on which scientists agree – is that life on planet Earth is possible because the temperature is just right – not too hot, not too cold (and the comparison here is with other plants such as Venus and Mars; see, among others, Richter, 2014). Earth receives almost all of its heat or energy from the sun. Once this heat reaches the surface of the earth, it is radiated back into space but part of this heat is trapped by greenhouse gases found in the atmosphere – many of which are formed naturally such as by water vaporization and other gases. The amount of heat trapped in this way in the atmosphere above us is what ensures that temperature on earth is what it is.[8] Burning fossil fuels to generate energy for our daily use releases more gases in the atmosphere, which traps more heat and prevents it from escaping into space – thus causing the temperature on earth to increase, that is, global warming.

Now, the concern is that if this activity continues unchecked, it will upset the natural balance and cause a change in the climatic conditions which have hitherto allowed human civilization to thrive. The available data (see Hansen *et al.*, 2016) indicate that such changes in the climate are already happening and taking the form of prolonged droughts and desertification in some parts of the planet, melting of the glaciers and ice in the Arctic, rising sea levels and severe floods, all of which disturb the historic stability of human settlement on earth – leading, as it did (see IPCC, 2014), to the ongoing drama of mass exodus, famines and wars over the resources that are so necessary for life, be they fertile land, water, or other sources of energy such as oil and gas. Other practices, such as the use of fertilizers in agriculture and deforestation, exacerbate the situation, but, according to Richter (2014: 105), these are responsible for only about 30 per cent of the total emissions of greenhouse gases, whereas the rest is attributed to the burning of fossil fuels, namely coal, oil and gas.

As noted earlier, ever since the energy revolution revealed the connection between energy use and wealth creation, industrialized countries have been on some sort of a wild shopping spree, acquiring and burning as much fossil fuel as seems required to boost their economic growth. Apart from the tricky convoluted ways of finance, energy has hitherto proven to be the uncontested source of wealth creation, and the huge rise in the demand for it worldwide is driven by what is now a stylized fact: countries with the highest use of energy per capita are also countries that enjoy the highest income per capita – a standard measure of well-being (see World Development Indicators: http://wdi.worldbank.org/table/3.6). Some might argue about the direction of causality and disagree that levels of energy consumption would make one rich or poor, but think of it this way: everyone needs a certain amount of energy just to stay alive, and the more of it one has, the better off one is. Today, the poorest of the poor have no access to lighting, refrigeration or any other type of commercial energy even though many of them live in resource-rich countries. As Richter (2014) noted, any policy that would allow the poor direct access to these sources of energy would greatly improve their living standards, an issue to which we will return in the next section.

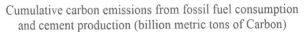

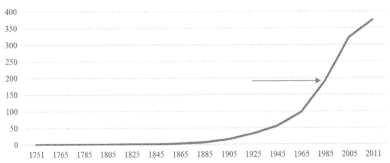

Figure 7.1 The stock of carbon emissions doubled since the mid-1980s.

Source: based on data provided by the US Department of Energy (2015).

In any case, the race to higher energy consumption has led to more emissions of greenhouse gases. According to the US Department of Energy (2015), the concentration of greenhouse gases in the atmosphere is growing so fast that the worldwide stock of emissions since 1750 has doubled during the last 30 years (see Figure 7.1; see also IPCC, 2014). Richter (2014: table 8.1) estimates that the dirty old coal still contributes 40 per cent to the current level of world CO_2 emissions whereas oil contributes 40 per cent and gas 20 per cent.

What is the problem if there is so much concentration of greenhouse gases in the atmosphere? In 2014, the Intergovernmental Panel on Climate Change[9] released its fifth assessment report (IPCC, 2014), which it called "the most comprehensive assessment of scientific knowledge on climate change". The report asserted three main things, which the scientific community considers as facts:

1   Climate change is unequivocal and the atmosphere and ocean are indeed warmer now than "they have been over the last 1400 years"; the amounts of snow and ice have diminished and the sea level has risen.
2   Human influence on climate change is clear and anthropogenic, or human-induced, emissions of greenhouse gases are the main cause of global warming.
3   Changes in the climate have had impacts on both natural and human systems.

The impact on the natural and human systems is what concerns us here directly. The IPCC (2014) report put particular emphasis on the impacts of climate change on natural systems and noted that, in addition to ocean acidification, hydrological systems have been altered in many regions and that as a consequence "many terrestrial, freshwater and marine species have shifted their geographic ranges, seasonal activities, migration patterns, abundances and species interactions in response to ongoing climate change". In addition, the report also emphasized extreme changes in all the components of the climate system, resulting in severe heat waves and prolonged droughts, water scarcity, cyclones and floods – all of which have serious impacts on the human systems because they directly affect areas of food production and force displacement of people, thus increasing vulnerability of the poor and causing more tensions and violent conflicts. Note, for instance, that as a direct result in Africa alone, the number of the poor has increased by at least 100 million people since 1990 (see World Bank, 2016).

Although science seems to have just discovered the links between changes in the natural systems and the human systems, this has been an established truth, for centuries and perhaps millennia, in the wisdom of the elders in many civilizations around the globe. Indeed, prior to the prevalence of the current view of the world, which is based on what we referred to earlier as techno progress and hard science, human attitudes towards Mother Nature were largely characterized by fear, respect and even reverence – something still found in the remnants of the disappearing 'old' civilizations. In this regard, it can be said that throughout their history, humans have always been seeking to understand their natural environment and that the entire progress achieved by humanity can in fact be defined as a better understanding of the forces of nature as a result of the advance in knowledge derived from physics, chemistry and other sciences. Ironically, however, as this knowledge improved, humans felt empowered and began seeking to dominate nature and bring all of its constituents into their dominion so that these could be selfishly exploited to satisfy their desires and enhance their well-being (see Leiss, 1994). The logic of capitalist exploitation provided the philosophical justification, and the industrial revolution was the beginning of a new era that marked a rift in the relationship between humans and nature (see Magdoff and Bellamy Foster, 2011).

Scientists have another name for that rift. They call it the *Anthropocene* (see Crutzen, 2002). The term was coined towards the turn of the twenty-first century and is used to mark the end of the *Holocene* era and the beginning of a new geologic epoch in which human activities are playing an important and perhaps decisive role in forcing ecological and geological changes (see Steffen *et al.*, 2007; Clark, 2015). As mentioned earlier, this coincides roughly with the industrial revolution but has intensified recently with a 'Great Acceleration' (see Figure 7.1 above) because of the rapid progress in technological capability and the heavy reliance on the use of fossil fuels as a source of energy (see Bellamy Foster *et al.*, 2011). The term Anthropocene then refers to all the impacts of humans on the earth system such as those discussed earlier resulting in climate change and the related environmental destruction and is clearly intended to emphasize the fact that humanity has become – and will remain – a major environmental force.

The green economy as alternative

The predominant view is that the enhanced power of humans to exploit nature's resources has greatly benefited humanity and that there is nothing to worry about – thus suggesting to just ignore the dangers of climate change and continue with business as usual (BAU). Yet, if we examine the evolution of humanity from the perspective of a geological eye and the concern of scientists, we realize that the BAU agenda is not sustainable for several reasons. The most obvious one is that the quantity of fossil fuels is finite and non-renewable, which calls for the need for alternative sources of energy. The second reason, which is the concern of climate scientists and environmentalists in general, is inherent in the process of energy extraction itself since the burning of these fossils releases gases into the atmosphere and causes the much-talked about climate change. The cumulative nature of these gases (most of which have a very long life span) has led some scientists to talk about the existence of 'tipping points' beyond which environmental dangers could no longer be avoided. Other environmentalists such as the authors of the report of the Club of Rome pleaded for a change in the BAU agenda and called for *limits to growth* (see Meadows *et al.*, 1972, 2005) while Daly (1977, 1996) argued for a *steady-state economy* as an alternative to "growthmania", whose *costs* should not be underestimated (Mishan, 1967). A good review of the economics literature on the environmental question is given by Kula (1998) in his *History of Environmental Economic Thought*.

The environmental crisis is obviously a planetary phenomenon and the negative effects of industrial activity in one corner of the globe are felt everywhere. But what is the fault of a poor African farmer using his muscles to plough his vegetable pitch? Billions of people in the poorest countries make no use of fossil energy and thus bear no responsibility in the emissions of greenhouse gases that drive climate change. According to the World Bank, there are today about 3 billion people – or 40 per cent of world population – who still rely on wood and charcoal for cooking and heating[10] and almost 2 billion people have no access to any type of commercial energy. As a result, per capita energy consumption in the least developed countries is less than one-tenth of that in the OECD countries.[11]

The pursuit of growth and industrial development through the massive exploitation of fossil fuels for more than two centuries has resulted in the creation of an unprecedented wealth and plenitude, but the benefits are far from universal: wealth is highly concentrated in the hands of a minority of super-rich individuals who are overseeing the reproduction of the capitalist system and the perpetuation of its individualistic principles. In the meanwhile, some of the poorest countries in Africa, such as Ghana, have become notorious dumping grounds for electronic toxic waste from the most industrialized nations (see the documentary *Toxicity*, 2016). The gross inequality in the distribution of these benefits and the widespread poverty raise yet another objection to the sustainability of the BAU agenda.

Still, the most damning objection to the BAU agenda is the criticism levelled against the whole idea of progress achieved by humanity during all these years – that is, millennia. Here again, looking at human history from a geological perspective is illuminating. Several thousand years since humans first discovered farming and herding, there appeared widespread deforestation and soil erosion as a result of the application of new techniques to intensify production and supply a higher output for the ever-growing population. Earlier civilizations like the Sumerians were successful in increasing the yield of their crops and creating prosperity for a while thanks to their progress, but failed to sustain it because the new techniques caused degradation of the soil. Trapped between the environmental damage of their own making and the external constraint of organic energy, these civilizations exhausted their growth potential and came to their logical fate: collapse. This was one of humanity's first *progress traps*[12] (see Wright, 2004). Fast-forwarding to the Anthropocene era, the parallels are there for those who care to see them. Our industrial civilization, based as it is on energy from fossil fuels and emissions of greenhouse gases, is disturbing the unusual climate stability within which it developed, and the next progress trap lies ahead, maybe not too far away, if the BAU agenda runs on unfettered.

Environmentalists, including scientists, have developed a certain sense of fatalism about the coming of the green economy – seeing it as the logical succession to the earlier switch from the organic economy to the fossil economy. Philosophers and spiritual thinkers have started a debate on the role of scientific and technological progress in society and have surmised that it is about time that humans have a spiritual reconnect with Mother Nature, arguing that some technologies are best left unrealized – pointing to the many progress traps, from the destruction of food sources (e.g. ocean acidification, soil degradation) to the atomic bomb. The general population seems to have taken the advice seriously and started behaving in an ecologically correct manner. Governments have enacted laws to protect the environment and imposed targets of lower emissions of greenhouse gases. Shrewd capitalists have responded by labelling their products 'environmentally friendly' and bio-products and 'green' businesses have appeared as a profitable niche. Even big oil companies have jumped on board and run aggressive marketing campaigns presenting themselves as leaders of the change towards a green economy.

With the exception of a few skeptics (see Zehner, 2012; Moran, 2015), there is now what appears to be universal agreement about the wisdom of the transition to a green economy. The IPCC, which is the leading international organization providing scientific explanations about – and recommendations on – climate change has more member countries (195) than the United Nations (193)! However, beneath this apparent accord, there lie some serious contradictions and conflicts about how to achieve this goal. To start at the official level, we note that, for instance, governments of the least developing countries are arguing that climate change is no fault of theirs and charge that the rich countries are kicking the ladder away but only after having relied on fossil fuel energy for centuries to achieve the kind of prosperity they are now enjoying. These claims are part of what is called the 'climate debt' or 'ecological debt', which industrialized countries ought to pay for the damage they have inflicted on everyone else. The rise of some NICs (newly industrialized countries) like China, India or Brazil with their heavy consumption of fossil fuels to boost their industrialization is reinforcing the veracity of this claim and inciting everyone else to follow their path – thus making the agreements on climate change, from Kyoto (1997) to Paris (2015), look more like diplomatic promises.

The energy revolution will fully deserve its name only if succeeds in moving beyond fossil fuels and creating an economy based on social and economic justice. The first possibility has now become clearly feasible and achievable in a relatively short run, but all the odds are that the question of unequal distribution will remain a characteristic of the new economy – now dubbed 'green' capitalism. For this reason, many moderate environmentalists who have the power to influence policymaking are willing to go at a slower pace and therefore accept an 'energy mix' that would comprise fossil fuels for a still long time, often with the added condition that efficiency should be increased in order to lower emissions of greenhouse gases. The bet here is to make fossil fuels 'as green as possible' and eventually emissions-free by the power of technology – hence the delay in the transition to the green economy. Digging a bit deeper reveals some of the hidden forces of inertia:

1   Capitalists need to exhaust their returns on existing capital investments in fossil energy and that may take decades if not longer, particularly when we consider the constant need for investments in new technology in order to keep up with competition in the industry,
2   As argued in Chapter 5, private corporations, by their nature, are reluctant to engage in basic research or venture into path-breaking projects that could speed up discoveries and improvements in the implementation of green energy. They are relying on government-financed research; as is the case in other areas,
3   The slow process allows private corporations to avoid high risk and high capital costs and then move in securely only when green technology has matured.

The vested interests of the super-rich – revealed through their various green initiatives (Branson, Buffet, Bloomberg, Gates)[13] – not only raise suspicion but also alert us to the real objectives behind their philanthropy and pretence to save the earth and its ecosystems. A careful examination of the current proposals and green projects reveals that the transition towards a green economy is being framed within the same socioeconomic system, and efforts are being deployed to make sure that change is contained and that the transition does not lead to the opening of a Pandora's box. To this effect, for instance, private investors have just built in the south of Morocco what has been called the biggest solar plant in the world, financed by the European Investment Bank, the World Bank, the African Development Bank, l'Agence Française de Développement and other international financial institutions. The project is owned and managed by the Moroccan Agency for Solar Energy, known as MASEN, which is a private-public partnership that includes the Saudi group ACWA power international. MASEN also received important subsidies in kind (communal and public land) and was permitted to acquire any real estate assets deemed necessary for its operations, including by means of expropriation. Electricity is produced by ACWA power international and sold to MASEN at a set price of 1.6 dirhams per KWh, which is higher than the market price. MASEN then resells electricity at a loss to the Office National de l'Électricité (ONE), which distributes it to the general population through private corporations, and the difference between the purchase price and the sale price is subsidized by a loan from the World Bank and guaranteed by the Moroccan government.[14] It sounds like a complicated scheme, but this is 'green' capitalism at work: creating wealth for the wealthy.

The transition to a green economy is really inspiring and has the potential of being transformative. Inspiring because it brings with it all sorts of exciting new ideas, and transformative because it can change the existing socioeconomic relations. The new technologies inspired by the green economy will certainly lead to new sectors and activities that will attract resources from old ones and lead to a 'creative destruction'. Fossil fuels energy empowered the nascent capitalist class and destroyed the older forms of aristocratic power and authority. The transition to a green economy is an opportunity to do away with some of the ills of our current, unegalitarian capitalist system, but the egalitarian society will not emerge as a simple by-product of that transition. The new green economy needs new institutions. The history of capitalism clearly shows that the capitalist class was successful in forging a change "by acquiring a power of action from within the new energy system" – and that is a lesson for the anti-capitalist movement (Mitchell, 2011: 12). The proponents of zero growth or de-growth, for instance, are not necessarily after an economy that does not grow. Their worry is motivated by two interrelated concerns: unequal distribution of the benefits of growth and the impact of the latter on climate change; that is, they are seeking a growth which is consistent with eliminating gas emissions but also with an egalitarian distribution (see Victor, 2008; Jackson and Victor, 2016). In *Greening the Global Economy*, Pollin (2015a) has detailed a policy agenda that can actually achieve both of those goals. As argued by Pollin (2015a, 2015b), one of the strengths of green energy is that it can be labour-intensive and therefore has the potential of creating more jobs – an essential component of the project of an egalitarian economy.

From our perspective, and in line with the thesis of this book, the ideal solution is a change of system and not only a change of the source from which we draw the energy to power the system. Otherwise, solar plants generating clean energy will simply replace what would then look like abandoned monuments of dirty coal and oil, but will serve the same function. Hence, the alternative is a cooperative system based on socioeconomic justice and respect for the environment – a system that eliminates poverty and guarantees full employment while pursuing the search for, and development of, what Ishida and Furukawa (2013: 124) call *Nature Technology*, that is, a technology which is designed to "intelligently [harness] the amazing powers of nature" and to "support a new lifestyle that is both environmentally sound and spiritually uplifting". In previous chapters, we argued that the struggle for economic and social democracy has become, now more than ever before, an absolute necessity; a precondition for the fulfilment of human ideals of joy and happiness. All of us, as individuals, instinctively reject inequality if the outcome negatively affects our lives, because that makes us unhappy.[15] If we remain sober and adopt this behaviour in all of our dealings with other humans, the logical and optimal result is the building of a community in which "The interests of society are paramount to individual interests, and [in which] the two must be brought into just and harmonious relation", Morgan (1877: 552).

The establishment of worker owned and managed enterprises powered by green energy – described in Chapter 4 – is perhaps the best embodiment of such a society, which necessarily requires the elimination of economic and social inequalities among all its members.

However, because we live according to the ideology of the dominant class, we have been taught that it is rational to be selfish. We have been conditioned to reject equality in the social realm as unnatural, illusionary and utopian. In consequence, we have built a competitive society that does not care about those who cannot survive the competition and end up falling by the wayside. As Graeber (2016) put it "Today we are seeing the effects of a relentless war against the very idea of working-class politics or working-class community" and that "Generations of political manipulation have finally turned that sense of solidarity into a scourge". We have developed an economic system whose dynamic requires the exploitation of other humans (as well as animals and nature) and whose ethic accepts and justifies exclusion.

Those who benefit from such a system obviously hope that it would last for ever. The dominant class has a nagging fear about losing its privileged position, so naturally it resists any change (to the social order) that has the potential of eroding its power and domination. Ideologues write books to convince us that capitalism and its democracy are the *end of history* – meaning that this is as best as it can ever get for humanity (see Fukuyama, 1992).[16] This is why the reordering of social relations is a slow and arduous process. It requires a change in culture and mentality, a change in ideology and strategy. But as is often the case, it is only when injustice becomes too intolerable to bear that the necessity of change enters the social psyche.

In the meanwhile, however, there are important steps that can be taken immediately to reduce the negative impact on the environment. Lowering the ecological footprint is a good thing even if the reduction in emissions is marginal. The additional benefits of ecologically correct behaviour follow from the increased awareness of the population, which encourages the need for, and development of, alternative green technologies for powering homes, transportation and so on. Democracy in government – because it gives more power to the people – is perhaps the most important lever in this transformation process. The democratic state that emerges from such a political process (see Chapter 2) shall impose binding restrictions on the emissions of greenhouse gases, use taxation in an intelligent way to phase out polluting industries and encourage harmonious behaviour with nature – thus gradually paving the way towards the ultimate goal of changing the current regime of capitalist accumulation.

Conclusion

In recent years, climate change has become a major concern for scientists, policymakers and ordinary citizens. Most environmentalists are willing to forsake economic growth and pursue instead a sustainable development. This strategy is consistent with the longer goal of the transition from an economy based on fossil fuels to a green economy. However, critics of the current regime of capitalist accumulation argue that changing the source of energy will do nothing to solve the pernicious problem of unequal distribution of wealth and income, and therefore advocate the creation of an alternative system based on social and economic justice that can flourish in a harmonious relationship with nature. The reasoning behind this proposal is based on the idea that the essence of human existence is simply about the realization of fulfilling lives, which give joy and happiness to individuals who instinctively yearn for a strong sense of belonging to their community and to nature. The conservative ideology is trying to undermine the confidence in anything other than capitalism as a way of organizing the economy and society, but a different, better world is certainly possible. The transition towards the green economy is an opportunity to work for that change and to make it happen.

Notes

1 In this context, it must be noted that property rights now extend to outer space. The US Congress and Senate have approved the so-called Space Act (H. R. 2262) in 2015, which was signed into law by the President, allowing US corporations "engaged in commercial recovery of an asteroid resource or a space resource [to] be entitled to any asteroid resource or space resource obtained, including to possess, own, transport, use, and sell it according to applicable law . . .". See details of the Act on the Congress website: www.congress.gov/bill/114th-congress/house-bill/2262, accessed 20 May 2016.

2 There are many controversies involving industrial products and chemicals that are harmful to human health, the well-being of other species and the ecosystems. A notorious case is a pesticide produced by Monsanto and licensed for use in Canada in 1969. It was later found to present an unacceptable health risk to humans and was banned in 1985, but Monsanto appealed the decision and brought forth evidence supplied by *International Biotest Laboratories*, a private firm doing laboratory analysis under contract. The decision was reversed and the pesticide was back on the market. For more details, see Leiss (1990: 145).

3 The word 'organic' is commonly used to mean environmentally friendly products or processes, but that is not necessarily the meaning attached to an 'organic economy'. In an organic economy, energy is principally derived from plant photosynthesis, which relies on burning a lot of woods – and that may lead to deforestation. By contrast, a 'fossil economy' draws its energy from the use of fossil fuels by digging them from the underground and the consumption of these fossil fuels, namely coal, oil and natural gas, results in the emissions of carbon dioxide and other gases that are widely believed to be causing climate change (see Malm, 2016).

4 Levasseur (1889: 74) considered steam engines to be (true slaves, the most sober, docile and tireless that one could ever imagine): "de véritables esclaves, les plus sobres, les plus dociles, les plus infatigables que l'imagination puisse rêver", also quoted in Wrigley (2010: 28).

5 Mokyr (1999: 20) thinks that the steam engine was "conceptually one of the most radical inventions ever made".

6 Climate scientists agree that there has been an unusual climate stability during this period. Nordhaus (2013) has made the interesting observation that the rise of our civilization coincides with this climatic stability and that any dramatic change in the climate – such as through global warming – will bring about chaos and instability, which may threaten not only civilization but the flourishing of life and the existence of humanity itself.

7 Wrigley (2010: 242) estimates that "The rate of growth in coal consumption varied only slightly over the whole period [1560s–1850s], averaging about 1.3 per cent per annum, which implies a doubling roughly every half-century. With organic raw materials, a rate of growth as high as this would very soon cause intolerable pressure upon the land and a sharp rise in price. If, for example, wood use were to rise at a similar rate, it would require sixteen times as much land to be devoted to forest after two centuries of growth as had been needed at the start of the period, since a doubling every half-century implies this scale of expansion. In organic economies growth of this kind is physically impossible".

8 Richter (2014: 20) has summarized this process as follows "Our planet's average temperature is determined by a balance that is struck between the energy coming from the Sun and the energy radiated back out into space. What comes in depends on the temperature of the Sun, and what goes out depends on the Earth's surface temperature and on what things in the atmosphere block parts of the radiation", adding that "Over the history of the Earth, the average temperature has varied considerably as the amount of greenhouse gases in the atmosphere has changed and as the output of the Sun has changed. Today, the concern about global warming focuses on human activity that causes an increase in some greenhouse gases. The logic is simple: greenhouse gases are known to increase the temperature, and if we add more of what increases the temperature, we will increase the temperature more. How much more is the question that thousands of scientists are trying to answer" (Richter, 2014: 25–6).

9 The Intergovernmental Panel on Climate Change (IPCC) was set up by the United Nations Environment Programme and the World Meteorological Organization in 1988 and has become the leading international organization providing scientific explanations to climate change and its environmental and socio-economic impacts. According to its website, the IPCC counts 195 countries as members and thousands of scientists from around the world contribute to its work: www.ipcc.ch/, accessed 20 March 2016.

10 Even though cutting trees and shrubs for fuel is for mere survival, in Africa, for instance, it is one of the serious factors contributing to land degradation and desertification.

11 See the World Bank website: http://data.worldbank.org/topic/energy-and-mining, accessed 20 March 2016.

12 Wright (2004: 5) talks about many progress traps and invites humans to learn from their past. He wrote, "Progress has an internal logic that can lead beyond reason to catastrophe. A seductive trail of successes may end in a trap. Take weapons, for example. Ever since the Chinese invented gunpowder, there has been great progress in the making of bangs: from the firecracker to the cannon, from the petard to the high explosive shell. And just when high explosives were reaching a state of perfection, progress found the infinitely bigger bang in the atom. But when the bang we can make can blow up our world, we have made rather too much progress". In this regard, it is important to note that Albert Einstein, one of the inventors of the atomic bomb, was strongly opposed to it and to war in general – warning of catastrophe and advocating the destruction of this weapon (see Einstein, 1949: 6–7).

13 Several billionaires started their own initiatives, supposedly green but in fact designed to boost the profitability of their own businesses, see Klein (2014: chapter 7). The latest initiative by Bill Gates dubbed *The Breakthrough Energy Coalition* includes other billionaires whose mission is to supply the world with "energy that is reliable, affordable and that does not produce carbon". online: www.breakthroughenergycoalition.com/en/index.html, accessed 20 March 2016.

14 For details, see the website of l'Agence Française de Développement: www.afd.fr/home/pays/mediterranee-et-moyen-orient/geo/maroc?actuCtnId=89653, accessed 20 March 2016.

15 Psychologists have conducted experiments by giving two individuals a fixed amount of money to divide among themselves. The rules are such that one person proposes a division and the second can either accept or reject it. If the division is accepted, then

each individual gets the proposed share. If the division is rejected, then the money is taken away from them and no one gets anything. As the Mexican adage goes, he who divides and distributes is expected to keep the biggest share for himself, say 9 out of 10, whereas the second person is expected to accept whatever little is given to him, say 1, because it is free and better than nothing. However, empirical evidence shows that most people reject such unequal divisions on the principle of fairness: the second person would obviously accept a 5 – 5 division but failing that, most people opt for 0 – 0 rather than 9 – 1 (see Pressman, 2016: 42 and references therein).

16 Wright (2004: 6) noted that "Fukuyama's naive triumphalism strengthened a belief, mainly on the political right, that those who have not chosen the true way forward should be made to do so for their own good – by force, if necessary". This is the philosophy of the neo-cons who use military power to invade countries and systematically destroy their millennia-old civilizations, claiming to help them adopt democratic values (e.g. Iraq, Syria, Libya, etc.).

References

Acemoglu, D., U. Akcigit, D. Hanley and W. Kerr (2016) "Transition to Clean Technology", *Journal of Political Economy*, Vol. 124, No. 1, pp. 52–104.

Ackerman, F. (2008) "Climate Economics in Four Easy Pieces", *Development*, Vol. 51, pp. 325–31.

Barnett, S. A. and H. Barnett (1895) *Practicable Socialism: Essays on Social Reform, revised edition* (London: Longmans).

Bator, M. F. (1958) *"The Anatomy of Market Failure"*, *Quarterly Journal of Economics*, Vol. 7, pp. 351–79.

Bellamy Foster, J., B. Clark and R. York (2011) *The Ecological Rift: Capitalism's War on Earth* (New York: Monthly Review Press).

Clark, T. (2015) *Ecocriticism on the Edge: The Anthropocene as a Threshold Concept* (London: Bloomsbury Academic).

Coase, R. (1960) "The Problem of Social Cost", *Journal of Law and Economics*, Vol. 3, pp. 1–44.

Crutzen, P. J. (2002) "Geology of Mankind: The Anthropocene", *Nature*, Vol. 415 (January 3), p. 23.

Daly, H. E. (1991 [1977]) *Steady-State Economics*, 2nd edition (Washington, DC: Island Press).

Daly, H. E. (1996) *Beyond Growth: The Economics of Sustainable Development* (Boston, MA: Beacon Press).

Einstein, A. (1984 [1949]) *The World As I see It* (New York: Citadel Press).

Fukuyama, F. (1992) *The End of History and the Last Man* (New York: Free Press).

Graeber, D. (2016) "Caring Too Much. That's the Curse of the Working Classes", online: www.theguardian.com/commentisfree/2014/mar/26/caring-curse-working-class-austerity-solidarity-scourge, accessed 16 May 2016

Hansen, J. *et al.* (2016) "Ice Melt, Sea Level Rise and Superstorms: Evidence from Paleoclimate Data, Climate Modeling, and Modern Observations that 2°C Global Warming Could be Dangerous", *Atmospheric Chemistry and Physics*, Vol. 16, No. 6, pp. 3761–812.

IPCC (2014) *Climate Change 2014: Synthesis Report* (Geneva: Intergovernmental Panel on Climate Change), online: http://ar5-syr.ipcc.ch/, accessed 5 February 2016.

Ishida, E. H. and R. Furukawa (2013) *Nature Technology: Creating a Fresh Approach to Technology and Lifestyle* (Tokyo: Springer).

Jackson, T. and P. A. Victor (2016) "Does Slow Growth Lead to Rising Inequality? Some Theoretical Reflections and Numerical Simulations", *Ecological Economics*, Vol. 121, pp. 206–19.

Klein, N. (2014) *This Changes Everything: Capitalism Vs. The Climate* (New York: Simon & Schuster Paperbacks).

Kula, E. (1998) *History of Environmental Thought* (New York: Routledge).

Leiss, W. (1990) *Under Technology's Thumb* (Montreal: McGill-Queen's University Press).

Leiss, W. (1994) *The Domination of Nature* (Montreal: McGill-Queen's University Press).

Levasseur, E. (1889) *La population française* (Paris : Rousseau).

Magdoff, F. and J. Bellamy Foster (2011) *What Every Environmentalist Needs to Know about Capitalism: A Citizen's Guide to Capitalism and the Environment* (New York: Monthly Review Press).

Malm, A. (2016) *Fossil Capital: The Rise of Steam Power and the Roots of Global Warming* (London: Verso).

Mantoux, P. (1961 [1928]) *The Industrial Revolution in the Eighteenth Century* (London: University Paperbacks).

Meadows, D. H., J. Randers and D. L., Meadows (2005) *Limits to Growth: The 30- Year Update* (London: Earthscan).

Meadows, D. H., D. L. Meadows, J. Randers and W. W. Behrens III (1972) *The Limits to Growth: A Report for the Club of Rome Project on the Predicament of Mankind* (New York: Universe Books).

Mishan, E. J. (1967) *The Costs of Economic Growth* (Harmondsworth, UK: Penguin Books Ltd).

Mitchell, T. (2011) *Carbon Democracy: Political Power in the Age of Oil* (London: Verso)

Mokyr, J. (ed.) (1999) *The British Industrial Revolution: An Economic Perspective*, 2nd edition (Boulder, CO: Westview Press).

Moran, A. (ed.) (2015) *Climate Change: The Facts* (Woodsville, NH: Stockade Books).

Morgan, L. H. (1877) *Ancient Society: Or Researches in the Lines of Human Progress from Savagery through Barbarism to Civilization*, New York: Holt & Co., online from the *Internet Archive*: https://archive.org/details/ancientsociety00morg, accessed 20 March 2016.

Nell, E. J. (1998) *The General Theory of Transformational Growth: Keynes After Sraffa* (Cambridge, UK: Cambridge University Press).

Nordhaus, W. D. (2013) *The Climate Casino: Risk, Uncertainty, and Economics for a Warming World* (New Haven, CT: Yale University Press).

Pollin, R. (2015a) *Greening the Global Economy* (Boston, MA: MIT Press).

Pollin, R. (2015b) "Think We Can't Stabilize the Climate While Fostering Growth? Think Again", *The Nation*, (November 16), online: www.thenation.com/article/think-we-cant-stabilize-the-climate-while-fostering-growth-think-again/, accessed 20 March 2016.

Pressman, S. (2016) *Understanding Piketty's Capital in the Twenty-First Century* (London: Routledge).

Richter, B. (2014) *Beyond Smoke and Mirrors: Climate Change and Energy in the 21st Century*, 2nd edition (Cambridge, UK: Cambridge University Press).

Steffen, W., P. J. Crutzen, and J. R. McNeil (2007) "The Anthropocene: Are Humans Now Overwhelming the Great Forces of Nature", *Ambio*, Vol. 36, No. 8 (December), pp. 614–621.

Toxicity (2016) *Documentary: The Story of a Graveyard for Electronics and . . . People*, online: www.rt.com/shows/documentary/317644-toxic-city-chemicals-poverty/, accessed 30 March 2016.

United Nations (2014) "7 Million Premature Deaths Annually Linked To Air Pollution", *The UN and Climate Change*, www.un.org/climatechange/blog/2014/03/7-million-premature-deaths-annually-linked-to-air-pollution/, accessed 20 May 2016.

US Department of Energy (2015) *Global, Regional, and National Fossil-Fuel CO_2 Emissions*, authored by Boden, T. A., G. Marland, and R. J. Andres, Carbon Dioxide Information Analysis Center (Oak Ridge National Laboratory: US Department of Energy, Oak Ridge, TN), online: http://cdiac.ornl.gov/trends/emis/tre_glob_2011.html, accessed 5 February 2016.

Victor, P. A. (2008) *Managing Without Growth* (Cheltenham, UK: Edward Elgar).

World Bank (2016) *Poverty in a Rising Africa: Africa Poverty Report*, authored by Beegle, K., L. Christiaensen, A. Dabalen, and I. Gaddis (Washington, DC: The World Bank).

World Health Organization (2015) *Climate Change and Health*, Fact sheet N° 266, online: www.who.int/mediacentre/factsheets/fs266/en/, accessed 20 May 2016.

Wright, R. (2011 [2004]) *A Short History of Progress* (Toronto: House of Anansi Press, Inc.).

Wrigley, E. A. (2010) *Energy and the English Industrial Revolution* (Cambridge, UK: Cambridge University Press).

Zehner, O. (ed.) (2012) *Green Illusions: The Dirty Secrets of Clean Energy and the Future of Environmentalism* (Lincoln, NE: University of Nebraska Press).

Index

Note: 'n' denotes chapter notes; bold denotes tables; italics denote figures.

For Product Safety Concerns and Information please contact our EU
representative GPSR@taylorandfrancis.com Taylor & Francis Verlag GmbH,
Kaufingerstraße 24, 80331 München, Germany

Printed and bound by CPI Group (UK) Ltd, Croydon, CR0 4YY
01/05/2025
01858450-0007